CLEP-42 COLLEGE-LEVEL EXAMINATION
PROGRAM SERIES

This is your
PASSBOOK for...

Principles of/ Introductory Micro- and Macroeconomics

Test Preparation Study Guide
Questions & Answers

COPYRIGHT NOTICE

This book is SOLELY intended for, is sold ONLY to, and its use is RESTRICTED to individual, bona fide applicants or candidates who qualify by virtue of having seriously filed applications for appropriate license, certificate, professional and/or promotional advancement, higher school matriculation, scholarship, or other legitimate requirements of education and/or governmental authorities.

This book is NOT intended for use, class instruction, tutoring, training, duplication, copying, reprinting, excerption, or adaptation, etc., by:

1) Other publishers
2) Proprietors and/or Instructors of "Coaching" and/or Preparatory Courses
3) Personnel and/or Training Divisions of commercial, industrial, and governmental organizations
4) Schools, colleges, or universities and/or their departments and staffs, including teachers and other personnel
5) Testing Agencies or Bureaus
6) Study groups which seek by the purchase of a single volume to copy and/or duplicate and/or adapt this material for use by the group as a whole without having purchased individual volumes for each of the members of the group
7) Et al.

Such persons would be in violation of appropriate Federal and State statutes.

PROVISION OF LICENSING AGREEMENTS – Recognized educational, commercial, industrial, and governmental institutions and organizations, and others legitimately engaged in educational pursuits, including training, testing, and measurement activities, may address request for a licensing agreement to the copyright owners, who will determine whether, and under what conditions, including fees and charges, the materials in this book may be used them. In other words, a licensing facility exists for the legitimate use of the material in this book on other than an individual basis. However, it is asseverated and affirmed here that the material in this book CANNOT be used without the receipt of the express permission of such a licensing agreement from the Publishers. Inquiries re licensing should be addressed to the company, attention rights and permissions department.

All rights reserved, including the right of reproduction in whole or in part, in any form or by any means, electronic or mechanical, including photocopying, recording, or by any information storage and retrieval system, without permission in writing from the Publisher.

Copyright © 2025 by
National Learning Corporation

212 Michael Drive, Syosset, NY 11791
(516) 921-8888 • www.passbooks.com
E-mail: info@passbooks.com

PASSBOOK® SERIES

THE *PASSBOOK® SERIES* has been created to prepare applicants and candidates for the ultimate academic battlefield – the examination room.

At some time in our lives, each and every one of us may be required to take an examination – for validation, matriculation, admission, qualification, registration, certification, or licensure.

Based on the assumption that every applicant or candidate has met the basic formal educational standards, has taken the required number of courses, and read the necessary texts, the *PASSBOOK® SERIES* furnishes the one special preparation which may assure passing with confidence, instead of failing with insecurity. Examination questions – together with answers – are furnished as the basic vehicle for study so that the mysteries of the examination and its compounding difficulties may be eliminated or diminished by a sure method.

This book is meant to help you pass your examination provided that you qualify and are serious in your objective.

The entire field is reviewed through the huge store of content information which is succinctly presented through a provocative and challenging approach – the question-and-answer method.

A climate of success is established by furnishing the correct answers at the end of each test.

You soon learn to recognize types of questions, forms of questions, and patterns of questioning. You may even begin to anticipate expected outcomes.

You perceive that many questions are repeated or adapted so that you can gain acute insights, which may enable you to score many sure points.

You learn how to confront new questions, or types of questions, and to attack them confidently and work out the correct answers.

You note objectives and emphases, and recognize pitfalls and dangers, so that you may make positive educational adjustments.

Moreover, you are kept fully informed in relation to new concepts, methods, practices, and directions in the field.

You discover that you are actually taking the examination all the time: you are preparing for the examination by "taking" an examination, not by reading extraneous and/or supererogatory textbooks.

In short, this PASSBOOK®, used directedly, should be an important factor in helping you to pass your test.

NONTRADITIONAL EDUCATION

Students returning to school as adults bring more varied experience to their studies than do the teenagers who begin college shortly after graduating from high school. As a result, there are numerous programs for students with nontraditional learning curves. Hundreds of colleges and universities grant degrees to people who cannot attend classes at a regular campus or have already learned what the college is supposed to teach.

You can earn nontraditional education credits in many ways:
- Passing standardized exams
- Demonstrating knowledge gained through experience
- Completing campus-based coursework, and
- Taking courses off campus

Some methods of assessing learning for credit are objective, such as standardized tests. Others are more subjective, such as a review of life experiences.

With some help from four hypothetical characters – Alice, Vin, Lynette, and Jorge – this article describes nontraditional ways of earning educational credit. It begins by describing programs in which you can earn a high school diploma without spending 4 years in a classroom. The college picture is more complicated, so it is presented in two parts: one on gaining credit for what you know through course work or experience, and a second on college degree programs. The final section lists resources for locating more information.

Earning High School Credit

People who were prevented from finishing high school as teenagers have several options if they want to do so as adults. Some major cities have back-to-school programs that allow adults to attend high school classes with current students. But the more practical alternatives for most adults are to take the General Educational Development (GED) tests or to earn a high school diploma by demonstrating their skills or taking correspondence classes.

Of course, these options do not match the experience of staying in high school and graduating with one's friends. But they are viable alternatives for adult learners committed to meeting and, often, continuing their educational goals.

GED Program

Alice quit high school her sophomore year and took a job to help support herself, her younger brother, and their newly widowed mother. Now an adult, she wants to earn her high school diploma – and then go on to college. Because her job as head cook and her family responsibilities keep her busy during the day, she plans to get a high school equivalency diploma. She will study for, and take, the GED tests. Every year, about half a million adults earn their high school credentials this way. A GED diploma is accepted in lieu of a high school one by more than 90 percent of employers, colleges, and universities, so it is a good choice for someone like Alice.

The GED testing program is sponsored by the American Council on Education and State and local education departments. It consists of examinations in five subject areas: Writing, science, mathematics, social studies, and literature and the arts. The tests also measure skills such as analytical ability, problem solving, reading comprehension, and ability to understand and apply information. Most of the questions are multiple choice; the writing test includes an essay section on a topic of general interest.

Eligibility rules for taking the exams vary, but some states require that you must be at least 18. Tests are given in English, Spanish, and French. In addition to standard print, versions in large print, Braille, and audiocassette are also available. Total time allotted for the tests is 7 1/2 hours.

The GED tests are not easy. About one-fourth of those who complete the exams every year do not pass. Passing scores are established by administering the tests to a sample of graduating high school seniors. The minimum standard score is set so that about one-third of graduating seniors would not pass the tests if they took them.

Because of the difficulty of the tests, people need to prepare themselves to take them. Often, they start by taking the Official GED Practice Tests, usually available through a local adult education center. Centers are listed in your phone book's blue pages under "Adult Education," "Continuing Education," or "GED." Adult education centers also have information about GED preparation classes and self-study materials. Classes are generally arranged to accommodate adults' work schedules. National Learning Corporation publishes several study guides that aim to thoroughly prepare test-takers for the GED.

School districts, colleges, adult education centers, and community organizations have information about GED testing schedules and practice tests. For more information, contact them, your nearest GED testing center, or:

GED Testing Service
One Dupont Circle, NW, Suite 250
Washington, DC 20036-1163
1(800) 62-MY GED (626-9433)
(202) 939-9490

Skills Demonstration

Adults who have acquired high school level skills through experience might be eligible for the National External Diploma Program. This alternative to the GED does not involve any direct instruction. Instead, adults seeking a high school diploma must demonstrate mastery of 65 competencies in 8 general areas: Communication; computation; occupational preparedness; and self, social, consumer, scientific, and technological awareness.

Mastery is shown through the completion of the tasks. For example, a participant could prove competency in computation by measuring a room for carpeting, figuring out the amount of carpet needed, and computing the cost.

Before being accepted for the program, adults undergo an evaluation. Tests taken at one of the program's offices measure reading, writing, and mathematics abilities. A take-home segment includes a self-assessment of current skills, an individual skill evaluation, and an occupational interest and aptitude test.

Adults accepted for the program have weekly meetings with an assessor. At the meeting, the assessor reviews the participant's work from the previous week. If the task has not been completed properly, the assessor explains the mistake. Participants continue to correct their errors until they master each competency. A high school diploma is awarded upon proven mastery of all 65 competencies.

Fourteen States and the District of Columbia now offer the External Diploma Program. For more information, contact:

External Diploma Program
One Dupont Circle, NW, Suite 250
Washington, DC 20036-1193
(202) 939-9475

Correspondence and Distance Study
Vin dropped out of high school during his junior year because his family's frequent moves made it difficult for him to continue his studies. He promised himself at the time he dropped out that he would someday finish the courses needed for his diploma. For people like Vin, who prefer to earn a traditional diploma in a nontraditional way, there are about a dozen accredited courses of study for earning a high school diploma by correspondence, or distance study. The programs are either privately run, affiliated with a university, or administered by a State education department.

Distance study diploma programs have no residency requirements, allowing students to continue their studies from almost any location. Depending on the course of study, students need not be enrolled full time and usually have more flexible schedules for finishing their work. Selection of courses ranges from vo-tech to college prep, and some programs place different emphasis on the types of diplomas offered. University affiliated schools, for example, allow qualified students to take college courses along with their high school ones. Students can then apply the college credits toward a degree at that university or transfer them to another institution.

Taking courses by distance study is often more challenging and time consuming than attending classes, especially for adults who have other obligations. Success depends on each student's motivation. Students usually do reading assignments on their own. Written exercises, which they complete and send to an instructor for grading, supplement their reading material.

A list of some accredited high schools that offer diplomas by distance study is available free from the Distance Education and Training Council, formerly known as the National Home Study Council. Request the "DETC Directory of Accredited Institutions" from:

The Distance Education and Training Council
1601 18th Street, NW.
Washington, DC 20009-2529
(202) 234-5100

Some publications profiling nontraditional college programs include addresses and descriptions of several high school correspondence ones. See the Resources section at the end of this article for more information.

Getting College Credit For What You Know
Adults can receive college credit for prior coursework, by passing examinations, and documenting experiential learning. With help from a college advisor, nontraditional students should assess their skills, establish their educational goals, and determine the number of college credits they might be eligible for.

Even before you meet with a college advisor, you should collect all your school and training records. Then, make a list of all knowledge and abilities acquired through experience, no matter how irrelevant they seem to your chosen field. Next, determine your educational goals: What specific field do you wish to study? What kind of a degree do you want? Finally, determine how your past work fits into the field of study. Later on, you will evaluate educational programs to find one that's right for you.

People who have complex educational or experiential learning histories might want to have their learning evaluated by the Regents Credit Bank. The Credit Bank, operated by Regents College of the University of the State of New York, allows people to consolidate credits earned through college, experience, or other methods. Special assessments are available for Regents College enrollees whose knowledge in a specific field cannot be adequately evaluated by standardized exams. For more information, contact the Regents Credit Bank at:

Regents College
7 Columbia Circle
Albany, NY 12203-5159
(518) 464-8500

Credit For Prior College Coursework

When Lynette was in college during the 1970s, she attended several different schools and took a variety of courses. She did well in some classes and poorly in others. Now that she is a successful business owner and has more focus, Lynette thinks she should forget about her previous coursework and start from scratch. Instead, she should start from where she is.

Lynette should have all her transcripts sent to the colleges or universities of her choice and let an admissions officer determine which classes are applicable toward a degree. A few credits here and there may not seem like much, but they add up. Even if the subjects do not seem relevant to any major, they might be counted as elective credits toward a degree. And comparing the cost of transcripts with the cost of college courses, it makes sense to spend a few dollars per transcript for a chance to save hundreds, and perhaps thousands, of dollars in books and tuition.

Rules for transferring credits apply to all prior coursework at accredited colleges and universities, whether done on campus or off. Courses completed off campus, often called extended learning, include those available to students through independent study and correspondence. Many schools have extended learning programs; Brigham Young University, for example, offers more than 300 courses through its Department of Independent Study. One type of extended learning is distance learning, a form of correspondence study by technological means such as television, video and audio, CD-ROM, electronic mail, and computer tutorials. See the Resources section at the end of this article for more information about publications available from the National University Continuing Education Association.

Any previously earned college credits should be considered for transfer, no matter what the subject or the grade received. Many schools do not accept the transfer of courses graded below a C or ones taken more than a designated number of years ago. Some colleges and universities also have limits on the number of credits that can be transferred and applied toward a degree. But not all do. For example, Thomas Edison State College, New Jersey's State college for adults, accepts the transfer of all 120 hours of credit required for a baccalaureate degree – provided all the credits are transferred from regionally accredited schools, no more than 80 are at the junior college level, and the student's grades overall and in the field of study average out to C.

To assign credit for prior coursework, most schools require original transcripts. This means you must complete a form or send a written, signed request to have your transcripts released directly to a college or university. Once you have chosen the schools you want to apply to, contact the schools you attended before. Find out how much each transcript costs, and ask them to send your transcripts to the ones you are applying to. Write a letter that includes your name (and names used during attendance, if different) and dates of attendance, along with the names and addresses of the schools to which your transcripts should be sent. Include payment and mail to the registrar at the schools you have attended. The registrar's office will process your request and send an official transcript of your coursework to the colleges or universities you have designated.

Credit For Noncollege Courses

Colleges and universities are not the only ones that offer classes. Volunteer organizations and employers often provide formal training worth college credit. The American Council on Education has two programs that assess thousands of specific courses and make recommendations on the amount of college credit they are worth. Colleges and universities accept the recommendations or use them as guidelines.

One program evaluates educational courses sponsored by government agencies, business and industry, labor unions, and professional and voluntary organizations. It is the Program on Noncollegiate Sponsored Instruction (PONSI). Some of the training seminars Alice has participated in covered topics such as food preparation, kitchen safety, and nutrition. Although she has not yet earned her GED, Alice can earn college credit because of her completion of these formal job-training seminars. The number of credits each seminar is worth does not hinge on Alice's current eligibility for college enrollment.

The other program evaluates courses offered by the Army, Navy, Air Force, Marines, Coast Guard, and Department of Defense. It is the Military Evaluations Program. Jorge has never attended college, but the engineering technology classes he completed as part of his military training are worth college credit. And as an Army veteran, Jorge is eligible for a service that takes the evaluations one step further. The Army/American Council on Education Registry Transcript System (AARTS) will provide Jorge with an individualized transcript of American Council on Education credit recommendations for all courses he completed, the military occupational specialties (MOS's) he held, and examinations he passed while in the Army. All Army and National Guard enlisted personnel and veterans who enlisted after October 1981 are eligible for the transcript. Similar services are being considered by the Navy and Marine Corps.

To obtain a free transcript, see your Army Education Center for a 5454R transcript request form. Include your name, Social Security number, basic active service date, and complete address where you want the transcript sent. Mail your request to:
AARTS Operations Center
415 McPherson Ave.
Fort Leavenworth, KS 66027-1373

Recommendations for PONSI are published in *The National Guide to Educational Credit for Training Programs;* military program recommendations are in *The Guide to the Evaluation of Educational Experiences in the Armed Forces.* See the Resources section at the end of this article for more information about these publications.

Former military personnel who took a foreign language course through the Defense Language Institute may request course transcripts by sending their name, Social Security number, course title, duration of the course, and graduation date to:

    Commandant, Defense Language Institute
    Attn: ATFL-DAA-AR
    Transcripts
    Presidio of Monterey
    Monterey, CA 93944-5006

Not all of Jorge's and Alice's courses have been assessed by the American Council on Education. Training courses that have no Council credit recommendation should still be assessed by an advisor at the schools they want to attend. Course descriptions, class notes, test scores, and other documentation may be helpful for comparing training courses to their college equivalents. An oral examination or other demonstration of competency might also be required.

There is no guarantee you will receive all the credits you are seeking – but you certainly won't if you make no attempt.

Credit By Examination

Standardized tests are the best-known method of receiving college credit without taking courses. These exams are often taken by high school students seeking advanced placement for college, but they are also available to adult learners. Testing programs and colleges and universities offer exams in a number of subjects. Two U.S. Government institutes have foreign language exams for employees that also may be worth college credit.

It is important to understand that receiving a passing score on these exams does not mean you get college credit automatically. Each school determines which test results it will accept, minimum scores required, how scores are converted for credit, and the amount of credit, if any, to be assigned. Most colleges and universities accept the American Council on Education credit recommendations, published every other year in the 250-page *Guide to Educational Credit by Examination*. For more information, contact:

    The American Council on Education
    Credit by Examination Program
    One Dupont Circle, Suite 250
    Washington, DC 20036-1193
    (202) 939-9434

Testing programs:

You might know some of the five national testing programs by their acronyms or initials: CLEP, ACT PEP: RCE, DANTES, AP, and NOCTI. (The meanings of these initialisms are explained below.) There is some overlap among programs; for example, four of them have introductory accounting exams. Since you will not be awarded credit more than once for a specific subject, you should carefully evaluate each program for the subject exams you wish to take. And before taking an exam, make sure you will be awarded credit by the college or university you plan to attend.

CLEP (College-Level Examination Program), administered by the College Board, is the most widely accepted of the national testing programs; more than 2,800 accredited schools award credit for passing exam scores. Each test covers material taught in basic undergraduate courses. There are five general exams – English composition, humanities, college mathematics, natural sciences, and social sciences and history – and many subject exams. Most exams are entirely multiple-choice, but English composition exams may include an essay section. For more information, contact:

    CLEP
    P.O. Box 6600
    Princeton, NJ 08541-6600
    (609) 771-7865

ACT PEP: RCE (American College Testing Proficiency Exam Program: Regents College Examinations) tests are given in 38 subjects within arts and sciences, business, education, and nursing. Each exam is recommended for either lower- or upper-level credit. Exams contain either objective or extended response questions, and are graded according to a standard score, letter grade, or pass/fail. Fees vary, depending on the subject and type of exam. For more information or to request free study guides, contact:

    ACT PEP: Regents College Examinations
    P.O. Box 4014
    Iowa City, IA 52243
    (319) 337-1387
    (New York State residents must contact Regents College directly.)

DANTES (Defense Activity for Nontraditional Education Support) standardized tests are developed by the Educational Testing Service for the Department of Defense. Originally administered only to military personnel, the exams have been available to the public since 1983. About 50 subject tests cover business, mathematics, social science, physical science, humanities, foreign languages, and applied technology. Most of the tests consist entirely of multiple-choice questions. Schools determine their own administering fees and testing schedules. For more information or to request free study sheets, contact:

    DANTES Program Office
    Mail Stop 31-X
    Educational Testing Service
    Princeton, NJ 08541
    1(800) 257-9484

The AP (Advanced Placement) Program is a cooperative effort between secondary schools and colleges and universities. AP exams are developed each year by committees of college and high school faculty appointed by the College Board and assisted by consultants from the Educational Testing Service. Subjects include arts and languages, natural sciences, computer science, social sciences, history, and mathematics. Most tests are 2 or 3 hours long and include both multiple-choice and essay questions. AP courses are available to help students prepare for exams, which are offered in the spring. For more information about the Advanced Placement Program, contact:

    Advanced Placement Services
    P.O. Box 6671
    Princeton, NJ 08541-6671
    (609) 771-7300

NOCTI (National Occupational Competency Testing Institute) assessments are designed for people like Alice, who have vocational-technical skills that cannot be evaluated by other tests. NOCTI assesses competency at two levels: Student/job ready and teacher/experienced worker. Standardized evaluations are available for occupations such as auto-body repair, electronics, mechanical drafting, quantity food preparation, and upholstering. The tests consist of multiple-choice questions and a performance component. Other services include workshops, customized assessments, and pre-testing. For more information, contact:

NOCTI
500 N. Bronson Ave.
Ferris State University
Big Rapids, MI 49307
(616) 796-4699

Colleges and universities:

Many colleges and universities have credit-by-exam programs, through which students earn credit by passing a comprehensive exam for a course offered by the institution. Among the most widely recognized are the programs at Ohio University, the University of North Carolina, Thomas Edison State College, and New York University.

Ohio University offers about 150 examinations for credit. In addition, you may sometimes arrange to take special examinations in non-laboratory courses offered at Ohio University. To take a test for credit, you must enroll in the course. If you plan to transfer the credit earned, you also need written permission from an official at your school. Books and study materials are available, for a cost, through the university. Exams must be taken within 6 months of the enrollment date; most last 3 hours. You may arrange to take the exam off campus if you do not live near the university.

Ohio University is on the quarter-hour system; most courses are worth 4 quarter hours, the equivalent of 3 semester hours. For more information, contact:

Independent Study
Tupper Hall 302
Ohio University
Athens, OH 45701-2979
1(800) 444-2910
(614) 593-2910

The University of North Carolina offers a credit-by-examination option for 140 independent study (correspondence) courses in foreign languages, humanities, social sciences, mathematics, business administration, education, electrical and computer engineering, health administration, and natural sciences. To take an exam, you must request and receive approval from both the course instructor and the independent studies department. Exams must be taken within six months of enrollment, and you may register for no more than two at a time. If you are not near the University's Chapel Hill campus, you may take your exam under supervision at an accredited college, university, community college, or technical institute. For more information, contact:

Independent Studies
CB #1020, The Friday Center
UNC-Chapel Hill
Chapel Hill, NC 27599-1020
1(800) 862-5669 / (919) 962-1134

The Thomas Edison College Examination Program offers more than 50 exams in liberal arts, business, and professional areas. Thomas Edison State College administers tests twice a month in Trenton, New Jersey; however, students may arrange to take their tests with a proctor at any accredited American college or university or U.S. military base. Most of the tests are multiple choice; some also include short answer or essay questions. Time limits range from 90 minutes to 4 hours, depending on the exam. For more information, contact:

> Thomas Edison State College
> TECEP, Office of Testing and Assessment
> 101 W. State Street
> Trenton, NJ 08608-1176
> (609) 633-2844

New York University's Foreign Language Program offers proficiency exams in more than 40 languages, from Albanian to Yiddish. Two exams are available in each language: The 12-point test is equivalent to 4 undergraduate semesters, and the 16-point exam may lead to upper level credit. The tests are given at the university's Foreign Language Department throughout the year.

Proof of foreign language proficiency does not guarantee college credit. Some colleges and universities accept transcripts only for languages commonly taught, such as French and Spanish. Nontraditional programs are more likely than traditional ones to grant credit for proficiency in other languages.

For an informational brochure and registration form for NYU's foreign language proficiency exams, contact:

> New York University
> Foreign Language Department
> 48 Cooper Square, Room 107
> New York, NY 10003
> (212) 998-7030

Government institutes:

The Defense Language Institute and Foreign Service Institute administer foreign language proficiency exams for personnel stationed abroad. Usually, the tests are given at the end of intensive language courses or upon completion of service overseas. But some people – like Jorge, who knows Spanish – speak another language fluently and may be allowed to take a proficiency exam in that language before completing their tour of duty. Contact one of the offices listed below to obtain transcripts of those scores. Proof of proficiency does not guarantee college credit, however, as discussed above.

To request score reports from the Defense Language Institute for Defense Language Proficiency Tests, send your name, Social Security number, language for which you were tested, and, most importantly, when and where you took the exam to:

> Commandant, Defense Language Institute
> Attn: ATFL-ES-T
> DLPT Score Report Request
> Presidio of Monterey
> Monterey, CA 93944-5006

To request transcripts of scores for Foreign Service Institute exams, send your name, Social Security number, language for which you were tested, and dates or year of exams to:

Foreign Service Institute
Arlington Hall
4020 Arlington Boulevard
Rosslyn, VA 22204-1500
Attn: Testing Office (Send your request to the attention of the testing office of the foreign language in which you were tested)

Credit For Experience

Experiential learning credit may be given for knowledge gained through job responsibilities, personal hobbies, volunteer opportunities, homemaking, and other experiences. Colleges and universities base credit awards on the knowledge you have attained, not for the experience alone. In addition, the knowledge must be college level; not just any learning will do. Throwing horseshoes as a hobby is not likely to be worth college credit. But if you've done research on how and where the sport originated, visited blacksmiths, organized tournaments, and written a column for a trade journal – well, that's a horseshoe of a different color.

Adults attempting to get credit for their experience should be forewarned: Having your experience evaluated for college credit is time-consuming, tedious work – not an easy shortcut for people who want quick-fix college credits. And not all experience, no matter how valuable, is the equivalent of college courses.

Requesting college credit for your experiential learning can be tricky. You should get assistance from a credit evaluations officer at the school you plan to attend, but you should also have a general idea of what your knowledge is worth. A common method for converting knowledge into credit is to use a college catalog. Find course titles and descriptions that match what you have learned through experience, and request the number of credits offered for those courses.

Once you know what credit to ask for, you must usually present your case in writing to officials at the college you plan to attend. The most common form of presenting experiential learning for credit is the portfolio. A portfolio is a written record of your knowledge along with a request for equivalent college credit. It includes an identification and description of the knowledge for which you are requesting credit, an explanatory essay of how the knowledge was gained and how it fits into your educational plans, documentation that you have acquired such knowledge, and a request for college credit. Required elements of a portfolio vary by schools but generally follow those guidelines.

In identifying knowledge you have gained, be specific about exactly what you have learned. For example, it is not enough for Lynette to say she runs a business. She must identify the knowledge she has gained from running it, such as personnel management, tax law, marketing strategy, and inventory review. She must also include brief descriptions about her knowledge of each to support her claims of having those skills.

The essay gives you a chance to relay something about who you are. It should address your educational goals, include relevant autobiographical details, and be well organized, neat, and convey confidence. In his essay, Jorge might first state his goal of becoming an engineer. Then he would explain why he joined the Army, where he got hands-on training and experience in developing and servicing electronic equipment.

This, he would say, led to his hobby of creating remote-controlled model cars, of which he has built 20. His conclusion would highlight his accomplishments and tie them to his desire to become an electronic engineer.

Documentation is evidence that you've learned what you claim to have learned. You can show proof of knowledge in a variety of ways, including audio or video recordings, letters from current or former employers describing your specific duties and job performance, blueprints, photographs or artwork, and transcripts of certifying exams for professional licenses and certification – such as Alice's certification from the American Culinary Federation. Although documentation can take many forms, written proof alone is not always enough. If it is impossible to document your knowledge in writing, find out if your experiential learning can be assessed through supplemental oral exams by a faculty expert.

Earning a College Degree

Nontraditional students often have work, family, and financial obligations that prevent them from quitting their jobs to attend school full time. Can they still meet their educational goals? Yes.

More than 150 accredited colleges and universities have nontraditional bachelor's degree programs that require students to spend little or no time on campus; over 300 others have nontraditional campus-based degree programs. Some of those schools, as well as most junior and community colleges, offer associate's degrees nontraditionally. Each school with a nontraditional course of study determines its own rules for awarding credit for prior coursework, exams, or experience, as discussed previously. Most have charges on top of tuition for providing these special services.

Several publications profile nontraditional degree programs; see the Resources section at the end of this article for more information. To determine which school best fits your academic profile and educational goals, first list your criteria. Then, evaluate nontraditional programs based on their accreditation, features, residency requirements, and expenses. Once you have chosen several schools to explore further, write to them for more information. Detailed explanations of school policies should help you decide which ones you want to apply to.

Get beyond the printed word – especially the glowing words each school writes about itself. Check out the schools you are considering with higher education authorities, alumni, employers, family members, and friends. If possible, visit the campus to talk to students and instructors and sit in on a few classes, even if you will be completing most or all of your work off campus. Ask school officials questions about such things as enrollment numbers, graduation rate, faculty qualifications, and confusing details about the application process or academic policies. After you have thoroughly investigated each prospective college or university, you can make an informed decision about which is right for you.

Accreditation

Accreditation is a process colleges and universities submit to voluntarily for getting their credentials. An accredited school has been investigated and visited by teams of observers and has periodic inspections by a private accrediting agency. The initial review can take two years or more.

Regional agencies accredit entire schools, and professional agencies accredit either specialized schools or departments within schools. Although there are no national accrediting standards, not just any accreditation will do. Countless "accreditation associations" have been invented by schools, many of which have no academic programs and sell phony degrees, to accredit themselves. But 6 regional and about 80 professional accrediting associations in the United States are recognized by the U.S. Department of Education or the Commission on Recognition of Postsecondary Accreditation. When checking accreditation, these are the names to look for. For more information about accreditation and accrediting agencies, contact:

> Institutional Participation Oversight Service Accreditation and State Liaison Division
> U.S. Department of Education
> ROB 3, Room 3915
> 600 Independence Ave., SW
> Washington, DC 20202-5244
> (202) 708-7417

Because accreditation is not mandatory, lack of accreditation does not necessarily mean a school or program is bad. Some schools choose not to apply for accreditation, are in the process of applying, or have educational methods too unconventional for an accrediting association's standards. For the nontraditional student, however, earning a degree from a college or university with recognized accreditation is an especially important consideration. Although nontraditional education is becoming more widely accepted, it is not yet mainstream. Employers skeptical of a degree earned in a nontraditional manner are likely to be even less accepting of one from an unaccredited school.

Program Features

Because nontraditional students have diverse educational objectives, nontraditional schools are diverse in what they offer. Some programs are geared toward helping students organize their scattered educational credits to get a degree as quickly as possible. Others cater to those who may have specific credits or experience but need assistance in completing requirements. Whatever your educational profile, you should look for a program that works with you in obtaining your educational goals.

A few nontraditional programs have special admissions policies for adult learners like Alice, who plan to earn their GEDs but want to enroll in college in the meantime. Other features of nontraditional programs include individualized learning agreements, intensive academic counseling, cooperative learning and internship placement, and waiver of some prerequisites or other requirements – as well as college credit for prior coursework, examinations, and experiential learning, all discussed previously.

Lynette, whose primary goal is to finish her degree, wants to earn maximum credits for her business experience. She will look for programs that do not limit the number of credits awarded for equivalency exams and experiential learning. And since well-documented proof of knowledge is essential for earning experiential learning credits, Lynette should make sure the program she chooses provides assistance to students submitting a portfolio.

Jorge, on the other hand, has more credits than he needs in certain areas and is willing to forego some. To become an engineer, he must have a bachelor's degree; but because he is accustomed to hands-on learning, Jorge is interested in getting experience as he gains more technical skills. He will concentrate on finding schools with strong cooperative education, supervised fieldwork, or internship programs.

Residency Requirements

Programs are sometimes deemed nontraditional because of their residency requirements. Many people think of residency for colleges and universities in terms of tuition, with in-state students paying less than out-of-state ones. Residency also may refer to where a student lives, either on or off campus, while attending school.

But in nontraditional education, residency usually refers to how much time students must spend on campus, regardless of whether they attend classes there. In some nontraditional programs, students need not ever step foot on campus. Others require only a very short residency, such as one day or a few weeks. Many schools have standard residency requirements of several semesters but schedule classes for evenings or weekends to accommodate working adults.

Lynette, who previously took courses by independent study, prefers to earn credits by distance study. She will focus on schools that have no residency requirement. Several colleges and universities have nonresident degree completion programs for adults with some college credit. Under the direction of a faculty advisor, students devise a plan for earning their remaining credits. Methods for earning credits include independent study, distance learning, seminars, supervised fieldwork, and group study at arranged sites. Students may have to earn a certain number of credits through the degree-granting institution. But many programs allow students to take courses at accredited schools of their choice for transfer toward their degree.

Alice wants to attend lectures but has an unpredictable schedule. Her best course of action will be to seek out short residency programs that require students to attend seminars once or twice a semester. She can take courses that are televised and videotape them to watch when her schedule permits, with the seminars helping to ensure that she properly completes her coursework. Many colleges and universities with short residency requirements also permit students to earn some credits elsewhere, by whatever means the student chooses.

Some fields of study require classroom instruction. As Jorge will discover, few colleges and universities allow students to earn a bachelor's degree in engineering entirely through independent study. Nontraditional residency programs are designed to accommodate adults' daytime work schedules. Jorge should look for programs offering evening, weekend, summer, and accelerated courses.

Tuition and Other Expenses

The final decisions about which schools Alice, Jorge, and Lynette attend may hinge in large part on a single issue: Cost. And rising tuition is only part of the equation. Beginning with application fees and continuing through graduation fees, college expenses add up.

Traditional and nontraditional students have some expenses in common, such as the cost of books and other materials. Tuition might even be the same for some courses, especially for colleges and universities offering standard ones at unusual times. But for nontraditional programs, students may also pay fees for services such as credit or transcript review, evaluation, advisement, and portfolio assessment.

Students are also responsible for postage and handling or setup expenses for independent study courses, as well as for all examination and transcript fees for transferring credits. Usually, the more nontraditional the program, the more detailed the fees. Some schools charge a yearly enrollment fee rather than tuition for degree completion candidates who want their files to remain active.

Although tuition and fees might seem expensive, most educators tell you not to let money come between you and your educational goals. Talk to someone in the financial aid department of the school you plan to attend or check your library for publications about financial aid sources. The U.S. Department of Education publishes a guide to Federal aid programs such as Pell Grants, student loans, and work-study. To order the free 74-page booklet, *The Student Guide: Financial Aid from the U.S. Department of Education,* contact:

Federal Student Aid Information Center
P.O. Box 84
Washington, DC 20044
1 (800) 4FED-AID (433-3243)

Resources

Information on how to earn a high school diploma or college degree without following the usual routes is available from several organizations and in numerous publications. Information on nontraditional graduate degree programs, available for master's through doctoral level, though not discussed in this article, can usually be obtained from the same resources that detail bachelor's degree programs.

National Learning Corporation publishes study guides for all of these exams, for both general examinations and tests in specific subject areas. To order study guides, or to browse their catalog featuring more than 5,000 titles, visit NLC online at www.passbooks.com, or contact them by phone at (800) 632-8888.

Organizations

Adult learners should always contact their local school system, community college, or university to learn about programs that are readily available. The following national organizations can also supply information:

American Council on Education
One Dupont Circle
Washington, DC 20036-1193
(202) 939-9300

Within the American Council on Education, the Center for Adult Learning and Educational Credentials administers the National External Diploma Program, the GED Program, the Program on Noncollegiate Sponsored Instruction, the Credit by Examination Program, and the Military Evaluations Program.

College-Level Examination Program (CLEP)

1. WHAT IS CLEP?

CLEP stands for the College-Level Examination Program, sponsored by the College Board. It is a national program of credit-by-examination that offers you the opportunity to obtain recognition for college-level achievement. No matter when, where, or how you have learned – by means of formal or informal study – you can take CLEP tests. If the results are acceptable to your college, you can receive credit.

You may not realize it, but you probably know more than your academic record reveals. Each day you, like most people, have an opportunity to learn. In private industry and business, as well as at all levels of government, learning opportunities continually occur. If you read widely or intensively in a particular field, think about what you read, discuss it with your family and friends, you are learning. Or you may be learning on a more formal basis by taking a correspondence course, a television or radio course, a course recorded on tape or cassettes, a course assembled into programmed tests, or a course taught in your community adult school or high school.

No matter how, where, or when you gained your knowledge, you may have the opportunity to receive academic credit for your achievement that can be counted toward an undergraduate degree. The College-Level Examination Program (CLEP) enables colleges to evaluate your achievement and give you credit. A wide range of college-level examinations are offered by CLEP to anyone who wishes to take them. Scores on the tests are reported to you and, if you wish, to a college, employer, or individual.

2. WHAT ARE THE PURPOSES OF THE COLLEGE-LEVEL EXAMINATION PROGRAM?

The basic purpose of the College-Level Examination Program is to enable individuals who have acquired their education in nontraditional ways to demonstrate their academic achievement. It is also intended for use by those in higher education, business, industry, government, and other fields who need a reliable method of assessing a person's educational level.

Recognizing that the real issue is not how a person has acquired his education but what education he has, the College Level Examination Program has been designed to serve a variety of purposes. The basic purpose, as listed above, is to enable those who have reached the college level of education in nontraditional ways to assess the level of their achievement and to use the test results in seeking college credit or placement.

In addition, scores on the tests can be used to validate educational experience obtained at a nonaccredited institution or through noncredit college courses.

Some colleges and universities may use the tests to measure the level of educational achievement of their students, and for various institutional research purposes.

Other colleges and universities may wish to use the tests in the admission, placement, and guidance of students who wish to transfer from one institution to another.

Businesses, industries, governmental agencies, and professional groups now accept the results of these tests as a basis for advancement, eligibility for further training, or professional or semi-professional certification.

Many people are interested in the examination simply to assess their own educational progress and attainment.

The college, university, business, industry, or government agency that adopts the tests in the College-Level Examination Program makes its own decision about how it will use and interpret the test scores. The College Board will provide the tests, score them, and report the results either to the individuals who took the tests or the college or agency that administered them. It does NOT, and cannot, award college credit, certify college equivalency, or make recommendations regarding the standards these institutions should establish for the use of the test results.

Therefore, if you are taking the tests to secure credit from an institution, you should FIRST ascertain whether the college or agency involved will accept the scores. Each institution determines which CLEP tests it will accept for credit and the amount of credit it will award. If you want to take tests for college credit, first call, write, or visit the college you wish to attend to inquire about its policy on CLEP scores, as well as its other admission requirements.

The services of the program are also available to people who have been requested to take the tests by an employer, a professional licensing agency, a certifying agency, or by other groups that recognize college equivalency on the basis of satisfactory CLEP scores. You may, of course, take the tests SOLELY for your own information. If you do, your scores will be reported only to you.

While neither CLEP nor the College Board can evaluate previous credentials or award college credit, you will receive, with your scores, basic information to help you interpret your performance on the tests you have taken.

3. WHAT ARE THE COLLEGE-LEVEL EXAMINATIONS?

In order to meet different kinds of curricular organization and testing needs at colleges and universities, the College-Level Examination Program offers 35 different subject tests falling under five separate general categories: Composition and Literature, Foreign Languages, History and Social Sciences, Science and Mathematics, and Business.

4. WHAT ARE THE SUBJECT EXAMINATIONS?

The 35 CLEP tests offered by the College Board are listed below:

COMPOSITION AND LITERATURE:
- American Literature
- Analyzing and Interpreting Literature
- English Composition
- English Composition with Essay
- English Literature
- Freshman College Composition
- Humanities

FOREIGN LANGUAGES
- French
- German
- Spanish

HISTORY AND SOCIAL SCIENCES
- American Government
- Introduction to Educational Psychology
- History of the United States I: Early Colonization to 1877
- History of the United States II: 1865 to the Present
- Human Growth and Development
- Principles of Macroeconomics
- Principles of Microeconomics
- Introductory Psychology
- Social Sciences and History
- Introductory Sociology
- Western Civilization I: Ancient Near East to 1648
- Western Civilization II: 1648 to the Present

SCIENCE AND MATHEMATICS
- College Algebra
- College Algebra-Trigonometry
- Biology
- Calculus
- Chemistry
- College Mathematics
- Natural Sciences
- Trigonometry
- Precalculus

BUSINESS
- Financial Accounting
- Introductory Business Law
- Information Systems and Computer Applications
- Principles of Management
- Principles of Marketing

CLEP Examinations cover material taught in courses that most students take as requirements in the first two years of college. A college usually grants the same amount of credit to students earning satisfactory scores on the CLEP examination as it grants to students successfully completing the equivalent course.

Many examinations are designed to correspond to one-semester courses; some, however, correspond to full-year or two-year courses.

Each exam is 90 minutes long and, except for English Composition with Essay, is made up primarily of multiple-choice questions. Some tests have several other types of questions besides multiple choice. To see a more detailed description of a particular CLEP exam, visit www.collegeboard.com/clep.

The English Composition with Essay exam is the only exam that includes a required essay. This essay is scored by college English faculty designated by CLEP and does not require an additional fee. However, other Composition and Literature tests offer optional essays, which some college and universities require and some do not. These essays are graded by faculty at the individual institutions that require them and require an additional $10 fee. Contact the particular institution to ask about essay requirements, and check with your test center for further details.

All 35 CLEP examinations are administered on computer. If you are unfamiliar with taking a test on a computer, consult the CLEP Sampler online at www.collegeboard.com/clep. The Sampler contains the same tutorials as the actual exams and helps familiarize you with navigation and how to answer different types of questions.

Points are not deducted for wrong or skipped answers – you receive one point for every correct answer. Therefore it is best that an answer is supplied for each exam question, whether it is a guess or not. The number of correct answers is then converted to a formula score. This formula, or "scaled," score is determined by a statistical process called *equating*, which adjusts for slight differences in difficulty between test forms and ensures that your score does not depend on the specific test form you took or how well others did on the same form. The scaled scores range from 20 to 80 – this is the number that will appear on your score report.

To ensure that you complete all questions in the time allotted, you would probably be wise to skip the more difficult or perplexing questions and return to them later. Although the multiple-choice items in these tests are carefully designed so as not to be tricky, misleading, or ambiguous, on the other hand, they are not all direct questions of factual information. They attempt, in their way, to elicit a response that indicates your knowledge or lack of knowledge of the material in question or your ability or inability to use or interpret a fact or idea. Thus, you should concentrate on answering the questions as they appear to be without attempting to out-guess the testmakers.

5. WHAT ARE THE FEES?

The fee for all CLEP examinations is $55. Optional essays required by some institutions are an additional $10.

6. WHEN ARE THE TESTS GIVEN?

CLEP tests are administered year-round. Consult the CLEP website (www.collegeboard.com/clep) and individual test centers for specific information.

7. WHERE ARE THE TESTS GIVEN?

More than 1,300 test centers are located on college and university campuses throughout the country, and additional centers are being established to meet increased needs. Any accredited collegiate institution with an explicit and publicly available policy of credit by examination can become a CLEP test center. To obtain a list of these centers, visit the CLEP website at www.collegeboard.com/clep.

8. HOW DO I REGISTER FOR THE COLLEGE-LEVEL EXAMINATION PROGRAM?

Contact an individual test center for information regarding registration, scheduling and fees. Registration/admission forms can also be obtained on the CLEP website.

9. MAY I REPEAT THE COLLEGE-LEVEL EXAMINATIONS?

You may repeat any examination providing at least six months have passed since you were last administered this test. If you repeat a test within a period of time less than six months, your scores will be cancelled and your fees forfeited. To repeat a test, check the appropriate space on the registration form.

10. WHEN MAY I EXPECT MY SCORE REPORTS?

With the exception of the English Composition with Essay exam, you should receive your score report instantly once the test is complete.

11. HOW SHOULD I PREPARE FOR THE COLLEGE-LEVEL EXAMINATIONS?

This book has been specifically designed to prepare candidates for these examinations. It will help you to consider, study, and review important content, principles, practices, procedures, problems, and techniques in the form of varied and concrete applications.

12. QUESTIONS AND ANSWERS APPEARING IN THIS PUBLICATION

The College-Level Examinations are offered by the College Board. Since copies of past examinations have not been made available, we have used equivalent materials, including questions and answers, which are highly recommended by us as an appropriate means of preparing for these examinations.

If you need additional information about CLEP Examinations, visit www.collegeboard.com/clep.

THE COLLEGE-LEVEL EXAMINATION PROGRAM

How The Program Works

CLEP examinations are administered at many colleges and universities across the country, and most institutions award college credit to those who do well on them. The examinations provide people who have acquired knowledge outside the usual educational settings the opportunity to show that they have learned college-level material without taking certain college courses.

The CLEP examinations cover material that is taught in introductory-level courses at many colleges and universities. Faculties at individual colleges review the tests to ensure that they cover the important material taught in their courses. Colleges differ in the examinations they accept; some colleges accept only two or three of the examinations while others accept nearly all of them.

Although CLEP is sponsored by the College Board and the examinations are scored by Educational Testing Service (ETS), neither of these organizations can award college credit. Only accredited colleges may grant credit toward a degree. When you take a CLEP examination, you may request that a copy of your score report be sent to the college you are attending or plan to attend. After evaluating your scores, the college will decide whether or not to award you credit for a certain course or courses, or to exempt you from them. If the college gives you credit, it will record the number of credits on your permanent record, thereby indicating that you have completed work equivalent to a course in that subject. If the college decides to grant exemption without giving you credit for a course, you will be permitted to omit a course that would normally be required of you and to take a course of your choice instead.

What the Examinations Are Like

The examinations consist mostly of multiple-choice questions to be answered within a 90-minute time limit. Additional information about each CLEP examination is given in the examination guide and on the CLEP website.

Where To Take the Examinations

CLEP examinations are administered throughout the year at the test centers of approximately 1,300 colleges and universities. On the CLEP website, you will find a list of institutions that award credit for satisfactory scores on CLEP examinations. Some colleges administer CLEP examinations to their own students only. Other institutions administer the tests to anyone who registers to take them. If your college does not administer the tests, contact the test centers in your area for information about its testing schedule.

Once you have been tested, your score report will be available instantly. CLEP scores are kept on file at ETS for 20 years; and during this period, for a small fee, you may have your transcript sent to another college or to anyone else you specify. (Your scores will never be sent to anyone without your approval.)

APPROACHING A COLLEGE ABOUT CLEP

The following sections provide a step-by-step approach to learning about the CLEP policy at a particular college or university. The person or office that can best assist students desiring CLEP credit may have a different title at each institution, but the following guidelines will lead you to information about CLEP at any institution.

Adults returning to college often benefit from special assistance when they approach a college. Opportunities for adults to return to formal learning in the classroom are now widespread, and colleges and universities have worked hard to make this a smooth process for older students. Many colleges have established special service offices that are staffed with trained professionals who understand the kinds of problems facing adults returning to college. If you think you might benefit from such assistance, be sure to find out whether these services are available at your college.

How to Apply for College Credit

STEP 1. Obtain the General Information Catalog and a copy of the CLEP policy from the colleges you are considering. If you have not yet applied for admission, ask for an admissions application form too.

Information about admissions and CLEP policies can be obtained by contacting college admissions offices or finding admissions information on the school websites. Tell the admissions officer that you are a prospective student and that you are interested in applying for admission and CLEP credit. Ask for a copy of the publication in which the college's complete CLEP policy is explained. Also get the name and the telephone number of the person to contact in case you have further questions about CLEP.

At this step, you may wish to obtain information from external degree colleges. Many adults find that such colleges suit their needs exceptionally well.

STEP 2. If you have not already been admitted to the college you are considering, look at its admission requirements for undergraduate students to see if you can qualify.

This is an important step because if you can't get into college, you can't get college credit for CLEP. Nearly all colleges require students to be admitted and to enroll in one or more courses before granting the students CLEP credit.

Virtually all public community colleges and a number of four-year state colleges have open admission policies for in-state students. This usually means that they admit anyone who has graduated from high school or has earned a high school equivalency diploma.

If you think you do not meet the admission requirements, contact the admissions office for an interview with a counselor. Colleges do sometimes make exceptions, particularly for adult applicants. State why you want the interview and ask what documents you should bring with you or send in advance. (These materials may include a high school transcript, transcript of previous college work, completed application for admission, etc.) Make an extra effort to have all the information requested in time for the interview.

During the interview, relax and be yourself. Be prepared to state honestly why you think you are ready and able to do college work. If you have already taken CLEP examinations and scored high enough to earn credit, you have shown that you are able to do college work. Mention this achievement to the admissions counselor because it may increase your chances of being accepted. If you have not taken a CLEP examination, you can still improve your chances of being accepted by describing how your job training or independent study has helped prepare you for college-level work. Tell the counselor what you have learned from your work and personal experiences.

STEP 3. Evaluate the college's CLEP policy.

Typically, a college lists all its academic policies, including CLEP policies, in its general catalog. You will probably find the CLEP policy statement under a heading such as Credit-by-Examination, Advanced Standing, Advanced Placement, or External Degree Program. These sections can usually be found in the front of the catalog.

Many colleges publish their credit-by-examination policies in a separate brochure, which is distributed through the campus testing office, counseling center, admissions office, or registrar's office. If you find a very general policy statement in the college catalog, seek clarification from one of these offices.

Review the material in the section of this guide entitled Questions to Ask About a College's CLEP Policy. Use these guidelines to evaluate the college's CLEP policy. If you have not yet taken a CLEP examination, this evaluation will help you decide which examinations to take and whether or not to take the free-response or essay portion. Because individual colleges have different CLEP policies, a review of several policies may help you decide which college to attend.

STEP 4. If you have not yet applied for admission, do so early.

Most colleges expect you to apply for admission several months before you enroll, and it is essential that you meet the published application deadlines. It takes time to process your application for admission; and if you have yet to take a CLEP examination, it will be some time before the college receives and reviews your score report. You will probably want to take some, if not all, of the CLEP examinations you are interested in before you enroll so you know which courses you need not register for. In fact, some colleges require that all CLEP scores be submitted before a student registers.

Complete all forms and include all documents requested with your application(s) for admission. Normally, an admissions decision cannot be reached until all documents have been submitted and evaluated. Unless told to do so, do not send your CLEP scores until you have been officially admitted.

STEP 5. Arrange to take CLEP examination(s) or to submit your CLEP score(s).

You may want to wait to take your CLEP examinations until you know definitely which college you will be attending. Then you can make sure you are taking tests your college will accept for credit. You will also be able to request that your scores be sent to the college, free of charge, when you take the tests.

If you have already taken CLEP examinations, but did not have a copy of your score report sent to your college, you may request the College Board to send an official transcript at any time for a small fee. Use the Transcript Request Form that was sent to you with your score report. If you do not have the form, you may find it online at www.collegeboard.com/clep.

Your CLEP scores will be evaluated, probably by someone in the admissions office, and sent to the registrar's office to be posted on your permanent record once you are enrolled. Procedures vary from college to college, but the process usually begins in the admissions office.

STEP 6. Ask to receive a written notice of the credit you receive for your CLEP score(s).

A written notice may save you problems later, when you submit your degree plan or file for graduation. In the event that there is a question about whether or not you earned CLEP credit, you will have an official record of what credit was awarded. You may also need this verification of course credit if you go for academic counseling before the credit is posted on your permanent record.

STEP 7. Before you register for courses, seek academic counseling.

A discussion with your academic advisor can prevent you from taking unnecessary courses and can tell you specifically what your CLEP credit will mean to you. This step may be accomplished at the time you enroll. Most colleges have orientation sessions for new students prior to each enrollment period. During orientation, students are usually assigned an academic advisor who then gives them individual help in developing long-range plans and a course schedule for the next semester. In conjunction with this counseling, you may be asked to take some additional tests so that you can be placed at the proper course level.

External Degree Programs

If you have acquired a considerable amount of college-level knowledge through job experience, reading, or noncredit courses, if you have accumulated college credits at a variety of colleges over a period of years, or if you prefer studying on your own rather than in a classroom setting, you may want to investigate the possibility of enrolling in an external degree program. Many colleges offer external degree programs that allow you to earn a degree by passing examinations (including CLEP), transferring credit from other colleges, and demonstrating in other ways that you have satisfied the educational requirements. No classroom attendance is required, and the programs are open to out-of-state candidates as well as residents. Thomas A. Edison State College in New Jersey and Charter Oaks College in Connecticut are fully accredited independent state colleges; the New York program is part of the state university system and is also fully accredited. If you are interested in exploring an external degree, you can write for more information to:

Charter Oak College
The Exchange, Suite 171
270 Farmington Avenue
Farmington, CT 06032-1909

Regents External Degree Program
Cultural Education Center
Empire State Plaza
Albany, New York 12230

Thomas A. Edison State College
101 West State Street
Trenton, New Jersey 08608

Many other colleges also have external degree or weekend programs. While they often require that a number of courses be taken on campus, the external degree programs tend to be more flexible in transferring credit, granting credit-by-examination, and allowing independent study than other traditional programs. When applying to a college, you may wish to ask whether it has an external degree or weekend program.

Questions to Ask About a College's CLEP Policy

Before taking CLEP examinations for the purpose of earning college credit, try to find the answers to these questions:

1. Which CLEP examinations are accepted by this college?

A college may accept some CLEP examinations for credit and not others - possibly not the one you are considering. The English faculty may decide to grant college English credit based on the CLEP English Composition examination, but not on the Freshman College Composition examination. Or, the mathematics faculty may decide to grant credit based on the College Mathematics to non-mathematics majors only, requiring majors to take an examination in algebra, trigonometry, or calculus to earn credit. For these reasons, it is important that you know the specific CLEP tests for which you can receive credit.

2. Does the college require the optional free-response (essay) section as well as the objective portion of the CLEP examination you are considering?

Knowing the answer to this question ahead of time will permit you to schedule the optional essay examination when you register to take your CLEP examination.

3. Is credit granted for specific courses? If so, which ones?

You are likely to find that credit will be granted for specific courses and the course titles will be designated in the college's CLEP policy. It is not necessary, however, that credit be granted for a specific course in order for you to benefit from your CLEP credit. For instance, at many liberal arts colleges, all students must take certain types of courses; these courses may be labeled the core curriculum, general education requirements, distribution requirements, or liberal arts requirements. The requirements are often expressed in terms of credit hours. For example, all students may be required to take at least six hours of humanities, six hours of English, three hours of mathematics, six hours of natural science, and six hours of social science, with no particular courses in these disciplines specified. In these instances, CLEP credit may be given as 6 hrs. English credit or 3 hrs. Math credit without specifying for which English or mathematics courses credit has been awarded. In order to avoid possible disappointment, you should know before taking a CLEP examination what type of credit you can receive and whether you will only be exempted from a required course but receive no credit.

4. How much credit is granted for each examination you are considering, and does the college place a limit on the total amount of CLEP credit you can earn toward your degree?

Not all colleges that grant CLEP credit award the same amount for individual tests. Furthermore, some colleges place a limit on the total amount of credit you can earn through CLEP or other examinations. Other colleges may grant you exemption but no credit toward your degree. Knowing several colleges' policies concerning these issues may help you decide which college you will attend. If you think you are capable of passing a number of CLEP examinations, you may want to attend a college that will allow you to earn credit for all or most of them. For example, the state external degree programs grant credit for most CLEP examinations (and other tests as well).

5. What is the required score for earning CLEP credit for each test you are considering?

Most colleges publish the required scores or percentile ranks for earning CLEP credit in their general catalog or in a brochure. The required score may vary from test to test, so find out the required score for each test you are considering.

6. What is the college's policy regarding prior course work in the subject in which you are considering taking a CLEP test?

Some colleges will not grant credit for a CLEP test if the student has already attempted a college-level course closely aligned with that test. For example, if you successfully completed English 101 or a comparable course on another campus, you will probably not be permitted to receive CLEP credit in that subject, too. Some colleges will not permit you to earn CLEP credit for a course that you failed.

7. Does the college make additional stipulations before credit will be granted?

It is common practice for colleges to award CLEP credit only to their enrolled students. There are other stipulations, however, that vary from college to college. For example, does the college require you to formally apply for or accept CLEP credit by completing and signing a form? Or does the college require you to validate your CLEP score by successfully completing a more advanced course in the subject? Answers to these and other questions will help to smooth the process of earning college credit through CLEP.

The above questions and the discussions that follow them indicate some of the ways in which colleges' CLEP policies can vary. Find out as much as possible about the CLEP policies at the colleges you are interested in so you can choose a college with a policy that is compatible with your educational goals. Once you have selected the college you will attend, you can find out which CLEP examinations your college recognizes and the requirements for earning CLEP credit.

DECIDING WHICH EXAMINATIONS TO TAKE

If You're Taking the Examinations for College Credit or Career Advancement:

Most people who take CLEP examinations do so in order to earn credit for college courses. Others take the examinations in order to qualify for job promotions or for professional certification or licensing. It is vital to most candidates who are taking the tests for any of these reasons that they be well prepared for the tests they are taking so that they can advance as rapidly as possible toward their educational or career goals.

It is usually advisable that those who have limited knowledge in the subjects covered by the tests they are considering enroll in the college courses in which that material is taught. Those who are uncertain about whether or not they know enough about a subject to do well on a particular CLEP test will find the following guidelines helpful.

There is no way to predict if you will pass a particular CLEP examination, but answers to the questions under the seven headings below should give you an indication of whether or not you are likely to succeed.

1. Test Descriptions

Read the description of the test provided. Are you familiar with most of the topics and terminology in the outline?

2. Textbooks

Examine the suggested textbooks and other resource materials following the test descriptions in this guide. Have you recently read one or more of these books, or have you read similar college-level books on this subject? If you have not, read through one or more of the textbooks listed, or through the textbook used for this course at your college. Are you familiar with most of the topics and terminology in the book?

3. Sample Questions

The sample questions provided are intended to be typical of the content and difficulty of the questions on the test. Although they are not an exact miniature of the test, the proportion of the sample questions you can answer correctly should be a rough estimate of the proportion of questions you will be able to answer correctly on the test.

Answer as many of the sample questions for this test as you can. Check your answers against the correct answers. Did you answer more than half the questions correctly?

Because of variations in course content at different institutions, and because questions on CLEP tests vary from easy to difficult - with most being of moderate difficulty - the average student who passes a course in a subject can usually answer correctly about half the questions on the corresponding CLEP examination. Most colleges set their passing scores near this level, but some set them higher. If your college has set its required score above the level required by most colleges, you may need to answer a larger proportion of questions on the test correctly.

4. Previous Study

Have you taken noncredit courses in this subject offered by an adult school or a private school, through correspondence, or in connection with your job? Did you do exceptionally well in this subject in high school, or did you take an honors course in this subject?

5. Experience

Have you learned or used the knowledge or skills included in this test in your job or life experience? For example, if you lived in a Spanish-speaking country and spoke the language for a year or more, you might consider taking the Spanish examination. Or, if you have worked at a job in which you used accounting and finance skills, Principles of Accounting would be a likely test for you to take. Or, if you have read a considerable amount of literature and attended many art exhibits, concerts, and plays, you might expect to do well on the Humanities exam.

6. Other Examinations

Have you done well on other standardized tests in subjects related to the one you want to take? For example, did you score well above average on a portion of a college entrance examination covering similar skills, or did you obtain an exceptionally high score on a high school equivalency test or a licensing examination in this subject? Although such tests do not cover exactly the same material as the CLEP examinations and may be easier, persons who do well on these tests often do well on CLEP examinations, too.

7. Advice

Has a college counselor, professor, or some other professional person familiar with your ability advised you to take a CLEP examination?

If your answer was yes to questions under several of the above headings, you probably have a good chance of passing the CLEP examination you are considering. It is unlikely that you would have acquired sufficient background from experience alone. Learning gained through reading and study is essential, and you will probably find some additional study helpful before taking a CLEP examination.

If You're Taking the Examinations to Prepare for College

Many people entering college, particularly adults returning to college after several years away from formal education, are uncertain about their ability to compete with other college students. They wonder whether they have sufficient background for college study, and those who have been away from formal study for some time wonder whether they have forgotten how to study, how to take tests, and how to write papers. Such people may wish to improve their test-taking and study skills prior to enrolling in courses.

One way to assess your ability to perform at the college level and to improve your test-taking and study skills at the same time is to prepare for and take one or more CLEP examinations. You need not be enrolled in a college to take a CLEP examination, and you may have your scores sent only to yourself and later request that a transcript be sent to a college if you then decide to apply for credit. By reviewing the test descriptions and sample questions, you may find one or several subject areas in which you think you have substantial knowledge. Select one examination, or more if you like, and carefully read at least one of the textbooks listed in the bibliography for the test. By doing this, you will get a better idea of how much you know of what is usually taught in a college-level course in that subject. Study as much material as you can, until you think you have a good grasp of the subject matter. Then take the test at a college in your area. It will be several weeks before you receive your results, and you may wish to begin reviewing for another test in the meantime.

To find out if you are eligible for credit for your CLEP score, you must compare your score with the score required by the college you plan to attend. If you are not yet sure which college you will attend, or whether you will enroll in college at all, you should begin to follow the steps outlined. It is best that you do this before taking a CLEP test, but if you are taking the test only for the experience and to familiarize yourself with college-level material and requirements, you might take the test before you approach a college. Even if the college you decide to attend does not accept the test you took, the experience of taking such a test will enable you to meet with greater confidence the requirements of courses you will take.

You will find information about how to interpret your scores in WHAT YOUR SCORES MEAN, which you will receive with your score report, and which can also be found online at the CLEP website. Many colleges follow the recommendations of the American Council on Education (ACE) for setting their required scores, so you can use this information as a guide in determining how well you did. The ACE recommendations are included in the booklet.

If you do not do well enough on the test to earn college credit, don't be discouraged. Usually, it is the best college students who are exempted from courses or receive credit-by-examination. The fact that you cannot get credit for your score means that you should probably enroll in a college course to learn the material. However, if your score was close to the required score, or if you feel you could do better on a second try or after some additional study, you may retake the test after six months. Do not take it sooner or your score will not be reported and your fee will be forfeited.

If you do earn the score required to earn credit, you will have demonstrated that you already have some college-level knowledge. You will also have a better idea whether you should take additional CLEP examinations. And, what is most important, you can enroll in college with confidence, knowing that you do have the ability to succeed.

PREPARING TO TAKE CLEP EXAMINATIONS

Having made the decision to take one or more CLEP examinations, most people then want to know if it is worthwhile to prepare for them - how much, how long, when, and how should they go about it? The precise answers to these questions vary greatly from individual to individual. However, most candidates find that some type of test preparation is helpful.

Most people who take CLEP examinations do so to show that they have already learned the important material that is taught in a college course. Many of them need only a quick review to assure themselves that they have not forgotten some of what they once studied, and to fill in some of the gaps in their knowledge of the subject. Others feel that they need a thorough review and spend several weeks studying for a test. A few wish to take a CLEP examination as a kind of final examination for independent study of a subject instead of the college course. This last group requires significantly more study than those who only need to review, and they may need some guidance from professors of the subjects they are studying.

The key to how you prepare for CLEP examinations often lies in locating those skills and areas of prior learning in which you are strong and deciding where to focus your energies. Some people may know a great deal about a certain subject area, but may not test well. These individuals would probably be just as concerned about strengthening their test-taking skills as they are about studying for a specific test. Many mental and physical skills are used in preparing for a test. It is important not only to review or study for the examinations, but to make certain that you are alert, relatively free of anxiety, and aware of how to approach standardized tests. Suggestions on developing test-taking skills and preparing psychologically and physically for a test are given. The following section suggests ways of assessing your knowledge of the content of a test and then reviewing and studying the material.

Using This Study Guide

Begin by carefully reading the test description and outline of knowledge and skills required for the examination, if given. As you read through the topics listed there, ask yourself how much you know about each one. Also note the terms, names, and symbols that are mentioned, and ask yourself whether you are familiar with them. This will give you a quick overview of how much you know about the subject. If you are familiar with nearly all the material, you will probably need a minimum of review; however, if less than half of it is familiar, you will probably require substantial study to do well on the test.

If, after reviewing the test description, you find that you need extensive review, delay answering the sample question until you have done some reading in the subject. If you complete them before reviewing the material, you will probably look for the answers as you study, and then they will not be a good assessment of your ability at a later date.

If you think you are familiar with most of the test material, try to answer the sample questions.

Apply the test-taking strategies given. Keeping within the time limit suggested will give you a rough idea of how quickly you should work in order to complete the actual test.

Check your answers against the answer key. If you answered nearly all the questions correctly, you probably do not need to study the subject extensively. If you got about half the questions correct, you ought o review at least one textbook or other suggested materials on the subject. If you answered less than half the questions correctly, you will probably benefit from more extensive reading in the subject and thorough study of one or more textbooks. The textbooks listed are used at many colleges but they are not the only good texts. You will find helpful almost any standard text available to you., such as the textbook used at your college, or earlier editions of texts listed. For some examinations, topic outlines and textbooks may not be available. Take the sample tests in this book and check your answers at the end of each test. Check wrong answers.

Suggestions for Studying

The following suggestions have been gathered from people who have prepared for CLEP examinations or other college-level tests.

1. Define your goals and locate study materials

First, determine your study goals. Set aside a block of time to review the material provided in this book, and then decide which test(s) you will take. Using the suggestions, locate suitable resource materials. If a preparation course is offered by an adult school or college in your area, you might find it helpful to enroll.

2. Find a good place to study

To determine what kind of place you need for studying, ask yourself questions such as: Do I need a quiet place? Does the telephone distract me? Do objects I see in this place remind me of things I should do? Is it too warm? Is it well lit? Am I too comfortable here? Do I have space to spread out my materials? You may find the library more conducive to studying than your home. If you decide to study at home, you might prevent interruptions by other household members by putting a sign on the door of your study room to indicate when you will be available.

3. Schedule time to study

To help you determine where studying best fits into your schedule, try this exercise: Make a list of your daily activities (for example, sleeping, working, and eating) and estimate how many hours per day you spend on each activity. Now, rate all the activities on your list in order of their importance and evaluate your use of time. Often people are astonished at how an average day appears from this perspective. They may discover that they were unaware how large portions of time are spent, or they learn their time can be scheduled in alternative ways. For example, they can remove the least important activities from their day and devote that time to studying or another important activity.

4. Establish a study routine and a set of goals

In order to study effectively, you should establish specific goals and a schedule for accomplishing them. Some people find it helpful to write out a weekly schedule and cross out each study period when it is completed. Others maintain their concentration better by writing down the time when they expect to complete a study task. Most people find short periods of intense study more productive than long stretches of time. For example, they may follow a regular schedule of several 20- or 30-minute study periods with short breaks between them. Some people like to allow themselves rewards as they complete each study goal. It is not essential that you accomplish every goal exactly within your schedule; the point is to be committed to your task.

5. Learn how to take an active role in studying.

If you have not done much studying for some time, you may find it difficult to concentrate at first. Try a method of studying, such as the one outlined below, that will help you concentrate on and remember what you read.

    a. First, read the chapter summary and the introduction. Then you will know what to look for in your reading.

    b. Next, convert the section or paragraph headlines into questions. For example, if you are reading a section entitled, The Causes of the American Revolution, ask yourself: *What were the causes of the American Revolution?* Compose the answer as you read the paragraph. Reading and answering questions aloud will help you understand and remember the material.

c. Take notes on key ideas or concepts as you read. Writing will also help you fix concepts more firmly in your mind. Underlining key ideas or writing notes in your book can be helpful and will be useful for review. Underline only important points. If you underline more than a third of each paragraph, you are probably underlining too much.

d. If there are questions or problems at the end of a chapter, answer or solve them on paper as if you were asked to do them for homework. Mathematics textbooks (and some other books) sometimes include answers to some or all of the exercises. If you have such a book, write your answers before looking at the ones given. When problem-solving is involved, work enough problems to master the required methods and concepts. If you have difficulty with problems, review any sample problems or explanations in the chapter.

e. To retain knowledge, most people have to review the material periodically. If you are preparing for a test over an extended period of time, review key concepts and notes each week or so. Do not wait for weeks to review the material or you will need to relearn much of it.

<u>Psychological and Physical Preparation</u>

Most people feel at least some nervousness before taking a test. Adults who are returning to college may not have taken a test in many years or they may have had little experience with standardized tests. Some younger students, as well, are uncomfortable with testing situations. People who received their education in countries outside the United States may find that many tests given in this country are quite different from the ones they are accustomed to taking.

Not only might candidates find the types of tests and the kinds of questions on them unfamiliar, but other aspects of the testing environment may be strange as well. The physical and mental stress that results from meeting this new experience can hinder a candidate's ability to demonstrate his or her true degree of knowledge in the subject area being tested. For this reason, it is important to go to the test center well prepared, both mentally and physically, for taking the test. You may find the following suggestions helpful.

1. Familiarize yourself, as much as possible, with the test and the test situation before the day of the examination. It will be helpful for you to know ahead of time:

a. How much time will be allowed for the test and whether there are timed subsections.

b. What types of questions and directions appear on the examination.

c. How your test score will be computed.

d. How to properly answer the questions on the computer (See the CLEP Sample on the CLEP website)

e. In which building and room the examination will be administered. If you don't know where the building is, locate it or get directions ahead of time.

f. The time of the test administration. You might wish to confirm this information a day or two before the examination and find out what time the building and room will be open so that you can plan to arrive early.

g. Where to park your car or, if you wish to take public transportation, which bus or train to take and the location of the nearest stop.

h. Whether smoking will be permitted during the test.

i. Whether there will be a break between examinations (if you will be taking more than one on the same day), and whether there is a place nearby where you can get something to eat or drink.

2. Go to the test situation relaxed and alert. In order to prepare for the test:

a. Get a good night's sleep. Last minute cramming, particularly late the night before, is usually counterproductive.

b. Eat normally. It is usually not wise to skip breakfast or lunch on the day of the test or to eat a big meal just before the test.

c. Avoid tranquilizers and stimulants. If you follow the other directions in this book, you won't need artificial aids. It's better to be a little tense than to be drowsy, but stimulants such as coffee and cola can make you nervous and interfere with your concentration.

d. Don't drink a lot of liquids before the test. Having to leave the room during the test will disturb your concentration and take valuable time away from the test.

e. If you are inclined to be nervous or tense, learn some relaxation exercises and use them before and perhaps during the test.

3. Arrive for the test early and prepared. Be sure to:

a. Arrive early enough so that you can find a parking place, locate the test center, and get settled comfortably before testing begins. Allow some extra time in case you are delayed unexpectedly.

b. Take the following with you:

- Your completed Registration/Admission Form
- Two forms of identification – one being a government-issued photo ID with signature, such as a driver's license or passport
- Non-mechanical pencil
- A watch so that you can time your progress (digital watches are prohibited)
- Your glasses if you need them for reading or seeing the chalkboard or wall clock

c. Leave all books, papers, and notes outside the test center. You will not be permitted to use your own scratch paper; it will be provided. Also prohibited are calculators, cell phones, beepers, pagers, photo/copy devices, radios, headphones, food, beverages, and several other items.

d. Be prepared for any temperature in the testing room. Wear layers of clothing that can be removed if the room is too hot but will keep you warm if it is too cold.

4. When you enter the test room:

a. Sit in a seat that provides a maximum of comfort and freedom from distraction.

b. Read directions carefully, and listen to all instructions given by the test administrator. If you don't understand the directions, ask for help before test timing begins. If you must ask a question after the test has begun, raise your hand and a proctor will assist you. The proctor can answer certain kinds of questions but cannot help you with the test.

c. Know your rights as a test taker. You can expect to be given the full working time allowed for the test(s) and a reasonably quiet and comfortable place in which to work. If a poor test situation is preventing you from doing your best, ask if the situation can be remedied. If bad test conditions cannot be remedied, ask the person in charge to report the problem in the Irregularity Report that will be sent to ETS with the answer sheets. You may also wish to contact CLEP. Describe the exact circumstances as completely as you can. Be sure to include the test date and name(s) of the test(s) you took. ETS will investigate the problem to make sure it does not happen again, and, if the problem is serious enough, may arrange for you to retake the test without charge.

TAKING THE EXAMINATIONS

A person may know a great deal about the subject being tested, but not do as well as he or she is capable of on the test. Knowing how to approach a test is an important part of the testing process. While a command of test-taking skills cannot substitute for knowledge of the subject matter, it can be a significant factor in successful testing.

Test-taking skills enable a person to use all available information to earn a score that truly reflects his or her ability. There are different strategies for approaching different kinds of test questions. For example, free-response questions require a very different tack than do multiple-choice questions. Other factors, such as how the test will be graded, may also influence your approach to the test and your use of test time. Thus, your preparation for a test should include finding out all you can about the test so that you can use the most effective test-taking strategies.

Before taking a test, you should know approximately how many questions are on the test, how much time you will be allowed, how the test will be scored or graded, what types of questions and directions are on the test, and how you will be required to record your answers.

Taking Multiple-Choice Tests

1. Listen carefully to the instructions given by the test administrator and read carefully all directions before you begin to answer the questions.

2. Note the time that the test administrator starts timing the test. As you proceed, make sure that you are not working too slowly. You should have answered at least half the questions in a section when half the time for that section has passed. If you have not reached that point in the section, speed up your pace on the remaining questions.

3. Before answering a question, read the entire question, including all the answer choices. Don't think that because the first or second answer choice looks good to you, it isn't necessary to read the remaining options. Instructions usually tell you to select the best answer. Sometimes one answer choice is partially correct, but another option is better; therefore, it is usually a good idea to read all the answers before you choose one.

4. Read and consider every question. Questions that look complicated at first glance may not actually be so difficult once you have read them carefully.

5. Do not puzzle too long over any one question. If you don't know the answer after you've considered it briefly, go on to the next question. Make sure you return to the question later.

6. Make sure you record your response properly.

7. In trying to determine the correct answer, you may find it helpful to cross out those options that you know are incorrect, and to make marks next to those you think might be correct. If you decide to skip the question and come back to it later, you will save yourself the time of reconsidering all the options.

8. Watch for the following key words in test questions:

all	generally	never	perhaps
always	however	none	rarely
but	may	not	seldom
except	must	often	sometimes
every	necessary	only	usually

When a question or answer option contains words such as always, every, only, never, and none, there can be no exceptions to the answer you choose. Use of words such as often, rarely, sometimes, and generally indicates that there may be some exceptions to the answer.

9. Do not waste your time looking for clues to right answers based on flaws in question wording or patterns in correct answers. Professionals at the College Board and ETS put

a great deal of effort into developing valid, reliable, fair tests. CLEP test development committees are composed of college faculty who are experts in the subject covered by the test and are appointed by the College Board to write test questions and to scrutinize each question that is included on a CLEP test. Committee members make every effort to ensure that the questions are not ambiguous, that they have only one correct answer, and that they cover college-level topics. These committees do not intentionally include trick questions. If you think a question is flawed, ask the test administrator to report it, or contact CLEP immediately.

Taking Free-Response or Essay Tests

If your college requires the optional free-response or essay portion of a CLEP Composition and Literature exams, you should do some additional preparation for your CLEP test. Taking an essay test is very different from taking a multiple-choice test, so you will need to use some other strategies.

The essay written as part of the English Composition and Essay exam is graded by English professors from a variety of colleges and universities. A process called holistic scoring is used to rate your writing ability.

The optional free-response essays, on the other hand, are graded by the faculty of the college you designate as a score recipient. Guidelines and criteria for grading essays are not specified by the College Board or ETS. You may find it helpful, therefore, to talk with someone at your college to find out what criteria will be used to determine whether you will get credit. If the test requires essay responses, ask how much emphasis will be placed on your writing ability and your ability to organize your thoughts as opposed to your knowledge of subject matter. Find out how much weight will be given to your multiple-choice test score in comparison with your free-response grade in determining whether you will get credit. This will give you an idea where you should expend the greatest effort in preparing for and taking the test.

Here are some strategies you will find useful in taking any essay test:

1. Before you begin to write, read all questions carefully and take a few minutes to jot down some ideas you might include in each answer.

2. If you are given a choice of questions to answer, choose the questions you think you can answer most clearly and knowledgeably.

3. Determine in what order you will answer the questions. Answer those you find the easiest first so that any extra time can be spent on the more difficult questions.

4. When you know which questions you will answer and in what order, determine how much testing time remains and estimate how many minutes you will devote to each question. Unless suggested times are given for the questions or one question appears to require more or less time than the others, allot an equal amount of time to each question.

5. Before answering each question, indicate the number of the question as it is given in the test book. You need not copy the entire question from the question sheet, but it will be helpful to you and to the person grading your test if you indicate briefly the topic you are addressing – particularly if you are not answering the questions in the order in which they appear on the test.

6. Before answering each question, read it again carefully to make sure you are interpreting it correctly. Underline key words, such as those listed below, that often appear in free-response questions. Be sure you know the exact meaning of these words before taking the test.

analyze	demonstrate	enumerate	list
apply	derive	explain	outline
assess	describe	generalize	prove
compare	determine	illustrate	rank
contrast	discuss	interpret	show
define	distinguish	justify	summarize

If a question asks you to outline, define, or summarize, do not write a detailed explanation; if a question asks you to analyze, explain, illustrate, interpret, or show, you must do more than briefly describe the topic.

For a current listing of CLEP Colleges

where you can get credit and be tested, write:

CLEP, P.O. Box 6600, Princeton, NJ 08541-6600

Or e-mail: clep@ets.org, or call: (609) 771-7865

PRINCIPLES OF MACROECONOMICS

Description of the Examination

The Principles of Macroeconomics examination covers material that is usually taught in a one-semester undergraduate course in this subject. This aspect of economics deals with principles of economics that apply to an economy as a whole, particularly the general price level, output and income, and interrelations among sectors of the economy. The test places particular emphasis on the determinants of aggregate demand and aggregate supply, and on monetary and fiscal policy tools that can be used to achieve particular policy objectives. Within this context, candidates are expected to understand measurement concepts such as gross domestic product, consumption, investment, unemployment, inflation, inflationary gap, and recessionary gap. Candidates are also expected to demonstrate knowledge of the institutional structure of the Federal Reserve Bank and the monetary policy tools it uses to stabilize economic fluctuations and promote long-term economic growth, as well as the tools of fiscal policy and their impacts on income, employment, price level, deficits, and interest rate. Basic understanding of foreign exchange markets, balance of payments, effects of currency, and appreciation and depreciation on a country's imports and exports are also expected.

The examination contains approximately 80 questions to be answered in 90 minutes. Some of these are pretest questions that will not be scored. Any time candidates spend on tutorials and providing personal information is in addition to the actual testing time.

Knowledge and Skills Required

Questions on the Principles of Macroeconomics examination require candidates to demonstrate one or more of the following abilities.

- Understanding of important economic terms and concepts
- Interpretation and manipulation of economic graphs
- Interpretation and evaluation of economic data
- Application of simple economic models
-

The subject matter of the Principles of Macroeconomics examination is drawn from the following topics. The percentages next to the main topics indicate the approximate percentage of exam questions on that topic.

8-12%   Basic Economic Concepts

- Scarcity, choice, and opportunity costs
- Production possibilities curve
- Comparative advantage, specialization, and exchange
- Demand, supply, and market equilibrium
- Macroeconomic issues: business cycle, unemployment, inflation, growth

12-16%   Measurement of Economic Performance

- National income accounts
    - Circular flow
    - Gross domestic product
    - Components of gross domestic product
    - Real versus nominal gross domestic product

- Inflation measurement and adjustment
    - Price indices
    - Nominal and real values
    - Costs of inflation

- Unemployment
    - Definition and measurement
    - Types of unemployment
    - Natural rate of unemployment

10-15%   **National Income and Price Determination**
- Aggregate demand
    - Determinants of aggregate demand
    - Multiplier and crowding-out effects

- Aggregate supply
    - Short-run and long-run analyses
    - Sticky versus flexible wages and prices
    - Determinants of aggregate supply

- Macroeconomic equilibrium
    - Real output and price level
    - Short and long run
    - Actual versus full-employment output
    - Economic fluctuations

15-20%   **Financial Sector**
- Money, banking, and financial markets
    - Definition of financial assets: money, stocks, bonds
    - Time value of money (present and future value)
    - Measures of money supply
    - Banks and creation of money
    - Money demand
    - Money market
    - Loanable funds market

- Central bank and control of the money supply
    - Tools of central bank policy
    - Quantity theory of money
    - Real versus nominal interest rate

20-30%   **Inflation, Unemployment, and Stabilization Policies**
- Fiscal and monetary policies
    - Demand-side effects
    - Supply-side effects
    - Policy mix
    - Government deficits and debt

- Inflation and unemployment
  - Types of inflation
  - Demand-pull inflation
  - Cost-push inflation
  - The Phillips curve: short run versus long run
  - Role of expectations

5-10%   **Economic Growth and Productivity**
- Investment in human capital
- Investment in physical capital
- Research and development, and technological progress
- Growth policy

10-15%   **Open Economy: International Trade and Finance**
- Balance of payments accounts
  - Balance of trade
  - Current account
  - Capital account

- Foreign exchange market
  - Demand for and supply of foreign exchange
  - Exchange rate determination
  - Currency appreciation and depreciation

- Net exports and capital flows
- Links to financial and goods markets

ECONOMISTS

NATURE OF THE WORK

Economists study the ways a society uses scarce resources such as land, labor, raw materials, and machinery to produce goods and services. They analyze the costs and benefits of distributing and consuming these goods and services. Their research might focus on topics such as energy costs, electronic components production, farm prices, or imports.

Some economists who are primarily theoreticians may develop theories through the use of mathematical models to explain the causes of business cycles and inflation or the effects of unemployment and tax policy. Most economists, however, are concerned with practical applications of economic policy in a particular area, such as finance, labor, agriculture, transportation, energy, or health. They use their understanding of economic relationships to advise business firms, insurance companies, banks, securities firms, industry associations, labor unions, government agencies, and others.

Depending on the topic under study, economists devise methods and procedures for obtaining data they need. For example, sampling techniques may be used to conduct a survey, and econometric modeling techniques may be used to develop projections. Preparing reports usually is an important part of the economist's job. He or she may be called upon to review and analyze all the relevant data, prepare tables and charts, and write up the results in clear, concise language.

Being able to present economic and statistical concepts in a meaningful way is particularly important for economists whose research is policy directed. Market research analysts who work for business firms may be asked to provide management with information to make decisions on marketing and pricing of company products; to look at the advisability of adding new lines of merchandise, opening new branches, or diversifying the company's operations; to analyze the effect of changes in the tax, laws; or to prepare economic and business forecasts. Business economists working for firms that carry on operations abroad may be asked to prepare forecasts of foreign economic conditions.

Economists who work for government agencies assess economic conditions in the United States and abroad and estimate the economic impact of specific changes in legislation or public policy. For example, they may study how changes in the minimum wage affect teenage unemployment. Most government economists are in the fields of agriculture, business, finance, labor, transportation, utilities, urban economics, or international trade. For example, economists in the U.S. Department of Commerce study domestic production, distribution, and consumption of commodities or services; those in the Federal Trade Commission prepare industry analyses to assist in enforcing Federal statutes designed to eliminate unfair, deceptive, or monopolistic practices in interstate commerce; and those in the Bureau of Labor Statistics analyze data on prices, wages, employment, and productivity.

WORKING CONDITIONS

Economists working for government agencies and private firms have structured work schedules. They may work alone writing reports, preparing statistical charts, and using computers and calculators. Or they may be an integral part of a research team. Most work under pressure of deadlines and tight schedules, and sometimes must work overtime. Their routine may be interrupted by special requests for data, letters, meetings, or conferences. Travel may be necessary to collect data or attend conferences.

Economics faculty has flexible work schedules, dividing their time among teaching, research, consulting, and administrative responsibilities.

EMPLOYMENT

Economists hold about 15,000 jobs. Private industry -- particularly economic and market research firms, management consulting firms, advertising firms, banks, and securities, investment, and insurance companies -- employed over two-thirds of all salaried economists. The remainders were employed by a wide range of government agencies, primarily in the Federal Government. The Department of Labor, Agriculture, and State are the largest Federal employers. About one out of every five economists runs his or her own consulting business. A number of economists combine a full-time job in government or business with part-time or - consulting work in another setting.

Employment of economists is concentrated in large cities. The largest numbers are in New York City and Washington, D.C. Some work abroad for companies with major international operations; for the Department of State and other U.S. Government agencies; and for international organizations.

Besides the jobs described above, an estimated 30,000 persons held economics and marketing faculty positions in colleges and universities.

TRAINING, OTHER QUALIFICATIONS, AND ADVANCEMENT

A bachelor's degree with a major in economics or marketing is sufficient for many beginning research, administrative, management trainee, and sales jobs. The undergraduate curriculum includes courses such as microeconomics, macroeconomics, business cycles, economic and business history, and economic development of selected areas, money and banking, international economics, public finance, industrial organization, labor economics, comparative economic systems, economics of national planning, urban economic problems, marketing, and consumer behavior analysis. Courses in related disciplines, such as political science, psychology, organizational behavior, sociology, finance, business law, and international relations, are suggested. Because of the importance of quantitative skills to economists, courses in mathematics, business and economic statistics, sampling theory and survey design, and computer science are highly recommended.

Graduate training increasingly is required for most economist jobs and for advancement to more responsible positions. Areas of specialization at the graduate level include advanced economic theory, mathematical economics, econometrics, history of economic thought, and comparative economic systems and planning. Other areas include economic history, economic development, environmental and natural resource economics, industrial organization, marketing, institutional economics, international economics, labor economics, monetary economics, public finance, regional and urban economics, and social policy. Students should select graduate schools strong in specialties in which they are interested. Some schools help graduate students find internships or part-time employment in government agencies, economic consulting firms, financial institutions, or market research firms. Work experience and contacts can be useful in testing career preference and learning about the job market for economists.

In the Federal Government, candidates for entrance positions generally need a college degree with a minimum of 21 semester hours of economics and 3 hours of statistics, accounting, or calculus. However, because competition is keen, additional education or experience may be required.

For a job as a college instructor in many junior colleges and small 4-year schools, a master's degree generally is the minimum requirement. In some colleges and universities, however, a Ph.D. and extensive publication are required for a professorship and for tenure, which are increasingly difficult to obtain.

In government, industry, research organizations, and consulting firms, economists who have a graduate degree usually can qualify for more responsible research and administrative positions. A Ph.D. is necessary for top positions in many organizations. Many corporation and government executives have a strong background in economics or marketing.

Over 1,200 colleges and universities offer bachelor's degree programs in economics and marketing; over 600, masters and about 130, doctoral programs.

Persons considering careers as economists should be able to work accurately with detail since much time is spent on data analysis. Patience and persistence are necessary because economists may spend long hours on independent study and problem solving. At the same time, they must be able to work well with others. Economists must be objective and systematic in their work and be able to express themselves effectively both orally and in writing. Creativity and intellectual curiosity are essential for success in this field, just as they are in other areas of scientific endeavor.

JOB OUTLOOK

Employment of economists is expected to grow at a slower rate than the average for all occupations in the next decade. Most job openings, however, will result from the need to replace experienced economists who transfer to other occupations, or retire or leave the labor force for other reasons.

Opportunities should be best in manufacturing, financial services, advertising agencies, research organizations, and consulting firms, reflecting the complexity of the domestic and international economies and increased reliance on quantitative methods of analyzing business trends, forecasting sales, and planning of purchasing and production. The continued need for economic analyses by lawyers, accountants, engineers, health service administrators, urban and regional planners, environmental scientists, and others will also increase the number of jobs for economists. Little or no change is expected in the employment of economists in the Federal Government – in line with the rate of growth projected for the Federal work force as a whole. Employment of economists in State and local government combined is expected to grow more slowly than the average.

A strong background in economic theory, statistics, and econometrics provides the tools for acquiring any specialty within the field. Those skilled in quantitative techniques and their application to economic modeling and forecasting and market research, including the use of computers, should have the best job opportunities.

Persons who graduate with a bachelor's degree in economics should face very keen competition for the limited number of economist positions for which they qualify. However, many will find employment in government, industry, and business as management or sales trainees, or as research or administrative assistants. Those with strong backgrounds in mathematics, statistics, survey design, and computer science may be hired by private firms for market research work. Those who meet State certification requirements may become high school economics teachers. (For additional information, see the statement on secondary school teachers elsewhere in the Handbook.)

Candidates who hold master's degrees in economics face very strong competition, particularly for teaching positions in colleges and universities. However, some may gain positions in junior and community colleges. Those with a strong background in marketing and finance may have the best prospects in business, banking, advertising, and management consulting firms.

Ph.D.'s are likely to face competition for academic positions, although top graduates from leading universities should have little difficulty in acquiring teaching jobs. Some will have to accept jobs at smaller or lower paying institutions. Ph.D.'s should have favorable opportunities to work as economists in government, industry, educational and research organizations, and consulting firms.

RELATED OCCUPATIONS

Economists are concerned with understanding and interpreting financial matters, among other subjects. Others with jobs in this area include financial managers, financial analysts, accountants and auditors, underwriters, actuaries, securities and financial services sales workers, credit analysts" loan officers, and budget officers.

SOURCES OF ADDITIONAL INFORMATION

National Association for Business Economics,
1223 20th St. NW, Suite 505, Washington, DC 20036 (Internet: http://www.nabe.com)

HOW TO TAKE A TEST

You have studied long, hard and conscientiously.

With your official admission card in hand, and your heart pounding, you have been admitted to the examination room.

You note that there are several hundred other applicants in the examination room waiting to take the same test.

They all appear to be equally well prepared.

You know that nothing but your best effort will suffice. The "moment of truth" is at hand: you now have to demonstrate objectively, in writing, your knowledge of content and your understanding of subject matter.

You are fighting the most important battle of your life—to pass and/or score high on an examination which will determine your career and provide the economic basis for your livelihood.

What extra, special things should you know and should you do in taking the examination?

I. YOU MUST PASS AN EXAMINATION

A. WHAT EVERY CANDIDATE SHOULD KNOW
Examination applicants often ask us for help in preparing for the written test. What can I study in advance? What kinds of questions will be asked? How will the test be given? How will the papers be graded?

B. HOW ARE EXAMS DEVELOPED?
Examinations are carefully written by trained technicians who are specialists in the field known as "psychological measurement," in consultation with recognized authorities in the field of work that the test will cover. These experts recommend the subject matter areas or skills to be tested; only those knowledges or skills important to your success on the job are included. The most reliable books and source materials available are used as references. Together, the experts and technicians judge the difficulty level of the questions.
Test technicians know how to phrase questions so that the problem is clearly stated. Their ethics do not permit "trick" or "catch" questions. Questions may have been tried out on sample groups, or subjected to statistical analysis, to determine their usefulness.
Written tests are often used in combination with performance tests, ratings of training and experience, and oral interviews. All of these measures combine to form the best-known means of finding the right person for the right job.

II. HOW TO PASS THE WRITTEN TEST

A. BASIC STEPS

1) Study the announcement

How, then, can you know what subjects to study? Our best answer is: "Learn as much as possible about the class of positions for which you've applied." The exam will test the knowledge, skills and abilities needed to do the work.

Your most valuable source of information about the position you want is the official exam announcement. This announcement lists the training and experience qualifications. Check these standards and apply only if you come reasonably close to meeting them. Many jurisdictions preview the written test in the exam announcement by including a section called "Knowledge and Abilities Required," "Scope of the Examination," or some similar heading. Here you will find out specifically what fields will be tested.

2) Choose appropriate study materials

If the position for which you are applying is technical or advanced, you will read more advanced, specialized material. If you are already familiar with the basic principles of your field, elementary textbooks would waste your time. Concentrate on advanced textbooks and technical periodicals. Think through the concepts and review difficult problems in your field.

These are all general sources. You can get more ideas on your own initiative, following these leads. For example, training manuals and publications of the government agency which employs workers in your field can be useful, particularly for technical and professional positions. A letter or visit to the government department involved may result in more specific study suggestions, and certainly will provide you with a more definite idea of the exact nature of the position you are seeking.

3) Study this book!

III. KINDS OF TESTS

Tests are used for purposes other than measuring knowledge and ability to perform specified duties. For some positions, it is equally important to test ability to make adjustments to new situations or to profit from training. In others, basic mental abilities not dependent on information are essential. Questions which test these things may not appear as pertinent to the duties of the position as those which test for knowledge and information. Yet they are often highly important parts of a fair examination. For very general questions, it is almost impossible to help you direct your study efforts. What we can do is point out some of the more common of these general abilities needed in public service positions and describe some typical questions.

1) General information

Broad, general information has been found useful for predicting job success in some kinds of work. This is tested in a variety of ways, from vocabulary lists to questions about current events. Basic background in some field of work, such as sociology or economics, may be sampled in a group of questions. Often these are principles which have become familiar to most persons through exposure rather than through formal training. It is difficult to advise you how to study for these questions; being alert to the world around you is our best suggestion.

2) Verbal ability

An example of an ability needed in many positions is verbal or language ability. Verbal ability is, in brief, the ability to use and understand words. Vocabulary and grammar tests are typical measures of this ability. Reading comprehension or paragraph interpretation questions are common in many kinds of civil service tests. You are given a paragraph of written material and asked to find its central meaning.

IV. KINDS OF QUESTIONS

1. Multiple-choice Questions

Most popular of the short-answer questions is the "multiple choice" or "best answer" question. It can be used, for example, to test for factual knowledge, ability to solve problems or judgment in meeting situations found at work.

A multiple-choice question is normally one of three types:
- It can begin with an incomplete statement followed by several possible endings. You are to find the one ending which best completes the statement, although some of the others may not be entirely wrong.
- It can also be a complete statement in the form of a question which is answered by choosing one of the statements listed.
- It can be in the form of a problem – again you select the best answer.

Here is an example of a multiple-choice question with a discussion which should give you some clues as to the method for choosing the right answer:

When an employee has a complaint about his assignment, the action which will best help him overcome his difficulty is to
- A. discuss his difficulty with his coworkers
- B. take the problem to the head of the organization
- C. take the problem to the person who gave him the assignment
- D. say nothing to anyone about his complaint

In answering this question, you should study each of the choices to find which is best. Consider choice "A" – Certainly an employee may discuss his complaint with fellow employees, but no change or improvement can result, and the complaint remains unresolved. Choice "B" is a poor choice since the head of the organization probably does not know what assignment you have been given, and taking your problem to him is known as "going over the head" of the supervisor. The supervisor, or person who made the assignment, is the person who can clarify it or correct any injustice. Choice "C" is, therefore, correct. To say nothing, as in choice "D," is unwise. Supervisors have and interest in knowing the problems employees are facing, and the employee is seeking a solution to his problem.

2. True/False

3. Matching Questions

Matching an answer from a column of choices within another column.

V. RECORDING YOUR ANSWERS

Computer terminals are used more and more today for many different kinds of exams.

For an examination with very few applicants, you may be told to record your answers in the test booklet itself. Separate answer sheets are much more common. If this separate answer sheet is to be scored by machine – and this is often the case – it is highly important that you mark your answers correctly in order to get credit.

VI. BEFORE THE TEST

YOUR PHYSICAL CONDITION IS IMPORTANT

If you are not well, you can't do your best work on tests. If you are half asleep, you can't do your best either. Here are some tips:

1) Get about the same amount of sleep you usually get. Don't stay up all night before the test, either partying or worrying—DON'T DO IT!
2) If you wear glasses, be sure to wear them when you go to take the test. This goes for hearing aids, too.
3) If you have any physical problems that may keep you from doing your best, be sure to tell the person giving the test. If you are sick or in poor health, you relay cannot do your best on any test. You can always come back and take the test some other time.

Common sense will help you find procedures to follow to get ready for an examination. Too many of us, however, overlook these sensible measures. Indeed, nervousness and fatigue have been found to be the most serious reasons why applicants fail to do their best on civil service tests. Here is a list of reminders:

- Begin your preparation early – Don't wait until the last minute to go scurrying around for books and materials or to find out what the position is all about.
- Prepare continuously – An hour a night for a week is better than an all-night cram session. This has been definitely established. What is more, a night a week for a month will return better dividends than crowding your study into a shorter period of time.
- Locate the place of the exam – You have been sent a notice telling you when and where to report for the examination. If the location is in a different town or otherwise unfamiliar to you, it would be well to inquire the best route and learn something about the building.
- Relax the night before the test – Allow your mind to rest. Do not study at all that night. Plan some mild recreation or diversion; then go to bed early and get a good night's sleep.
- Get up early enough to make a leisurely trip to the place for the test – This way unforeseen events, traffic snarls, unfamiliar buildings, etc. will not upset you.
- Dress comfortably – A written test is not a fashion show. You will be known by number and not by name, so wear something comfortable.
- Leave excess paraphernalia at home – Shopping bags and odd bundles will get in your way. You need bring only the items mentioned in the official notice you received; usually everything you need is provided. Do not bring reference books to the exam. They will only confuse those last minutes and be taken away from you when in the test room.

- Arrive somewhat ahead of time – If because of transportation schedules you must get there very early, bring a newspaper or magazine to take your mind off yourself while waiting.
- Locate the examination room – When you have found the proper room, you will be directed to the seat or part of the room where you will sit. Sometimes you are given a sheet of instructions to read while you are waiting. Do not fill out any forms until you are told to do so; just read them and be prepared.
- Relax and prepare to listen to the instructions
- If you have any physical problem that may keep you from doing your best, be sure to tell the test administrator. If you are sick or in poor health, you really cannot do your best on the exam. You can come back and take the test some other time.

VII. AT THE TEST

The day of the test is here and you have the test booklet in your hand. The temptation to get going is very strong. Caution! There is more to success than knowing the right answers. You must know how to identify your papers and understand variations in the type of short-answer question used in this particular examination. Follow these suggestions for maximum results from your efforts:

1) Cooperate with the monitor

The test administrator has a duty to create a situation in which you can be as much at ease as possible. He will give instructions, tell you when to begin, check to see that you are marking your answer sheet correctly, and so on. He is not there to guard you, although he will see that your competitors do not take unfair advantage. He wants to help you do your best.

2) Listen to all instructions

Don't jump the gun! Wait until you understand all directions. In most civil service tests you get more time than you need to answer the questions. So don't be in a hurry. Read each word of instructions until you clearly understand the meaning. Study the examples, listen to all announcements and follow directions. Ask questions if you do not understand what to do.

3) Identify your papers

Civil service exams are usually identified by number only. You will be assigned a number; you must not put your name on your test papers. Be sure to copy your number correctly. Since more than one exam may be given, copy your exact examination title.

4) Plan your time

Unless you are told that a test is a "speed" or "rate of work" test, speed itself is usually not important. Time enough to answer all the questions will be provided, but this does not mean that you have all day. An overall time limit has been set. Divide the total time (in minutes) by the number of questions to determine the approximate time you have for each question.

5) Do not linger over difficult questions

If you come across a difficult question, mark it with a paper clip (useful to have along) and come back to it when you have been through the booklet. One caution if you do this – be sure to skip a number on your answer sheet as well. Check often to be sure that you have not lost your place and that you are marking in the row numbered the same as the question you are answering.

6) Read the questions

Be sure you know what the question asks! Many capable people are unsuccessful because they failed to read the questions correctly.

7) Answer all questions

Unless you have been instructed that a penalty will be deducted for incorrect answers, it is better to guess than to omit a question.

8) Speed tests

It is often better NOT to guess on speed tests. It has been found that on timed tests people are tempted to spend the last few seconds before time is called in marking answers at random – without even reading them – in the hope of picking up a few extra points. To discourage this practice, the instructions may warn you that your score will be "corrected" for guessing. That is, a penalty will be applied. The incorrect answers will be deducted from the correct ones, or some other penalty formula will be used.

9) Review your answers

If you finish before time is called, go back to the questions you guessed or omitted to give them further thought. Review other answers if you have time.

10) Return your test materials

If you are ready to leave before others have finished or time is called, take ALL your materials to the monitor and leave quietly. Never take any test material with you. The monitor can discover whose papers are not complete, and taking a test booklet may be grounds for disqualification.

VIII. EXAMINATION TECHNIQUES

1) Read the general instructions carefully. These are usually printed on the first page of the exam booklet. As a rule, these instructions refer to the timing of the examination; the fact that you should not start work until the signal and must stop work at a signal, etc. If there are any special instructions, such as a choice of questions to be answered, make sure that you note this instruction carefully.

2) When you are ready to start work on the examination, that is as soon as the signal has been given, read the instructions to each question booklet, underline any key words or phrases, such as least, best, outline, describe and the like. In this way you will tend to answer as requested rather than discover on reviewing your paper that you listed without describing, that you selected the worst choice rather than the best choice, etc.

3) If the examination is of the objective or multiple-choice type – that is, each question will also give a series of possible answers: A, B, C or D, and you are called upon to select the best answer and write the letter next to that answer on your answer paper – it is advisable to start answering each question in turn. There may be anywhere from 50 to 100 such questions in the three or four hours allotted and you can see how much time would be taken if you read through all the questions before beginning to answer any. Furthermore, if you

come across a question or group of questions which you know would be difficult to answer, it would undoubtedly affect your handling of all the other questions.

4) If the examination is of the essay type and contains but a few questions, it is a moot point as to whether you should read all the questions before starting to answer any one. Of course, if you are given a choice – say five out of seven and the like – then it is essential to read all the questions so you can eliminate the two that are most difficult. If, however, you are asked to answer all the questions, there may be danger in trying to answer the easiest one first because you may find that you will spend too much time on it. The best technique is to answer the first question, then proceed to the second, etc.

5) Time your answers. Before the exam begins, write down the time it started, then add the time allowed for the examination and write down the time it must be completed, then divide the time available somewhat as follows:
   - If 3-1/2 hours are allowed, that would be 210 minutes. If you have 80 objective-type questions, that would be an average of 2-1/2 minutes per question. Allow yourself no more than 2 minutes per question, or a total of 160 minutes, which will permit about 50 minutes to review.
   - If for the time allotment of 210 minutes there are 7 essay questions to answer, that would average about 30 minutes a question. Give yourself only 25 minutes per question so that you have about 35 minutes to review.

6) The most important instruction is to read each question and make sure you know what is wanted. The second most important instruction is to time yourself properly so that you answer every question. The third most important instruction is to answer every question. Guess if you have to but include something for each question. Remember that you will receive no credit for a blank and will probably receive some credit if you write something in answer to an essay question. If you guess a letter – say "B" for a multiple-choice question – you may have guessed right. If you leave a blank as an answer to a multiple-choice question, the examiners may respect your feelings but it will not add a point to your score. Some exams may penalize you for wrong answers, so in such cases only, you may not want to guess unless you have some basis for your answer.

7) Suggestions
   a. Objective-type questions
      1. Examine the question booklet for proper sequence of pages and questions
      2. Read all instructions carefully
      3. Skip any question which seems too difficult; return to it after all other questions have been answered
      4. Apportion your time properly; do not spend too much time on any single question or group of questions
      5. Note and underline key words – all, most, fewest, least, best, worst, same, opposite, etc.
      6. Pay particular attention to negatives
      7. Note unusual option, e.g., unduly long, short, complex, different or similar in content to the body of the question
      8. Observe the use of "hedging" words – probably, may, most likely, etc.

9. Make sure that your answer is put next to the same number as the question
10. Do not second-guess unless you have good reason to believe the second answer is definitely more correct
11. Cross out original answer if you decide another answer is more accurate; do not erase until you are ready to hand your paper in
12. Answer all questions; guess unless instructed otherwise
13. Leave time for review

b. Essay questions
   1. Read each question carefully
   2. Determine exactly what is wanted. Underline key words or phrases.
   3. Decide on outline or paragraph answer
   4. Include many different points and elements unless asked to develop any one or two points or elements
   5. Show impartiality by giving pros and cons unless directed to select one side only
   6. Make and write down any assumptions you find necessary to answer the questions
   7. Watch your English, grammar, punctuation and choice of words
   8. Time your answers; don't crowd material

8) Answering the essay question

Most essay questions can be answered by framing the specific response around several key words or ideas. Here are a few such key words or ideas:

M's: manpower, materials, methods, money, management
P's: purpose, program, policy, plan, procedure, practice, problems, pitfalls, personnel, public relations

a. Six basic steps in handling problems:
   1. Preliminary plan and background development
   2. Collect information, data and facts
   3. Analyze and interpret information, data and facts
   4. Analyze and develop solutions as well as make recommendations
   5. Prepare report and sell recommendations
   6. Install recommendations and follow up effectiveness

b. Pitfalls to avoid
   1. Taking things for granted – A statement of the situation does not necessarily imply that each of the elements is necessarily true; for example, a complaint may be invalid and biased so that all that can be taken for granted is that a complaint has been registered
   2. Considering only one side of a situation – Wherever possible, indicate several alternatives and then point out the reasons you selected the best one
   3. Failing to indicate follow up – Whenever your answer indicates action on your part, make certain that you will take proper follow-up action to see how successful your recommendations, procedures or actions turn out to be
   4. Taking too long in answering any single question – Remember to time your answers properly

EXAMINATION SECTION

EXAMINATION SECTION
TEST 1

DIRECTIONS: Each question or incomplete statement is followed by several suggested answers or completions. Select the one that BEST answers the question or completes the statement. *PRINT THE LETTER OF THE CORRECT ANSWER IN THE SPACE AT THE RIGHT.*

1. In the economy of the United States, the actual gross national product is most likely to be less than the potential GNP at full capacity whenever 1._____

    A. business investment is large
    B. consumer spending is rising
    C. government spending is falling
    D. total spending is falling

2. _____ would tend to reduce consumer spending. 2._____

    A. A reduction in personal income tax rates
    B. A decline in consumer incomes
    C. An expectation that prices will soon rise
    D. Increased government payments to individuals

3. When the economy fluctuates between boom and depression, the part of *total* spending that changes by the largest percent is 3._____

    A. spending by families on consumer goods and services
    B. business spending on factories, machinery, and inventories
    C. state and local government spending on all activities
    D. business spending on wages and salaries

4. If, when there is full employment, the federal government increases its spending WITHOUT increasing its tax revenues, *generally* 4._____

    A. a serious depression will occur
    B. an increase in unemployment will occur
    C. the national debt will decrease
    D. inflation will occur

5. A government budgetary deficit exists whenever 5._____

    A. the national debt is decreasing
    B. taxes are reduced
    C. government expenditures are increased
    D. total government spending exceeds receipts

6. When more money is created through government mints or through increased bank lending, the result is *generally* 6._____

    A. more spending
    B. less spending
    C. higher interest rates
    D. decreased savings

7. The Federal Reserve Board *generally* tries to increase the money supply when it wants to

   A. fight unemployment-during recessions
   B. fight inflation
   C. hold down the government debt
   D. make large profits

8. The limit of an economy's real output at any time is set by

   A. business demand for goods and services
   B. the quantity and quality of labor, capital, and natural resources
   C. government regulations and spending
   D. the amount of money in circulation

9. MOST of the funds on deposit in commercial banks originate through

   A. individuals depositing currency in banks
   B. the rise of our gold stock
   C. business firms extending credit to customers
   D. banks making loans and investments

10. A monetary policy is *often* ineffective when used to check a recession, because at such times

    A. banks lack reserves to make loans
    B. there may NOT be a strong demand for loans
    C. the Federal Reserve CANNOT engage in open-market conditions
    D. reserve requirements CANNOT be lowered

11. Rapidly growing economies differ from slowly growing economies in that the former are always characterized by a(n)

    A. slow rate of population growth
    B. abundant supply of natural resources
    C. high rate of investment
    D. balanced national budget

12. If effective demand (i.e., total spending) periodically falls short of productive capacity, the rate of growth of the economy over a long period will be _____ because

    A. higher; inefficient plants, equipment, and labor no longer need be employed
    B. higher; production will be concentrated on necessary goods rather than luxuries
    C. lower; some productive resources will not be employed
    D. lower; of a heavier reliance on the raw materials of foreign countries

13. Three of these statements are TRUE of the so-called underdeveloped economies. Which one is NOT?

    A. Approximately two-thirds of the world's population live in such areas.
    B. These areas would soon achieve developed economies if their domestic money supply could be greatly increased.
    C. Low income in these areas makes savings for economic growth difficult.
    D. Political and social conditions exist that hold back their economic development.

14. *Americans are a mixed-up people with no sense of ethical values. Everyone knows that baseball is far less necessary than food and steel, yet they pay ballplayers a lot more than farmers and steelworkers.*
    Why?

    A. Ballplayers are *really* entertainers rather than producers.
    B. Ballplayers are more skilled than persons who get less pay.
    C. Excellent baseball players are scarcer relative to the demand for their services.
    D. There are fewer professional ballplayers than farmers or steelworkers.

15. The median household income in the United States in 2013 was between _____ and _____.

    A. $20,000; $30,000
    B. $30,000; $40,000
    C. $40,000; $60,000
    D. $60,000; $80,000

16. In the United States, the high wages received by MOST workers depend *largely* on

    A. actions of the federal government
    B. the social responsibility shown by business
    C. our minimum wage laws
    D. the high output per worker

17. Labor unions in the United States have

    A. strengthened the bargaining position of laborers in relation to their employers
    B. substantially increased the real wages of organized labor as compared with those of unorganized labor
    C. increased the percent of Americans who earn their living by rendering labor services
    D. increased competition in the labor market

18. The government program for agriculture is BEST summarized in which statement?

    A. Output has been drastically reduced so that surpluses have not accumulated; thus, farm income and prices of farm products have been high.
    B. An attempt has been made to improve farm incomes by taking a variety of measures to raise the price of farm products above the free market price.
    C. The government pays farmers enough money to bring their yearly incomes after taxes up to the level of incomes received by average non-farm laborers.
    D. Ours has been a policy of laissez-faire – of expressing concern for the farmer but generally doing nothing to affect the level of his income.

19. Identify the FALSE explanation of the *farm problem* in the United States.

    A. The growth of agricultural productivity has been much less rapid than that of the rest of the economy.
    B. Technological change has made it economical to use less labor and more capital in agriculture.
    C. As our economy has grown, the total demand for agricultural products has increased much less than for industrial products.
    D. When farm prices fall, the consumption of agricultural products increases only slightly.

20. Of these features of capitalism, communism as practiced in the former Soviet Union functioned without

   A. prices
   B. capital goods
   C. private profit
   D. all of the above

21. Which point is characteristic of both communism as practiced in the U.S.S.R. and private enterprise as practiced in the United States?

   A. Nearly all capital goods and natural resources are owned by the state.
   B. Trade unions have an important role in setting wages and conditions of work.
   C. Market prices automatically reflect consumer demand.
   D. Differences in money wages and salaries are used as an economic incentive.

22. As compared with more orthodox, communism, democratic socialism (e.g., in the United Kingdom, Sweden, and India)

   A. has more extensive government control over wages
   B. uses wage incentives more for workers
   C. places more emphasis on rapid economic growth
   D. permits the people more influence over what is produced

Questions 23-25.

DIRECTIONS: Questions 23 to 25 refer to the three charts on the next page.

23. Judging from your inspection of the charts above, the MOST serious economic problem of the early 1960's seems to be the

   A. decline in the output of the economy
   B. rapid inflation
   C. unemployment
   D. increase of the gross national product to a new all-time high

24. The fact that the consumer price index on the chart was *approximately* 75 in 1947 means that the average price of consumer goods and services in 1947 was about

   A. 75¢ a unit
   B. 75% above the average level of prices since 1947
   C. 25% less than 1957-59 prices
   D. 75% lower than at present

25. On the charts above, note the behavior of the economy between 1956 and 1958. Which statement MOST correctly analyzes the situation and states the MOST appropriate monetary and fiscal policies for these years?

   A. With GNP moving to an all-time high, *no* change in policy is necessary to keep the economy stable.
   B. Unemployment is rising. A budgetary deficit and/or an easy money policy is called for.
   C. Inflation continues and accelerates. A budgetary surplus and/or a tight money policy is called for.
   D. A dilemma exists. The appropriate monetary-fiscal policy to reduce unemployment is *likely* to increase the inflation, and policies to check inflation may increase unemployment.

GROSS NATIONAL PRODUCT, PRICES AND UNEMPLOYMENT

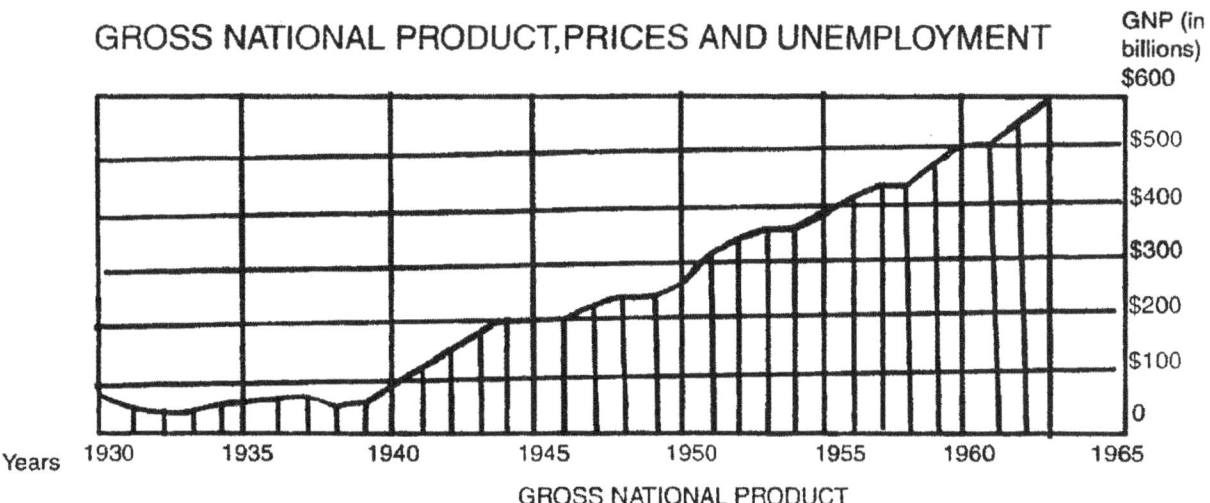

GROSS NATIONAL PRODUCT

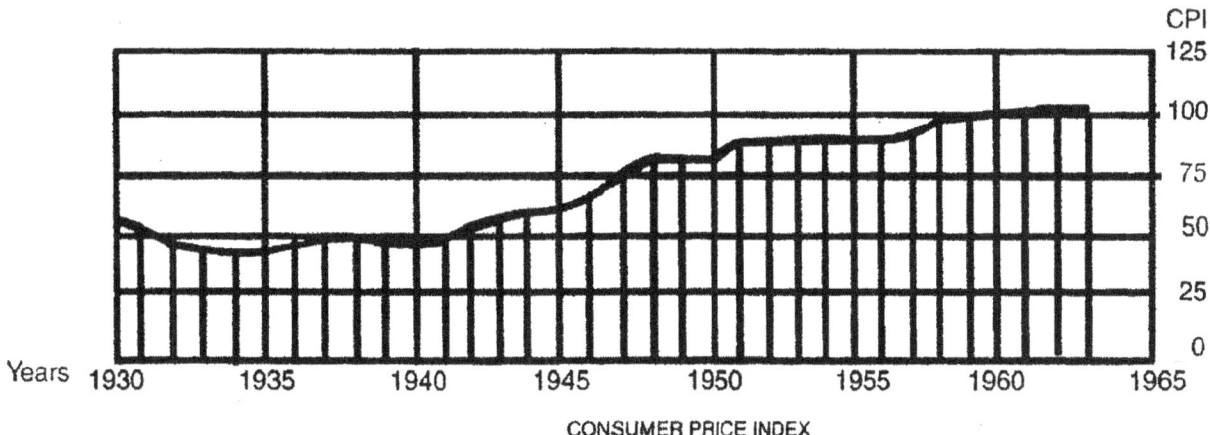

CONSUMER PRICE INDEX

(1957-59=100)

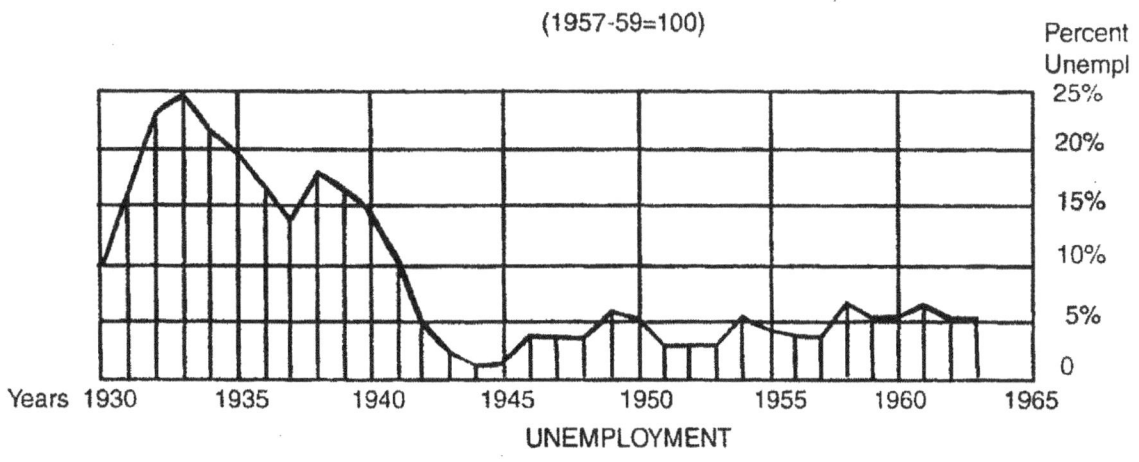

UNEMPLOYMENT
(Percent of civilion labor force)

KEY (CORRECT ANSWERS)

1. D
2. B
3. B
4. D
5. D

6. A
7. A
8. B
9. D
10. B

11. C
12. C
13. B
14. C
15. C

16. D
17. A
18. B
19. A
20. C

21. D
22. D
23. C
24. C
25. D

TEST 2

DIRECTIONS: Each question or incomplete statement is followed by several suggested answers or completions. Select the one that BEST answers the question or completes the statement. *PRINT THE LETTER OF THE CORRECT ANSWER IN THE SPACE AT THE RIGHT.*

1. When a nation's human and material resources are being fully and efficiently used, more of any one product

    A. cannot be produced
    B. cannot be produced unless private enterprise rather than government does so
    C. can be produced only if there is less production of some other products
    D. can be produced only if there is a general decrease in prices

    1.____

2. All economic systems (capitalist, communist, feudal, or any other) face similar economic problems.
    Which one of these questions would SOME but not all economies face?

    A. What will be produced and how?
    B. How can markets be kept competitive?
    C. How many resources will be devoted to maintaining and increasing future capacity?
    D. For whom will the goods be produced?

    2.____

3. In a basically private enterprise economy, which group exercises the PRINCIPAL influence on the choice of goods produced over a long period of time?

    A. Consumers   B. Government
    C. Big business   D. Labor unions

    3.____

4. Which is NOT a function of profits in a basically private enterprise economy?

    A. Providing an incentive for efficient production by businesses
    B. Rewarding producers who give consumers what they demand
    C. Inducing businessmen to assume necessary business risks
    D. Indicating to the government where wages are too low

    4.____

5. How does a family's saving MOST clearly influence capital formation?

    A. Saving means spending less; therefore, family saving hurts the seller and thus discourages capital formation.
    B. Savings are ALWAYS invested by the saver; therefore, an increase in family saving increases capital formation.
    C. A family's savings are normally channeled through financial institutions to firms that *usually* use the savings for capital formation.
    D. A family's savings lead to capital formation when they are used to pay off debts.

    5.____

6. In a basically private enterprise economy, the MAIN objective of businessmen is to

    A. provide good jobs for workers at reasonable wages
    B. secure government regulation that is favorable to business
    C. try to make profits
    D. provide highest-quality products

    6.____

7. If a consumer is to exercise his freedom of choice wisely in a private enterprise economy, he

   A. should know whether a product was produced by a monopolist
   B. MUST know where products are produced so that he may purchase those made locally, if possible
   C. should know what alternative goods and services are available as well as their qualities and prices
   D. MUST have sufficient income to permit him to purchase whatever he chooses

8. Assume that the demand increases for a commodity produced by many competitive firms.
   The resulting rise in price of the commodity will *usually* lead to

   A. less being produced
   B. more being produced
   C. no change in production
   D. elimination of inefficient businesses from the market

9. If the supply of a commodity increases at the same time the demand for it falls, in the absence of counteracting forces, its price will

   A. rise   B. fall
   C. stay the same D. be indeterminate

10. In a private enterprise economy, the public interest is served even when individuals pursue their own private economic goals.
    This is because of

    A. the social responsibility of private businessmen
    B. careful planning and coordination of economic activity
    C. the operation of competitive markets
    D. individuals who understand what is in the public interest

11. Under a private enterprise economy, the function of competition is to

    A. eliminate wasteful advertising
    B. eliminate interest and profits
    C. prevent large firms from driving small ones out of business
    D. force prices to the LOWEST level consistent with a reasonable profit

12. Of these factors, a(n) _____ is *not likely* to increase the demand for bricks.

    A. increase in the price of home construction
    B. increase in the incomes of potential home builders
    C. decrease in the price of mortar (i.e., a complementary commodity)
    D. increase in the price of lumber (i.e., a substitute for bricks)

13. Which of the following is the MOST basic economic objection to monopolies?

    A. Prices set by monopolies are *usually* too low.
    B. Monopolies exert disproportionate political power.
    C. When a monopoly fails, the effect upon our economy is far more serious than when a competitive enterprise fails.
    D. Economic resources will tend to be less efficiently allocated.

14. Identify the FALSE statement regarding the economy of the United States over the past fifty years.

    A. Monopoly has increased to the point where it controls more than half of our production.
    B. The average size of firms has grown substantially.
    C. Small firms and large firms have both increased in number.
    D. Improved transportation and communication have resulted in firms competing over larger markets.

15. The federal government attempts to eliminate monopolies MAINLY in order to

    A. ensure competition
    B. prevent small firms from decreasing
    C. expand public utilities
    D. prevent the growth of big business

16. In large business corporations, the common stockholders *generally* do NOT

    A. own the business
    B. receive a share of the profits
    C. vote for the board of directors
    D. manage the day-to-day business

17. The opportunity cost (or alternative cost) of a new public high school is the

    A. money cost of the new building
    B. other desirable economic goods that must be forgone to secure the school
    C. necessary increase in the annual tax rate
    D. cost of constructing it now as opposed to the cost of a new school at a later date

18. Government expenditures (federal, state, and local combined) *now* represent about what portion of the gross national product?

    A. A tenth B. A quarter
    C. Half   D. Three-fourths

19. The bulk of federal government expenditure during the Reagan-Bush years was for

    A. foreign aid
    B. the space program
    C. special benefits for the poor and unemployed
    D. national defense

20. In a basically private enterprise economy, a(n) _____ is *likely* to alter MOST the pattern of consumer choice among alternative products.

    A. general sales tax
    B. personal income tax
    C. excise tax on particular products
    D. tax on business profits

21. Specialization and exchange within a nation or between nations create which effect? 21.____

    A. A larger total quantity of wanted goods and services can be produced.
    B. The independence of both nations and individuals is increased.
    C. The danger of economic instability is reduced.
    D. All costs of production will rise, but not proportionately.

22. When a nation is running a deficit in its international balance of payments, it is ALWAYS currently 22.____

    A. exporting more goods than it is importing
    B. importing more goods than it is exporting
    C. paying more to other nations than others are paying to it
    D. helping less fortunate nations to develop economically

23. Reduced U.S. tariffs would *probably* 23.____

    A. lessen job opportunities in our export industries
    B. injure most farmers
    C. force some workers out of jobs in presently protected industries
    D. lower the average U.S. standard of living

24. When obtained at various intervals, which one of these four types of statistics will give the BEST measure of the economic growth of a nation? 24.____

    A. Balance of payments   B. Index of stock prices
    C. Total employment   D. Real income per capita

25. Annual gross national product is a measure of 25.____

    A. the quantity of goods and services produced by private businesses
    B. the value of a nation's total output of goods and services
    C. the price level of goods and services sold
    D. that part of production which is used by the government

KEY (CORRECT ANSWERS)

1. C		11. D
2. B		12. A
3. A		13. D
4. D		14. A
5. C		15. A
6. C		16. D
7. C		17. B
8. B		18. B
9. B		19. D
10. C		20. C

21. A
22. C
23. C
24. D
25. B

TEST 3

DIRECTIONS: Each question or incomplete statement is followed by several suggested answers or completions. Select the one that BEST answers the question or completes the statement. *PRINT THE LETTER OF THE CORRECT ANSWER IN THE SPACE AT THE RIGHT.*

1. The MAXIMUM gross national product a nation can produce in any one year is set by   1.____

   A. its natural resources
   B. families' demand for products
   C. the amount of money people have to spend
   D. its productive resources

2. Often an economy operates at less than full employment. This is *most likely* to occur when   2.____

   A. total spending is inadequate
   B. there is inflation
   C. there is a scarcity of unskilled labor
   D. ever competition is intense.

3. The *total* output of the economy is bought by which large group of spenders?   3.____

   A. Farmers, laborers, and housewives
   B. Consumers, business firms, and governments
   C. Investors, speculators, and bankers
   D. Corporations, households, and capitalists

4. In recessions in the United States since World War II, _____ has declined MOST sharply.   4.____

   A. family spending on consumer goods
   B. business firms' spending on plants, equipment, and inventories
   C. family spending on services
   D. government spending on goods and services

5. Increasing the government budgetary surplus or decreasing the deficit is particularly desirable in a period of   5.____

   A. inflation   B. mass unemployment
   C. depression   D. economic instability

6. The PRIMARY reason for the growth in federal debt over the last century has been government deficits caused by   6.____

   A. wasteful domestic expenditures and social welfare payments
   B. depressions and recessions
   C. declining tax receipts
   D. wars

7. An increase in the amount of money in the nation *usually* leads to higher prices EXCEPT when

   A. there is widespread unemployment of men and machines
   B. labor unions are strong
   C. the nation's gold reserves are adequate
   D. there is general prosperity

8. When commercial banks increase their loans to businesses and consumers, the result is a(n)

   A. decrease in the spending power of consumers and businesses
   B. increase in the nation's money supply
   C. increase in government control over the economy
   D. increase in the banks' excess reserves

9. In an inflationary period, an appropriate policy for the Federal Reserve would be to

   A. sell government securities on the open market
   B. lower legal reserve requirements
   C. decrease the discount rate
   D. encourage member banks to increase their loans

10. _____ are typically hurt the MOST by inflation.

    A. Farmers
    B. Debtors
    C. Government bondholders
    D. Businessmen

11. Assume our economy is operating at full capacity.
    Which policy would NOT be appropriate to increase our rate of economic growth?

    A. Encouraging an increase of private savings and investment in capital goods and equipment
    B. Improving the skill and knowledge of people through increased education
    C. Developing technology and managerial ability
    D. Encouraging an increase in personal consumption

12. If total demand declines relative to the productive capacity of the economy,

    A. the growth rate is *likely* to slow down, at least temporarily
    B. inflation is *likely* to occur
    C. a large government budgetary surplus is *likely* to occur
    D. employment is *likely* to increase

13. The average per capita income of the two-thirds of the world's population in the so-called underdeveloped nations is _____ of ours.

    A. less than one-tenth
    B. about one-quarter
    C. about one-half
    D. about three-fourths

14. The MOST general cause of low individual incomes in the United States is

    A. lack of valuable productive services to sell
    B. unwillingness to work
    C. automation
    D. discrimination against non-union employees

15. In the United States during the present decade, 15._____

    A. inequality in personal incomes has been *largely* eliminated
    B. the rich have become richer and the poor poorer
    C. average real family income after taxes has remained *generally* unchanged
    D. income inequality has been *somewhat* reduced

16. High wages in the United States are based on the high productivity of U.S. labor. 16._____
All of these factors contribute to this high productivity EXCEPT

    A. the skill and work habits of U.S. labor
    B. our accumulation of a large stock of capital goods
    C. our technological and managerial advances
    D. tariff protection from competition of low-paid foreign workers

17. Both featherbedding by unions and monopolistic practices by employers are *likely* to 17._____
result in

    A. an increase in average labor productivity for the nation as a whole
    B. a less efficient use of resources
    C. less labor being used in the industry affected
    D. a raising of average real wages in the nation as a whole

18. Identify the MOST obvious result of our governmental policy toward agriculture. 18._____

    A. The average farm income has been raised *almost* to the level of the average non-farm income.
    B. Large surpluses of farm commodities have been accumulated by the government.
    C. Capital and labor have turned to agriculture to take advantage of guaranteed high prices and profits.
    D. The family farm has been *almost* completely replaced by the large corporate farm.

19. Measures to increase economic security against unemployment will tend to increase 19._____
economic efficiency if

    A. one cannot transfer to better-paying jobs offered by other employers, to be eligible for benefits
    B. the security the measure provides tends to reduce one's incentive to produce
    C. the costs of the measures are borne equally by firms regardless of their record for causing economic insecurity
    D. the average output per worker is increased as a result of improved economic security

20. In the United States, in contrast to socialist/communist nations, 20._____

    A. the problem of scarcity has been eliminated
    B. consumer spending *largely* determines what commodities are produced
    C. incomes are unequally distributed
    D. government plays an insignificant role in economic life

4 (#3)

21. The interest rate charged on overnight loans from one member bank of the Federal Reserve System to another is known as

   A. overnight fund interest rate
   B. exdividend rate
   C. Federal funds rate
   D. fiscal debenture reserve rate

21.____

22. Compared with the U.S. economy, the democratic socialist economies of the United Kingdom, the Scandinavian countries, and India

   A. are considerably more productive
   B. have more government ownership and control
   C. demonstrate clearly that *only* private enterprise is compatible with democracy
   D. have been short-lived, for in two of the cases socialism has been abandoned

22.____

Questions 23-25.

DIRECTIONS: Questions 23-25 refer to the charts on the on the following page.

23. We desire a growing economy in which the price level is stable and employment reasonably high.
    The charts on the preceding page show that we have MOST fully approximated this ideal between _____ and _____.

   A. 1937; 1938   B. 1940; 1941
   C. 1946; 1947   D. 1955; 1956

23.____

24. Judging from your inspection of the three charts, the MOST serious economic problem of the immediate postwar period (1946-48) is

   A. decline in the output of the economy
   B. inflation
   C. unemployment
   D. declining output per worker

24.____

25. On the charts, note the behavior of the economy between 1950 and 1952.
    Identify the statement which MOST correctly analyzes the situation and states the MOST appropriate monetary and fiscal policies for these years.

   A. The GNP is moving to an all-time high and prices are stable; no change in policy is called for.
   B. Unemployment is rising; a budgetary deficit and/or an easy money policy is called for.
   C. It is a period of inflation; a budgetary surplus and/or a tight money policy is called for.
   D. Employment is falling and prices are rising; therefore, a budgetary deficit and/or a tight money policy is called for.

25.____

GROSS NATIONAL PRODUCT, PRICES AND UNEMPLOYMENT

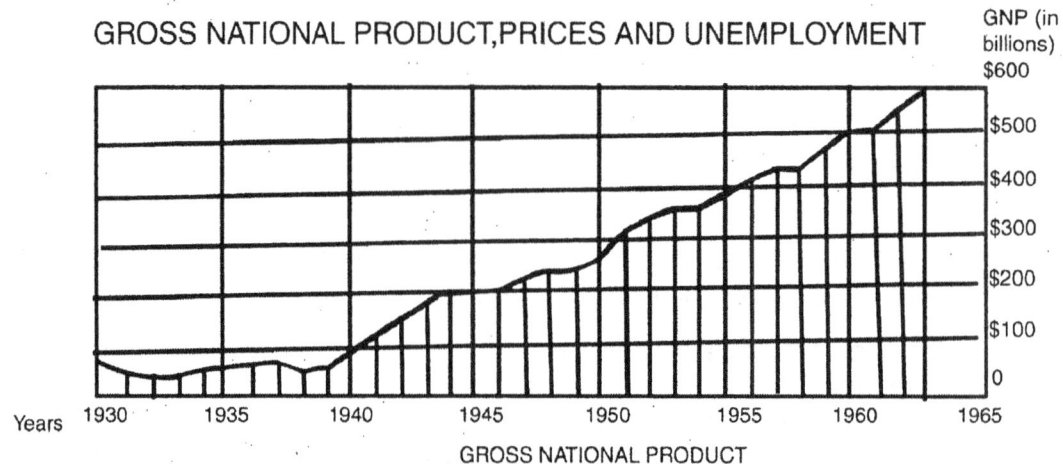

GROSS NATIONAL PRODUCT

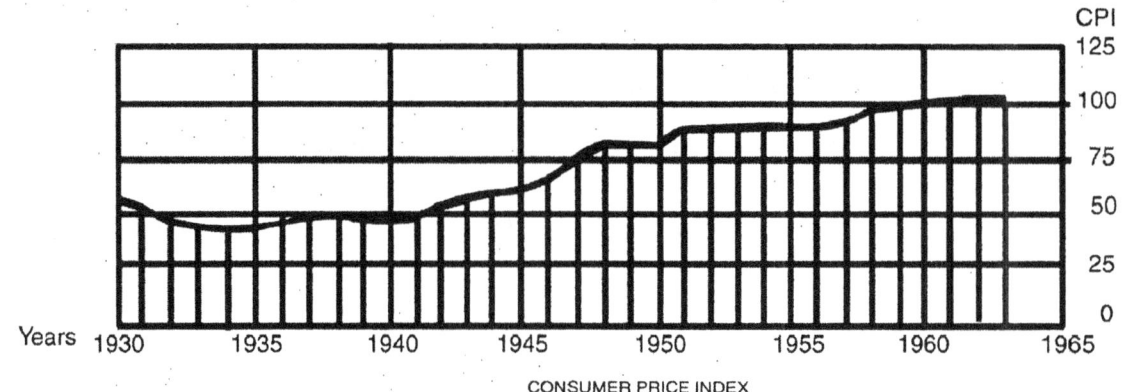

CONSUMER PRICE INDEX

(1957-59=100)

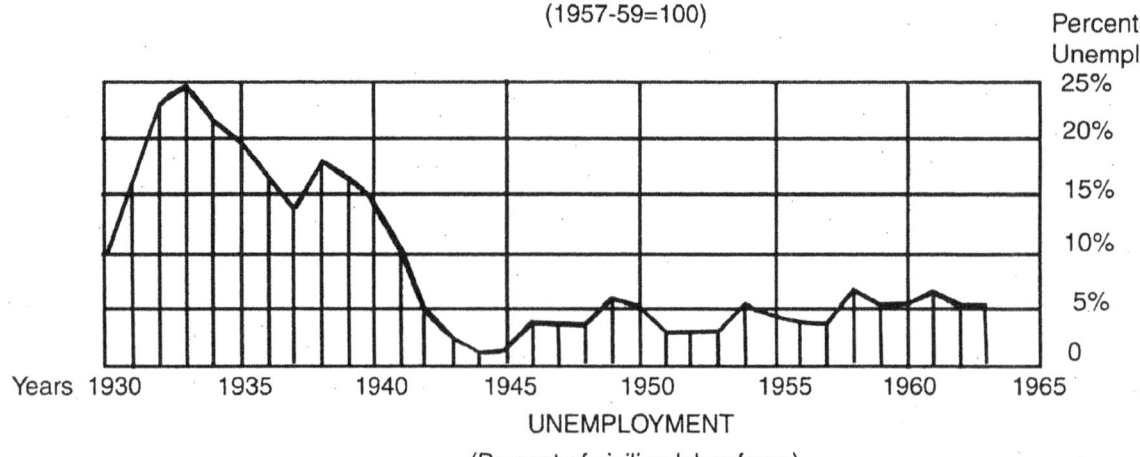

UNEMPLOYMENT
(Percent of civilion labor force)

KEY (CORRECT ANSWERS)

1. D
2. A
3. B
4. B
5. A

6. D
7. A
8. B
9. A
10. C

11. D
12. A
13. A
14. A
15. D

16. D
17. B
18. B
19. D
20. B

21. C
22. B
23. D
24. B
25. C

TEST 4

DIRECTIONS: Each question or incomplete statement is followed by several suggested answers or completions. Select the one that BEST answers the question or completes the statement. *PRINT THE LETTER OF THE CORRECT ANSWER IN THE SPACE AT THE RIGHT.*

1. Every economic system faces the need to economize. In this context, the BEST definition of *to economize* is to

    A. save money and thus reduce the national debt
    B. dispense with the production of luxuries
    C. balance the government's budget by reducing spending
    D. make the best use of scarce resources that have alternative uses

    1._____

2. What is meant by the assertion that *every* economic system (such as socialism, capitalism, communism) faces the fact of scarcity?

    A. There are insufficient productive resources to satisfy all wants of a society.
    B. There are times when some products can be had *only* by paying high prices.
    C. In the beginning, every society faces shortages, but a mature economy, such as our own, overcomes scarcity in time.
    D. All economies have depressions during which scarcities exist.

    2._____

3. Which point BEST characterizes the relation between producers, consumers, and government in a private enterprise economy?

    A. Producers decide what to produce, government how it shall be produced, and consumers who shall receive the product.
    B. Consumer spending leads producers to decide what shall be produced and how resources shall be used. Government seeks to maintain competition and the rights of private property.
    C. Consumers decide what should be produced, producers how BEST to produce it, and government who shall receive which products.
    D. Government ultimately decides what shall be produced and how. Consumers and producers, as voters, control the government.

    3._____

4. Three of the following are essential to the operation of a private enterprise economy. Which one might such an economy operate WITHOUT?

    A. Profit motive   B. Markets
    C. Corporations   D. Prices

    4._____

5. The principle of diminishing returns is BEST illustrated by

    A. small firms being driven out of business by large firms
    B. any decline in the average rate of profits
    C. a slowing rate of increase in output as a farmer adds increasing amounts of fertilizer to his land
    D. the decline in personal income as workers age

    5._____

6. Business firms wish to sell their products at a high price; households wish to buy products at low prices.
   In a private enterprise economy, this conflict of interests

   A. is reconciled by competitive markets
   B. is reconciled by government regulation
   C. does NOT exist; there is really *no* conflict of interest between households and firms
   D. is NOT reconciled; since all household heads are members of firms, the interests of firms prevail

7. In a private enterprise economy, government encourages freedom of choice by

   A. guaranteeing complete freedom of choice to households and firms
   B. limiting this freedom for some if their choices might reduce freedom of choice significantly for others
   C. requiring individuals and firms to use their freedom of choice wisely
   D. seeing that individuals and firms choose what the majority believes BEST

8. A rise in the price of _____ would be *likely* to increase the demand for butter.

   A. butter
   B. oleomargarine
   C. bread
   D. any of the above

9. Assuming that the supply of a product remains constant as the demand for it increases, its price will *normally*

   A. fall
   B. rise
   C. stay the same
   D. either rise or fall

10. _____ is MOST essential for a private enterprise economy.

    A. Active competition in the marketplace
    B. The functioning of labor unions
    C. Action by responsible business leaders
    D. Extensive government regulation

11. The price of shoes is *likely* to be increased by

    A. more capital investment by producers
    B. a decrease in the demand for shoes
    C. a decrease in the supply of shoes
    D. new machines reducing the cost of shoe production

12. If the government were to levy a tax of one dollar on every pair of shoes sold, a *most likely* result would be that

    A. consumers would pay a higher price for shoes and probably buy a smaller quantity
    B. suppliers would increase the quantity sold in order to offset the taxes paid to the government
    C. consumers would pay a higher price and, as a result, suppliers would make larger profits
    D. suppliers would sell more and charge a higher price

13. *Generally*, when a monopoly replaces private competitive enterprises,   13.____

    A. production efficiency is increased because of the larger scale of operation
    B. the market *no* longer tends to bring about the MOST efficient allocation of resources
    C. there is an increase in the number of firms making the product
    D. the monopolist controls both consumers and labor

14. The purpose of the Sherman and Clayton Antitrust Acts is to   14.____

    A. keep markets effectively competitive
    B. keep firms from becoming large
    C. prevent banks from becoming trusts
    D. protect the investing public

15. Common stocks, limited liability, and a charter are characteristic of   15.____

    A. individual proprietorships
    B. partnerships
    C. private business corporations
    D. most small business firms

16. Over the past fifty years, the share of the total U.S. market controlled by the hundred largest firms has   16.____

    A. changed by only a small amount
    B. risen substantially
    C. increased to more than 90 percent
    D. fallen steadily

17. These arguments have been used regarding the proposals for increased public expenditures on education.   17.____
    Which one shows the BEST use of economic reasoning, using the alternative (or opportunity cost) principle?

    A. Taxpayers should compare the probable sacrifices resulting from the added tax with the probable advantages of the new program.
    B. In real terms, the added school tax will cost us necessary food and clothing, adequate support of our churches, and essential medical care.
    C. Luxuries are the real alternative cost of the proposed educational improvements.
    D. Whenever a product is good, public or private expenditure on it is always desirable.

18. Government expenditure (federal, state, and local combined) is now the GREATEST for   18.____

    A. social services, including health and social security
    B. salaries of elected public officials, upkeep of public buildings, and cost of hearings, of the court system, and of highways
    C. public education - elementary, secondary, and higher
    D. national defense and related operations

19. Most taxes divert spending power; as a result, control over some resources passes from   19.____

    A. the government to individuals and businesses
    B. individuals and businesses to government

C. the federal government to the state government
D. gross national product to national income

20. Given our present pattern of government expenditure, the graduated or progressive income tax causes

   A. income after taxes to be more evenly distributed
   B. the rich to get richer and the poor to get poorer
   C. wage earners to pay more tax than property owners
   D. it to be impossible to inherit wealth

21. Specialization and division of labor by nations followed by increasing international trade *probably* would

   A. increase total world production of wanted goods and services
   B. lower living standards in the wealthy nations
   C. increase the likelihood of worldwide unemployment
   D. eliminate differences in standards of living among nations

22. A nation has a deficit in its international balance of payments when it

   A. buys more goods and services abroad than it sells
   B. makes more payments, excluding gold, to other countries than it receives from them
   C. has an unfavorable balance of trade
   D. owes more gold to other nations than it has

23. Each statement about tariffs is *likely* to be TRUE EXCEPT that tariffs

   A. preserve employment in domestic industries whose products they protect
   B. reduce the market for our exports by reducing our imports
   C. encourage the growth of our most efficient industries and eliminate the least efficient
   D. benefit some groups at the expense of the national standard of living

24. Inflation is *most likely* to benefit

   A. savings bank depositors
   B. debtors
   C. life insurance policyholders
   D. persons living on fixed pensions

25. The BEST single measure of the total economic output in the United States is the

   A. gross national product
   B. total amount of take-home pay
   C. consumer price index
   D. index of industrial production

KEY (CORRECT ANSWERS)

1.	D	11.	C
2.	A	12.	A
3.	B	13.	B
4.	C	14.	A
5.	C	15.	C
6.	A	16.	A
7.	B	17.	A
8.	B	18.	D
9.	B	19.	B
10.	A	20.	A

21. A
22. B
23. C
24. B
25. A

EXAMINATION SECTION
TEST 1

DIRECTIONS: Each question or incomplete statement is followed by several suggested answers or completions. Select the one that BEST answers the question or completes the statement. *PRINT THE LETTER OF THE CORRECT ANSWER IN THE SPACE AT THE RIGHT.*

1. Which of the following trends is a result of the other three?

   A. Shift of population away from rural areas
   B. Increased mechanization of agriculture
   C. Depletion of soil fertility
   D. Improvement in general business conditions

2. Which one of the following groupings includes laws which are MOST closely related to each other?

   A. Social Security Act, Wheeler-Rayburn Act, Fair Labor Standards Act
   B. National Labor Relations Act, Taft-Hartley Law, Webb-Pomerene Act
   C. Sherman Anti-Trust Act, Clayton Act, Robinson-Patman Act
   D. Walsh-Healey Act, Federal Reserve Act, Glass-Steagall Act

3. Which one of the following is NOT a plan for alleviating the effects of the business cycle?

   A. The Social Credit Program
   B. The compensated dollar
   C. Pump priming
   D. The International Stabilization Fund

4. When a nation such as Great Britain devalues its currency, the tendency is to

   A. increase imports
   B. decrease its tourist trade
   C. reduce its dollar shortage
   D. lower prices in Great Britain

5. Which one of the following objections to a steadily increasing public debt involves a fallacy?

   A. Interest must be paid by taxes or further borrowing.
   B. Our generation is spared at the expense of future generations.
   C. Fear of the debt may deter investment.
   D. Expenditure may be wasteful if no ceiling to the debt is enforced.

6. The *total value of all the goods and services produced during the year by all the producers in the nation* BEST describes

   A. national income
   C. real national income
   B. gross national product
   D. national wealth

7. Of the following, the one which is the BEST example of a trade association is the

   A. Newspaper Guild
   B. Brookings Institution
   C. Ford Foundation
   D. American Iron and Steel Institute

8. Labor economists report that the period 1945-1954 may well become known in the history of the labor movement in the United States as the one which saw the

   A. widespread growth of union welfare funds
   B. winning of the guaranteed annual wage in many industries
   C. increase in independent labor unions
   D. organization of the majority of American workers into labor unions

9. Fundamental reasons for the change from laissez-faire to federal government regulation in the United States include all of the following EXCEPT

   A. expansion of business combinations
   B. unfair business practices
   C. lax state corporation laws
   D. the gold standard

10. In each of the annual federal budgets that were submitted since World War II, the LARGEST single sum, apart from expenditure for national security programs, was expended for

    A. agricultural supports
    B. veterans' benefits
    C. interest on debt
    D. old age and unemployment payments

11. Each of the following is characteristic of current farm prosperity in the United States EXCEPT:

    A. There has been a sharp decrease in the number of farm units since 1935
    B. Farm tenancy has declined since 1935
    C. Farm income has averaged more than 20% of the national income in recent years
    D. An increasing volume of farm products is utilized for industrial production

12. Which one of the following is NOT based on the benefit theory of taxation?

    A. Social security taxes
    B. Special assessments
    C. Estate taxes
    D. License fees

13. During inflation, unearned benefits come to

    A. bondholders
    B. owners of life insurance
    C. pensioners
    D. stockholders

14. In economic analysis, the term *unearned increment* has been MOST commonly applied to

    A. rents
    B. profits
    C. interest
    D. bonuses

15. Which one of the following economic principles provides the basis for the Malthusian doctrine? Law of

    A. Diminishing Returns
    B. Comparative Costs
    C. Supply and Demand
    D. Monopoly Price

    15._____

16. A family's standard of living can MOST accurately be measured by its _____ income.

    A. money
    B. real
    C. take-home
    D. net

    16._____

17. Which one of the following conditions is MOST likely to counteract the tendency of the price of a product to rise following an increase in wages?

    A. The existence of competition in the industry
    B. A corresponding rise in productivity
    C. An accompanying reduction in hours of work
    D. The existence of inelastic demand for the product

    17._____

18. Which one of the following types of unemployment is MOST susceptible to control by the individual firm or industry?

    A. Seasonal
    B. Cyclical
    C. Technological
    D. Residual

    18._____

19. The MOST pervasive principal underlying the distribution of income in a capitalist society is

    A. social usefulness
    B. effort expended
    C. need
    D. productivity

    19._____

20. Which of the following types of legislation is designed to insure the free functioning of the price mechanism in the economic system?

    A. Laws regulating labor relations
    B. Anti-trust laws
    C. Protective tariffs
    D. Progressive taxes

    20._____

21. Which of the following items makes possible each of the other three?

    A. Retention of profits by a corporation instead of distributing them
    B. Issuance by a corporation of stock dividends as distinguished from cash dividends
    C. Reduction in the market price of a corporation's stock
    D. Concealment or minimization of the appearance of a corporation's profits

    21._____

22. Which of the following writings attacked Colbert's economic theories?

    A. Das Kapital
    B. Progress and Poverty
    C. Utopia
    D. Wealth of Nations

    22._____

23. Which of the following is the STRONGEST argument advanced for a protective tariff? It

    A. tends to promote national self-sufficiency
    B. increases total employment
    C. raises the general level of real wages
    D. yields substantial amounts of revenue

    23._____

24. In which of the following fields has the cooperative movement in the United States been MOST successful? 24.____

    A. Manufacturing and credit
    B. Marketing and credit
    C. Consumption and marketing
    D. Credit and consumption

25. The trust laws passed by the Federal Government between 1880-1914 attempted to protect the American public against the undesirable practices of Big Business by 25.____

    A. providing for fair competition
    B. establishing government ceilings in wages and hours
    C. regulating the output of industries producing strategic materials
    D. encouraging government ownership of industries in which private enterprise failed

KEY (CORRECT ANSWERS)

1.	A	11.	C
2.	C	12.	C
3.	D	13.	D
4.	C	14.	A
5.	B	15.	A
6.	B	16.	B
7.	D	17.	B
8.	A	18.	A
9.	D	19.	D
10.	C	20.	B

21.	B
22.	D
23.	A
24.	B
25.	A

TEST 2

DIRECTIONS: Each question or incomplete statement is followed by several suggested answers or completions. Select the one that BEST answers the question or completes the statement. *PRINT THE LETTER OF THE CORRECT ANSWER IN THE SPACE AT THE RIGHT.*

1. Which of the following *New Deal* laws constitute an innovation in the role played by the Federal government in the economic system?

    A. Food, Drug, and Cosmetic Act
    B. Public Utility Holding Company
    C. Banking Act of 1935
    D. Social Security Act

    1.____

2. Which of the following events occurred subsequent to the formation of the Congress of Industrial Organizations?

    A. Total trade union membership in the United States more than doubled.
    B. Agreement was reached on the respective jurisdictions of the C.I.O. and the A.F. of L.
    C. Virtually all workers in mining and railroading became affiliated with either the C.I.O. or the A.F. of L.
    D. The membership of the C.I.O. grew to twice that of the A.F. of L.

    2.____

3. In which of the following provisions is the Labor-Management Relations Act of 1947 (Taft-Hartley) MOST similar to the National Labor Relations Act of 1935?

    A. Jurisdictional strikes and secondary boycotts are prohibited.
    B. Employers may call for an election to determine which organization represents the majority of their employees.
    C. Unions and corporations are forbidden to make political contributions.
    D. Employers must bargain collectively with the duly certified representatives of their workers.

    3.____

4. Which one of the following conditions is common to the union shop and the closed shop?

    A. Union membership is restricted as a means of limiting the number of employees.
    B. The union has complete control over hiring and firing of employees.
    C. Regular employees are compelled to be union members.
    D. None of the above

    4.____

5. *Escalator* clauses in trade union contracts are based on the index of

    A. personal income   B. consumers' prices
    C. commodity prices   D. industrial production

    5.____

6. A corporation that owns, the majority of stock or securities of one or more other corporations for purposes of control rather than investment is known as a(n) _____ company.

    A. hypothecation
    B. indenture
    C. holding
    D. trust

    6.____

7. The trend toward geographical centralization of industry has been partially reversed in recent years by the
    I. development of hydro-electric power plants
    II. development of more efficient means of transportation
    III. lack of sufficient capital for large-scale industry
    IV. limitations on the size of firms specified in the anti-trust laws
   The CORRECT factors are:

   A. I, II   B. I, II, III   C. I, III, IV   D. II, IV

8. Which of the following common practices have been employed to facilitate control of a corporation by individuals who together own a small fraction of the total common stock of the corporation?
    I. Issuing non-voting common stock
    II. Providing for voting by proxy
    III. Granting the right to vote only to holders of a certain number of shares
    IV. Allowing a small fraction of the votes cast to elect the board of directors
   The practices commonly employed are:

   A. I, II   B. I, II, III   C. II, IV   D. III, IV

9. All of the following measures taken by the United States government during World War II were aimed at preventing inflation EXCEPT

   A. restricting installment buying
   B. freezing employer and employee contributions to old age insurance at the existing rate
   C. maintaining the little steel formula
   D. rationing scarce goods

10. The Employment Act of 1946 was significant as

    A. enactment into legislation of the requirements concerning fair employment practices that had been operative in government contracts for war production
    B. a substantial extension of federal activity in the field of unemployment insurance
    C. an approach to the problem of cyclical fluctuations in business activity
    D. a substantial extension of civil service positions in federal government departments

11. The doctrine of an objective just price belongs to the period of the

    A. prescientific era of economics
    B. German historical school
    C. laissez-faire era in England
    D. socialist-communist school

12. Which of the following represents the chronological order in which the various schools of economic thought developed?

    A. Mercantilism; Physiocracy; English Classical; Austrian; Neo-classical
    B. Physiocracy; Mercantilism; English Classical; Austrian; Neo-classical
    C. English classical; Mercantilism; Austrian; Neo-classical; Physiocracy
    D. Mercantilism; Physiocracy; Austrian; English Classical; Neo-classical

13. The British economist whose works may be said to mark the beginning of the neo-classical school of economic thought was

    A. Alfred Marshall
    B. John Maynard Keynes
    C. William Stanley Jevons
    D. John Stuart Mill

14. Which of these pairs are names of economists of the same school of economic thought?

    A. Karl Menger and Eugen von Bohm-Bawerk
    B. Thomas Mun and Francois Quesnay
    C. J.B. Say and Friedrich Engels
    D. William Jevons and John A. Hobson

15. The theory that the problem of finding an investment for savings becomes more serious as a community grows richer is a central doctrine in the writings of

    A. Marshall
    B. Keynes
    C. Adam Smith
    D. Hayek

16. Organized commodity exchanges are characterized by
    I. dealings in inspected and graded products
    II. one price for any given commodity at any one time
    III. considerable trading in futures
    IV. open trading
    The CORRECT answer is:

    A. II, III   B. I, IV   C. I, II, III   D. I, II, III, IV

17. Overhead costs are significant in modern industry because

    A. they accentuate the importance of volume of production in determining cost per unit
    B. industries with heavy overhead costs tend to have stable employment records
    C. they are directly dependent upon wage rates and hence on the strength of organized labor
    D. they vary with prices for raw materials

18. The general effect of a tariff on a given commodity is to raise the domestic price of that commodity

    A. by the exact amount of the tariff
    B. if it succeeds in reducing supply of the commodity
    C. by increasing the foreign price
    D. if there is no retaliation

19. Price stability is MOST likely to characterize the market for a commodity in which the demand is _____ and supply _____.

    A. elastic; elastic
    B. elastic; inelastic
    C. inelastic; inelastic
    D. inelastic; elastic

20. Price leadership is MOST common in industries
    I. producing standardized or nearly standardized goods
    II. where there are many sellers
    III. where there are relatively few sellers
    IV. where firms are large enough to make or break price by independent action
    The CORRECT answer is:

    A. I, II, III
    B. II, III, IV
    C. I, III, IV
    D. I, II, IV

21. Which one of the following is NOT an advantage of the corporate form of business organization?

    A. Limited liability
    B. Possibility of obtaining large amounts of capital
    C. Permanence of life
    D. Privileged position in taxation

22. The yield of any given security is

    A. the rate of interest or dividend it bears
    B. determined by the relationship between the income from the security and the purchase price
    C. determined by the accretion in market value of the security
    D. high or low, depending upon the degree of risk involved in the investment

23. The term *counterpart funds* refers to an aspect of the operation of the

    A. European Recovery Program
    B. Point Four Program
    C. International Trade Organization
    D. International Monetary Fund

24. The basic policy underlying the farm price legislation of the Truman administration was one of

    A. subsidies to farmers to make up the difference between competitively determined market prices and parity prices
    B. support of farm prices at levels fixed in the price legislation
    C. subsidies to farmers who enter into marketing agreements to control supply
    D. support of farm prices at levels determined on the principle of parity

25. The term *inflationary gap* is usually used to refer to the excess of

    A. government expenditures over receipts
    B. bank loans over liquid bank assets
    C. consumer incomes over goods available for purchase
    D. consumer savings over opportunities for profitable investment

KEY (CORRECT ANSWERS)

1. D
2. A
3. D
4. C
5. B

6. C
7. A
8. A
9. B
10. C

11. A
12. A
13. A
14. A
15. B

16. D
17. A
18. B
19. C
20. C

21. D
22. B
23. A
24. D
25. C

TEST 3

DIRECTIONS: Each question or incomplete statement is followed by several suggested answers or completions. Select the one that BEST answers the question or completes the statement. *PRINT THE LETTER OF THE CORRECT ANSWER IN THE SPACE AT THE RIGHT.*

1. Contemporary economic theory utilizes three of the following concepts that are closely related to one another.
   The one that is NOT so related is

   A. national income
   B. federal income
   C. gross national product
   D. net national product

   1._____

2. Which of the following series of items contain CORRECTLY associated terms?
   I. Tariffs—most favored nation treaties
   II. Taxation—capital gains
   III. C.I.O.—political action committee
   IV. Union contracts—basing point system
   The CORRECT answer is:

   A. I, III
   B. I, II, III
   C. II, IV
   D. I, II, III, IV

   2._____

3. The railroad industry is characterized by
   I. heavy fixed charges
   II. operation under conditions of decreasing costs
   III. rates based largely on bulk
   IV. rate classification as a device to attract business
   The CORRECT answer is:

   A. I, II, III
   B. I, II, IV
   C. I, III, IV
   D. II, III, IV

   3._____

4. The index number of consumer prices computed by the Bureau of Labor Statistics

   A. is frequently criticized because so few prices are taken into consideration
   B. avoids the use of a base year
   C. is a weighted index number
   D. is the average of the prices of many commodities

   4._____

5. Workers who are victims of technological unemployment are MOST likely to find re-employment within their own industry if that industry is

   A. competitive and its products have an inelastic demand
   B. affected with characteristics of monopoly
   C. competitive and its products have an elastic demand
   D. characterized by administered prices

   5._____

6. The reserves of the member banks of the Federal Reserve system in recent years have

   A. been so great that the rediscount rate has not been an effective instrument of credit control
   B. declined so sharply that the Board of Governors has had to enforce its minimum reserve requirements

   6._____

C. been at a point where credit control through the use of the rediscount rate has been effective
D. been too low to permit effective open market operations

7. According to business cycle theory, which one of the following does NOT pave the way for the end of the period of prosperity? 7._____

   A. Increase in supply as new productive capacity comes into operation
   B. Tempering of optimism as rising costs catch up with selling price
   C. Decline in new construction
   D. Increase in speculative buying

8. Which one of the following combinations of conditions is MOST likely to exist at the end of a period of depression? 8._____

   A. Bank reserves high-interest rates declining-inventories kept low
   B. Bank reserves high-business costs rising-interest rates declining
   C. Business costs declining-bank reserves low-inventories rising
   D. Business costs rising-interest rates declining-inventories kept low

9. Which one of the following results might reasonably be expected from a United States loan to Mexico, the proceeds of which are spent in hiring Mexican labor? 9._____

   A. Increased American exports to Mexico
   B. Increased American imports to Mexico
   C. No effect on trade since proceeds were not spent for goods
   D. Decreased Mexican total trade

10. Depreciation of the British pound would have the effect of 10._____

    A. raising the prices paid by British buyers for American products
    B. raising the prices paid by American buyers for British products
    C. lowering the prices paid by British buyers for American products
    D. raising the price for British pounds in American banks

11. Which one of the social functions listed below do interest and land rent perform? They 11._____

    A. act to withdraw resources from use in present consumption
    B. serve to direct their respective factors of production into the most valuable and useful channels
    C. stimulate increased supply of their respective factors
    D. help to maintain balance between the provision for present and future wants

12. Review of interest rates in specific countries over long periods of time reveals long-term trends of 12._____

    A. constancy, that can most reasonably be explained in terms of persistent traits of human psychology
    B. variability, that can be most correctly associated with changes in the productivity of capital

C. variability, that can be most correctly associated with cyclical fluctuations in the economy
D. constancy, that can most reasonably be explained in terms of consistent superiority of capitalistic methods of production over the techniques of less developed economics

13. Which of the following are CORRECT statements of modern economic theory as related to profit?   13.____
    I. Pure profit tends to disappear as a state of balanced competition is approached.
    II. Pure profit results from the imperfections of competition.
    III. Pure profit is the net income of a business as a whole, rather than the return for entrepreneurial service.
    IV. Scientific management and insurance have minimized the validity of the concept of profit as *compensation for risk-taking.*
    The CORRECT answer is:
    A. I, II, III, IV   B. I, II
    C. III, IV   D. I, III

14. Study of United States corporate financing practice during the period after World War II indicates more financing by   14.____

    A. bond issues than stock issues, partly due to the tax advantage involved in bond financing
    B. stock issues than by bond issues, partly due to the tax advantage involved in stock financing
    C. stock issues than by bond issues, due to the shortage of equity capital
    D. bond issues than by stock issues, due to the shortage of equity capital

15. Which one of the following statements concerning the control of monetary and credit conditions in the United States is NOT correct?   15.____

    A. The fact that the Federal Reserve Board supported the government securities market during World War II and after, which resulted in member banks becoming independent of Federal Reserve restraints
    B. The United States Treasury must work through the Federal Reserve System to effect its purposes in relation to money and credit supply
    C. Since the early 1920's, the Federal Reserve authorities have relied chiefly on open-market operation rather than rediscount rate changes as the method of credit control
    D. The policy of gold sterilization in the 1930's kept gold coming into the country from increasing the excess reserves then prevailing in the banks

16. Which of the following statements are CORRECT concerning the settlement of labor disputes in the United States?   16.____
    I. The Taft-Hartley Act prescribes conditions for reporting disputes to the Federal Mediation and Conciliation Service.
    II. Agents of the Federal Mediation and Conciliation Service may act as mediators or arbitrators, depending upon the circumstances of the case.

III. If disputants agree to submit a dispute to arbitration by the Service, the decision is binding and refusal to abide by the award is punishable by criminal penalties.
IV. The National Railroad Adjustment Board and the National Mediation Board handle railway labor disputes.
V. The law establishing machinery for settling railway labor disputes forbids strikes on the railroads.

The CORRECT answer is:

A. I, II, IV
B. I, IV
C. II, III, V
D. I, III, IV

17. In contemporary theory, the function of the entrepreneur in the corporation is

    A. assigned to the common stockholders
    B. assigned to a group of executive officers
    C. divided between a group of executive officers and the common stockholders
    D. divided between the common stockholders and all the other investors who bear the burden of uncertainty as to future income

18. The MOST important factor that now holds Government bonds at par or slightly above is the

    A. price support by the Federal Reserve System
    B. relatively high interest rates offered
    C. tax exemption for such bonds
    D. pressure by the Government to induce banks and insurance companies to invest in such bonds

19. Among the MOST conspicuous developments in commodity markets after World War II was the strong gain in prices registered by

    A. major farm products
    B. imported foodstuffs such as cocoa and sugar
    C. non-ferrous metals
    D. both natural and synthetic rubber

20. An important effect of the Taft-Hartley law was:

    A. All union security agreements were invalidated
    B. Membership in both the A.F. of L. and the C.I.O. declined
    C. More unfair labor practice charges had been filed against unions than against employers
    D. The NLRB refused to certify unions unless their officers filed non-Communist affidavits

KEY (CORRECT ANSWERS)

1.	B	11.	B
2.	B	12.	A
3.	B	13.	A
4.	C	14.	A
5.	C	15.	B
6.	A	16.	A
7.	D	17.	B
8.	A	18.	A
9.	A	19.	A
10.	A	20.	D

TEST 4

DIRECTIONS: Each question or incomplete statement is followed by several suggested answers or completions. Select the one that BEST answers the question or completes the statement. *PRINT THE LETTER OF THE CORRECT ANSWER IN THE SPACE AT THE RIGHT.*

1. Before the war, western Europe normally depended on its trade with and investment in the Far East, particularly southeast Asia, to provide it with the dollars to finance its import surplus from the Western Hemisphere.
   The importance of southeast Asia as a source of dollar supply resulted from the fact that

   A. the most productive areas in that region were under Western European control
   B. Western Europe bought more in that area than it sold in the Western Hemisphere
   C. it was the only major region with which the United States had an import surplus before the war
   D. the foreign trade and investments of the United States in that area were larger than in any other region

   1.____

2. The Monnet Plan in France closely resembled the

   A. program of nationalization of industry in England before World War II
   B. nationalization program of the British Labor party
   C. Marshall plan for European recovery
   D. Gosplan

   2.____

3. Early in 1948, the French Government put into effect a drastic devaluation of the franc. This measure had the approval of

   A. French exporters
   B. the British Labor party
   C. the International Monetary Fund
   D. the French Communist party

   3.____

4. Which of the following combinations of causes helps to explain the existing dollar shortages in Latin-American countries?

   I. Inability of European countries to buy goods from Latin America in prewar quantities
   II. Increase in Latin American exports to the United States in the war and postwar period
   III. Inconvertibility of currencies held by Latin American countries such as the sterling pound
   IV. Excess of imports from United States as compared to their exports to the United States in the postwar period
   V. Tariff policy of the United States toward Latin American products

   The CORRECT answer is:

   A. II, III, IV, V   B. I, II, V
   C. I, III, IV   D. I, II, III, IV, V

   4.____

37

5. Which of the following statements belong to a pattern of economic development which was formed in the South during 1865-1900?
   I. Cotton was perpetuated as the main crop through a crop-lien system of financing.
   II. Share-cropping provided a system of labor that enabled large numbers of plantations to continue.
   III. The great planters were successful in re-establishing agriculture on its former large-scale basis.
   IV. Small yeoman farmers with little funds bought up the choicest plots of bankrupted plantations.

   The CORRECT answer is:

   A. II, III, IV
   B. I, II, III
   C. I, II, IV
   D. I, III, IV

6. Which one of the following statements about farm income and prices since 1865 is FALSE?

   A. Since 1947, the number of farming units has increased steadily.
   B. After the Civil War, the farmer sold at low prices in the world market and bought at high prices in the protected home market.
   C. Acreage control and soil conservation have been used as a means of keeping farm prices steady by limiting production.
   D. Parity payments have attempted to adjust farmers' income to workers' income.

7. Which of the following are CORRECT statements regarding the American farm problem?
   I. In 1860, agriculture represented about half the national wealth.
   II. In 1880, a majority of American farmers owned their own land.
   III. The farmer received a decreasing share of the national income between 1860 and 1930.
   IV. Between 1890 and 1930, an increasing number of farms were mortgaged.

   The CORRECT answer is:

   A. I, II
   B. I, III, IV
   C. II, III, IV
   D. I, II, III, IV

8. The Brannan Plan differed from the farm policies under the New Deal in that under it,

   A. prices of perishable farm products would have been allowed to rise or fall according to the law of supply and demand
   B. parity prices would have been more flexible
   C. farmers would have had no voice in determining acreage allotments
   D. payments to the farmers would have to be greater during periods of prosperity than during periods of depression

9. The AFL differed from the Knights of Labor in that the AFL believed that

   A. the national structure should be built on strong local unions united into city and state federations
   B. unions should base their programs on Utopian objectives
   C. unions should not dissipate their energies in fighting for the improvement of the position of women in industry
   D. the unlimited immigration of European laborers would add to the strength of the American labor movement

10. Which statement concerning labor BEST describes the attitude of most Americans in the years immediately after the Civil War?

    A. They welcomed the entry of labor into politics.
    B. There was little hostility to the closed shop.
    C. Picketing and the boycott were regarded as legitimate weapons of labor.
    D. Public opinion tended to be more hostile to labor than to capital.

11. Organized labor at first opposed minimum wage legislation because they claimed such laws

    A. violated the fourteenth amendment
    B. were an undue exercise of the police power of the state
    C. interfered with labor's right to enter into contracts freely
    D. tended to lower the general wage scale

12. Which one of the following provisions of the Social Security Act is administered by the federal government exclusively?

    A. Old-age assistance
    B. Old-age and survivors insurance
    C. Unemployment compensation
    D. Assistance for dependent children

13. The CHIEF technological advance in the past ten years in the field of mass production has been

    A. in the application of atomic energy to industrial machines
    B. the harnessing of atomic energy to industrial machines
    C. the development of the *belt-line* system
    D. the development of automation using computerized robotics

14. The relationship of a stockholder to a corporation is that of a(n)

    A. owner   B. debtor   C. creditor   D. manager

15. In teaching the forms of business organization, which of the following terms would the teacher be LEAST likely to explain?

    A. Limited liability   B. Absentee ownership
    C. Equity capital   D. Reserve ratio

16. The statement that imperfect competition prevails in a given industry means that prices in that industry are determined

    A. by government regulation
    B. by a single firm with a monopoly position
    C. solely by conditions in the market
    D. by the competing firms' decisions

17. Which of the following was NOT an economic consequence of the Fordney-McCumber Tariff Act of 1921?

    A. It encouraged the growth of monopolies in the United States.

B. The tariff commission gave flexibility to the schedules, thereby equalizing production costs at home and abroad.
C. It prevented Europe from paying her war debt to us in the form of goods.
D. Foreign countries introduced retaliatory tariffs.

18. The tax in the United States which MOST closely meets the needs of a sound tax system is the _____ tax.

    A. personal income
    B. excess profits
    C. death and inheritance
    D. excise

19. In teaching the topic of exchange, a point of emphasis would be the fact that at least nine-tenths of all transactions (in terms of value) are accomplished by the use of

    A. Federal Reserve notes
    B. promissory notes
    C. checks
    D. bills of exchange

20. Which one of the following CANNOT be characterized as a *New Deal* reform measure?

    A. Labor was given the right to organize and bargain collectively through representatives of their own choosing.
    B. A government corporation was organized to give financial assistance to hard-pressed banks, insurance companies, farmers' associations, railroads, and other bona fide financial institutions.
    C. Minimum wages and maximum hours were established for industrial workers in interstate commerce.
    D. A system of social security was set up.

21. Which one of the following was NOT used as an argument against the Tennessee Valley Authority (T.V.A.) Act?

    A. It was a threat to the twelve billion dollar investment in private utilities.
    B. The act provided insufficient funds with which to carry out its purpose.
    C. It tended to *degeneration* and paved the way to socialism.
    D. It gave the President powers not authorized by the Constitution.

22. Which one of the following statements regarding the financing of World War II is NOT true?

    A. Nearly one-half of the cost of the war was financed by taxation.
    B. The withholding system in the taxation of individual incomes was introduced during World War II.
    C. The bulk of the war bonds was purchased by small investors.
    D. An excess profits tax of 90% was levied to eliminate war profiteering.

23. The United States Government prefers to sell defense bonds to individuals rather than to banks because the

    A. average person hoards his high wages in times of prosperity
    B. banks are reluctant to invest large sums of money in such bonds
    C. tendency of such sales is to avert inflation
    D. administration fears the domination of the Government by banking interests

24. When the President announced in January, 2007, a budget providing for an expenditure 24._____
of billions of dollars for the fiscal year of 2008, he indicated the amount of money

    A. he wished Congress to appropriate during fiscal 2008
    B. he expected federal agencies to spend during fiscal 2008
    C. the government was committed to spend under existing legislation
    D. that will be received under existing tax legislation

25. One effective way that the Federal Reserve handles inflation is to regulate the money 25._____
supply (MI or M2).
To reduce the money supply, the Federal Reserve will

    A. order the Treasury Department not to print any more money
    B. Increase the margin rate on stocks
    C. buy back Treasury Securities
    D. sell Treasury Securities on the market

KEY (CORRECT ANSWERS)

1.	A	11.	D
2.	D	12.	B
3.	C	13.	D
4.	C	14.	A
5.	C	15.	D
6.	A	16.	D
7.	D	17.	B
8.	A	18.	A
9.	A	19.	C
10.	D	20.	B

21. B
22. C
23. C
24. B
25. D

TEST 5

DIRECTIONS: Each question or incomplete statement is followed by several suggested answers or completions. Select the one that BEST answers the question or completes the statement. *PRINT THE LETTER OF THE CORRECT ANSWER IN THE SPACE AT THE RIGHT.*

1. Which of the following statements about international trade are TRUE?   1.____
   I. A nation must always have a favorable balance of trade to be financially sound.
   II. A nation cannot permanently buy in foreign markets if it cannot sell abroad.
   III. Services have the same effect as goods in foreign trade.
   IV. Adoption of a high tariff is a sound policy for a creditor nation.
   V. High tariffs were a cause of World War II
   The CORRECT answer is:

   A. I, II
   B. I, III, IV
   C. II
   D. II, III, V
   E. All of the above

2. Which one of the following groups gives three advantages of the Federal Reserve System?   2.____

   A. Elasticity of credit and currency, centralization of reserves, government ownership of most important banks
   B. Elasticity of credit, inelasticity of currency, centralization of reserves
   C. Inelasticity of credit, uniformity of currency, sound reserve policy
   D. Provision for control of credit, elasticity of currency, centralization of reserves
   E. Unrestricted credit, elasticity of currency, open-market operations

3. Which one of the following BEST illustrates practical application of the principle of diminishing returns?   3.____

   A. Abandonment of a copper mine before all the copper has been extracted
   B. Imposition of import quotas on copper
   C. Re-opening of a copper mine which had previously been abandoned
   D. Substitution of silver for copper in certain productive processes
   E. Use of improved machinery in copper mining

4. One of the functions of the Securities and Exchange Commission is the   4.____

   A. prevention of short-selling on exchanges
   B. registration of securities sold in interstate commerce
   C. registration of securities sold in intrastate commerce
   D. regulation of prices on commodity exchanges
   E. regulation of prices on stock and bond exchanges

5. Which one of the following pairs expresses a cause and effect relationship prevalent in the United States during World War I?   5.____

   A. High prices of agricultural products—increase in farm tenancy
   B. High prices of agricultural products—heavy imports of agricultural products
   C. High prices of agricultural products—utilization of grazing land for wheat growing

42

D. Low prices of agricultural products—increase in farm tenancy
E. Low prices of agricultural products—withdrawal of marginal farms from cultivation

6. A result of the ideas expressed in GENERAL THEORY OF EMPLOYMENT, INTEREST AND MONEY by John Maynard Keynes was a(n)

    A. comprehensive scheme of social insurance
    B. new concept of the role of government in the economic system
    C. plan for 100% money
    D. restatement of laissez-faire in terms of modern business practice
    E. indictment of socialist theories

6._____

7. On the commodity exchanges in the United States, the MAXIMUM limits for grain price drop in one day's trading are set by

    A. daily summary of the Federal Reserve Board
    B. Federal regulation
    C. law of supply and demand
    D. operators in the grain pit
    E. state regulation

7._____

8. An economic principle at issue in the monetary controversy preceding the national election of 1896 was that

    A. good money drives out bad money
    B. money issued by state banks lacks uniformity
    C. overvalued money tends to drive undervalued money out of circulation
    D. the value of money varies with its purchasing power
    E. the demand for money depends upon the supply of gold

8._____

9. Overhead costs include

    A. interest on bonds, rent, insurance
    B. interest on bonds, rent, wages
    C. rent, raw materials, salaries of officials
    D. wages, rent, insurance
    E. wages, rent, raw materials

9._____

10. Today in the United States, total bank deposits exceed the amount of money in circulation because

    A. bank deposits usually consist of checks
    B. loans create a large percentage of bank deposits
    C. people are hoarding money
    D. this is a period of inflation
    E. United States bank notes have been withdrawn from circulation

10._____

11. Which one of the following factors indicates the difference between a weighted index number of prices and a simple index number of prices?

    A. Current prices
    B. Prices adjusted for seasonal variations
    C. Prices in a normal year

11._____

D. Quantities produced
E. Quantities sold

12. Which one of the following items would appear on the liabilities' side of a bank's financial statement?

    A. Cash
    B. Customers' deposits
    C. Furniture and fixtures
    D. Government bonds
    E. Loans and discounts

13. Which one of the following statements is a conclusion from Engel's Law?

    A. A sales tax on food is desirable because it will reach all families.
    B. High income families spend the largest percentage of their income on food.
    C. Low income families are unable to provide adequately for education or health protection.
    D. Low income families do not budget wisely.
    E. Most American families have incomes over $4,500 per year.

14. Which one of the following is the MOST essential and basic characteristic of feudalism?

    A. Institution of chivalry
    B. Land-holding relationship of lord and vassal
    C. Taxation in the form of feudal dues
    D. Use of *ordeal* to determine justice
    E. Warfare among rival feudal lords

15. Federal laws safeguard the interests of consumers by each of the following EXCEPT

    A. permitting use of injunctions to stop the distribution of harmful products
    B. prohibiting use of deceptive containers
    C. prohibiting use of uncertified coal tar colors in foods
    D. requiring drugs liable to deteriorate to be so labeled
    E. requiring the Bureau of Standards to publish its test results in newspapers

16. Each of the following agencies is correctly paired with an important function EXCEPT

    A. Bank for International Settlements—reparations of World War II
    B. Export-Import Bank—loans to encourage foreign trade
    C. International Bank—loans for reconstruction abroad
    D. International Monetary Fund—currency stabilization
    E. Reconstruction Finance Corporation—domestic loans to banks and railroads

17. Each of the following statements concerning the socialist movement is valid EXCEPT:

    A. A basic tenet of scientific socialism is the labor theory of value.
    B. A basic weakness of Utopian socialism lay in its reliance upon the slow process of legislation to achieve reform.
    C. In the international conflicts of the 20th century, the international outlook of the socialist parties yielded to nationalist loyalties.

D. The Revisionists in the German Social Democratic Party stressed an evolutionary rather than a revolutionary approach to socialist goals.
E. While opposing the principles of scientific socialism, Catholic political parties in Europe in the early 20th century supported Socialists' efforts to obtain social reform.

18. Each of the following generalizations concerning the economic history of Europe is correct EXCEPT: The

    A. craft unions of today are the counterparts of the craft guilds of the medieval period
    B. distinctive characteristic of the first stage of the Industrial Revolution was the application of artificial power to the processes of production
    C. Industrial Revolution caused a shift in the industrial centers of England from the southern to the northern part of the country
    D. laissez-faire philosophy of Adam Smith was predicated on the operation of economic laws
    E. medieval growth of business and industry, by strengthening the middle class, increased the power of the kings at the expense of the nobles

19. A large deficit in a national budget is MOST likely to result in
    I. inflation
    II. deflation
    III. high, interest rates
    IV. low profits
    V. an unfavorable balance of trade
    The CORRECT answer is:

    A. I, III   B. III, V   C. I, IV   D. II, IV   E. IV, V

20. Which of the following combinations would be MOST likely to bring about deflation?

    A. More paper money in circulation, more use of credit, increased production of goods
    B. Less paper money in circulation, more saving, increased production of goods
    C. More use of credit, less saving, decreased production of goods
    D. Lowering the rediscount rate, buying on the open market by the Federal Reserve Banks, unchanged demand for consumers' goods
    E. Removal of price controls, lowering of taxes, a widespread drought

21. Which of the following MOST NEARLY retains its purchasing power when the value of money fluctuates?

    A. Bonds   B. Stocks
    C. Annuity payments   D. First mortages
    E. Life insurance premiums

22. The Federal Reserve System may curtail extension of credit by

    A. buying securities in the open market
    B. speeding up the process of clearing checks
    C. lowering the rediscount rate
    D. lowering the reserve requirements for member banks
    E. selling some of its holdings of government bonds to private investors

23. All of the following are true of the International Bank for Reconstruction and Development EXCEPT that it(s)

    A. is located in Washington, D.C.
    B. receives about one-third of its funds from the United States
    C. is administered independently of the United Nations
    D. may make direct loans to the governments of member nations for productive enterprises
    E. primary function is to stabilize international monetary systems

24. All of the following contributed to the rapid growth of industry in the United States after the Civil War EXCEPT the

    A. increase in number of consumers
    B. discovery of vast sources of raw materials
    C. employment of former slaves in factory work
    D. passage of legislation favorable to industry
    E. inventive genius of the American people

25. All of the following are true about government regulation of business EXCEPT that the

    A. Clayton Anti-Trust Act legalized peaceful strikes, picketing, and boycotts
    B. Robinson-Patman Act attempted to preserve competition among retailers
    C. Security Exchange Act is both regulatory and protective
    D. Supreme Court declared the National Industrial Recovery Act unconstitutional, partially because it interfered with states' rights
    E. Lea Act corrected a very serious defect in the corporate form of business

KEY (CORRECT ANSWERS)

1.	D	11.	E
2.	D	12.	B
3.	A	13.	C
4.	B	14.	B
5.	C	15.	E
6.	B	16.	A
7.	B	17.	B
8.	C	18.	A
9.	A	19.	A
10.	B	20.	B

21.	B
22.	E
23.	E
24.	C
25.	E

ECONOMICS

EXAMINATION SECTION
TEST 1

DIRECTIONS: Each question or incomplete statement is followed by several suggested answers or completions. Select the one that BEST answers the question or completes the statement. *PRINT THE LETTER OF THE CORRECT ANSWER IN THE SPACE AT THE RIGHT.*

1. The following is a complete and correct definition of the demand curve for commodity X. It shows, for a given market,

    A. how much X will be bought at the equilibrium price
    B. how, as people's incomes rise and they have more money to spend, their purchases of X will increase, and by how much
    C. how the amount of money people spend to purchase X changes as the price they must pay for it changes
    D. the amounts of X that will be bought each period, at each and any price, assuming other factors influencing demand (income, tastes, etc.) remain constant
    E. the amounts of X to be supplied in each period, at each and any price, assuming other factors influencing sale remain constant

    1._____

2. *A change in quantity demanded* (as distinct from *a change in demand*) means

    A. that buyers have decided to buy more (or less) than they are now buying, at the existing price
    B. the same thing as a change in demand
    C. a change in purchases resulting from some shift in the supply curve
    D. that the demand curve must have shifted in position
    E. that the demand curve has become more elastic than it previously was

    2._____

3. If the demand for any product is described as *elastic* (or *price-elastic*), it means specifically that

    A. it would be possible to sell more of the product than is now being sold at the present price
    B. with any increase in consumer income, buyers would buy substantially more than they are now buying
    C. following any reduction in price, consumers would buy a greater quantity of the product than they are now buying
    D. if supply were to be increased for any reason, causing a fall in price, the total money outlay of consumers for the product would then decrease
    E. if supply were to be increased for any reason, causing a fall in price, the total money outlay of consumers for the product would then increase

    3._____

4. If some commodity such as wheat is used as money in a society, then the amount of money (wheat) which a man will ask for a unit of some other good he has to sell will depend

    A. mainly upon the usefulness of wheat in feeding himself and his family
    B. upon the price of wheat in terms of gold or silver

    4._____

C. in no way upon the value of wheat, no matter how used
D. upon the prices of still other goods which he may hope to buy
E. upon his personal liking for, or dislike of, wheat as a food

5. If a commodity or substance is to be used successfully as money, the following (according to economists) is a necessary requirement:
It must

   A. possess inherent value-i.e., must be useful for its own sake, independent of its use as money
   B. be backed by one of the precious metals, preferably gold
   C. be a free good
   D. carry the stamp of approval of some government
   E. none of the above

5.____

6. In terms of numbers, the form of business unit MOST frequently found in the United States today is the

   A. individual, or single, proprietorship
   B. partnership
   C. small corporation
   D. giant corporation
   E. none of the above

6.____

7. The term *limited liability* is frequently used in describing the characteristics of a corporation.
It means the following:

   A. Any officer of the corporation is strictly limited in his ability to speak for the corporation and commit it to any liability
   B. Once a shareholder has paid for his stock, he has no further financial obligation, regardless of how much trouble the corporation gets into
   C. The corporation's liability to pay dividends to its stockholders is a limited one, since it is required to pay them only if it has earned a profit
   D. There are certain obligations which a corporation can legally refuse to pay
   E. The corporation has only a limited obligation to meet claims made by any single person or firm against it (provided it has acted within the scope of its charter), so that there is some protection for its assets and financial position

7.____

8. A corporation's obligation to pay interest on bonds it has issued is PROPERLY described as follows:

   A. Interest must be paid regardless of whether a profit has been earned or not
   B. Interest must be paid whenever a profit has been earned
   C. Interest need not be paid even if a profit has been earned, but it must be paid before any dividend is paid
   D. Normally interest ranks ahead of dividends, but there are some circumstances in which a dividend can be paid without payment of bond interest
   E. Interest ranks behind dividends and is paid only after dividends have been paid in full

8.____

9. The MAIN reason why indirect, or *capital-using*, methods of production have not displaced direct methods in economically underdeveloped areas of the world is that

   A. the governments of such areas have not issued enough money to finance indirect methods
   B. people do not realize that the indirect methods would produce more consumption goods
   C. there are no indirect methods that would actually produce more consumption goods
   D. such areas do not have a properly functioning price system
   E. the adoption of such indirect methods would involve a sacrifice of present consumption

10. The economic problem of how goods shall be produced is that of

    A. finding out how much product will be obtained when given quantities of factors of production are put to work together in the most effective known manner
    B. having a mechanism that will somehow reveal what goods people really want to be produced
    C. getting the existing factors of production distributed among different occupations to best produce whatever goods the community wants
    D. deciding how the goods that have been produced shall be distributed among the people who made those goods
    E. none of the above

11. If, with respect to the guns-and-butter-production-possibility diagram used in some books, the economy's actual output is marked by a point inside (to the southwest) of the production-possibility curve, this means that

    A. it is impossible to produce more guns without the sacrifice of some butter output
    B. either all available resources are not being fully employed or they are not being employed to the best advantage
    C. the law of diminishing returns cannot be in operation
    D. the diagram illustrates something which could not possibly happen
    E. the phenomenon of *increasing returns to scale* must be in operation

12. The law of diminishing returns notes the effect on output resulting from an increase in productive inputs. This effect depends on one assumption, without which the law does not apply.
    The assumption is that

    A. although the output increase results from an increase in productive inputs, at least one such input must remain fixed in supply during the process
    B. the supply of all productive inputs must increase proportionately to produce the increase in output
    C. all productive inputs except one must be held fixed in supply, and only that one input may be allowed to increase
    D. as successive units of the productive input are added, the inherent quality of that input must decline
    E. the physical quantity of output may increase in proportion to the increase in inputs, but the worth of that output in the eyes of consumers must decline

13. The use of a money pricing system is NOT expected to help settle the following economic problem:

    A. Determining the particular output of goods and services that is best for a community to have, regardless of the tastes of any or all individual consumers therein
    B. Distribution of money income between different individuals in the community
    C. Helping a consumer with given tastes and a limited income to decide how best to spend that income
    D. How much of the total available resource supply is to be occupied in making any given consumer good
    E. The particular kinds of resources (factors of Production) that should be used for the manufacture of any given consumer good

14. The *law of downward-sloping demand* says the following:

    A. An excess of supply over demand will induce price reductions
    B. As price falls, people spend more money to buy the commodity in question
    C. When a demand schedule is illustrated graphically, it runs from northeast to southwest
    D. When price falls, quantity purchased normally increases
    E. None of these

15. In a system of free private enterprise, the following must consciously assume responsibility for deciding how the three basic economic problems-What, How, and For Whom-are to be settled:

    A. The law-making branch of the government
    B. The general public
    C. One or more administrative agencies of the government
    D. All business firms engaged in production
    E. None of the above

16. In the following table, circle the letter showing the interval in which demand is elastic.

	P	q
	1	100
A.	3	60
B.	8	30
C.	15	10
D.	30	5
E.	50	4

17. Using the same table as in the above problem, circle the letter showing the interval in which demand is of unitary elasticity.

    A. A   B. B   C. C   D. D   E. E

18. Most of the very large U.S. federal debt outstanding arose as the result of

    A. war
    B. depressions
    C. borrowing to meet interest charges on previous debt
    D. borrowing from abroad
    E. none of the above

19. The C plus I plus G schedule would tend to be shifted up by 19._____

    A. an increase in taxes
    B. a decrease in government spending
    C. an increase in interest rates
    D. open-market sales by the central bank
    E. none of these

20. An expansionary monetary policy adopted by a central bank will be unsuccessful if 20._____

    A. prices do not increase
    B. saving on the part of the public does not decrease
    C. investment spending is not changed by a change in the interest rate
    D. the inflationary tendency which prompted this policy is not checked
    E. no decrease in the price of government bonds occurs

21. If the Federal Reserve authorities wished to pursue an expansionary monetary policy, it would be CORRECT for them to 21._____

    A. raise the Discount Rate to discourage hoarding by the public
    B. raise reserve requirements to eliminate any excess reserves held by the Member banks
    C. raise margin requirements to discourage wasteful speculation
    D. sell securities on the open market to drive interest rates down
    E. do none of the above

22. If the level of spending increases, with the quantity of money held constant, then 22._____

    A. the velocity of circulation of money must have increased
    B. the amount of real national output must have increased
    C. either the velocity of money circulation or the amount of real national output must have increased, or both
    D. the amount of real national output must have decreased
    E. either the velocity of money circulation must have increased, or the amount of real national output decreased, or both

23. One of the following statements is FALSE: 23._____

    A. Tax reduction tends to stimulate income
    B. Tax reduction tends to increase personal consumption
    C. Tax reduction tends to increase personal saving
    D. Whatever else tax reduction does, the increases in personal consumption resulting from tax reductions must stimulate income
    E. If tax reductions cause personal saving to increase, then Net National Product will fail

24. By *induced investment* is meant 24._____

    A. changes in investment which result from a change in Net National Product
    B. the fact that increased saving may sometimes result in increased investment
    C. investment made as a result of government orders
    D. an increase in investment which results from technological change
    E. none of the above

25. By the *Paradox of Thrift* is meant the fact that   25.____
    A. positive saving will always mean unemployment
    B. if changes in investment are induced by changes in Net National Product, then a decision on the part of people to save more might result in their actually saving less
    C. if the economy is at full employment, a decision on the part of people to save more might produce an inflationary gap
    D. saving stimulates investment spending so as to worsen an inflationary spiral
    E. saving must always equal investment

KEY (CORRECT ANSWERS)

1.	D	11.	B
2.	A	12.	A
3.	C	13.	A
4.	D	14.	D
5.	E	15.	E
6.	A	16.	C
7.	B	17.	D
8.	A	18.	C
9.	E	19.	E
10.	E	20.	B

21.	E
22.	A
23.	E
24.	A
25.	B

TEST 2

DIRECTIONS: Each question or incomplete statement is followed by several suggested answers or completions. Select the one that BEST answers the question or completes the statement. *PRINT THE LETTER OF THE CORRECT ANSWER IN THE SPACE AT THE RIGHT.*

1. The calculation of Net National Product does NOT include   1.____

   A. net interest payments
   B. depreciation allowances
   C. rental income of individuals
   D. payments made to all government employees
   E. corporate profits before taxes

2. A stationary economy is one where   2.____

   A. no factories or machines are ever built
   B. the economy is growing but at a fixed rate instead of an accelerating one
   C. the economy is eating up its capital stock and is, therefore, not growing
   D. the capital stock is maintained at a steady level
   E. there can be no divergence of Gross National Product from Net National Product

3. The *propensity-to-consume* of families refers to the   3.____

   A. amounts of consumption expenditure associated with different levels of income
   B. fraction of an extra dollar of income that would be spent on consumption
   C. manner in which the family allocates its consumption on food, shelter, clothing, etc.
   D. manner in which the family would allocate extra dollars of income on food, clothing, etc.
   E. incentive of a family to obtain more income in order to spend more

4. If a family saves $10,000 of a $50,000 income and its propensity-to-consume function has the typical shape and position, then its marginal propensity to consume should be   4.____

   A. less than 4/5
   B. 4/5
   C. greater than 4/5 but less than 1
   D. equal to 1
   E. any of the above-impossible to tell from the data given

5. The value of the housekeeping service of a wife is excluded from Net National Product because   5.____

   A. it is a transfer item
   B. no money payment is involved and, therefore, it must be excluded
   C. it does not represent a current contribution to a factor of production
   D. of the problem of measurement
   E. of none of these

6. Government share of national product is HIGHEST in   6.____

   A. India   B. Puerto Rico   C. United Kingdom
   D. Japan   E. United States

7. Government expenditures have been rising, but the rate of government expenditure to the increasing level of national income

   A. has been *remarkably* constant
   B. has shown generally a declining trend
   C. has shown a generally rising trend
   D. rose rapidly from 1975 to 1987, then declined
   E. none of these

8. One of the following industries would be much less vulnerable to the business cycle than the others:

   A. Food processing
   B. Building construction
   C. Shipbuilding
   D. Iron and steel manufacture
   E. None of these

9. By the *excess reserves* of a commercial bank is meant

   A. assets which, although not money, can be quickly converted into money by the bank should the need arise
   B. money and near-money assets possessed by the bank in excess of 100 percent of the amount of its demand deposits
   C. cash which must be kept on hand, not because the everyday needs of the bank demand it, but because of a legal requirement
   D. money held by the bank in excess of that fraction of its deposits which is required by law
   E. none of these

10. The economy's money supply will increase whenever commercial banks

    A. reduce their demand-deposit liabilities by paying out part of these accounts in the form of coins or bills
    B. increase their demand-deposit liabilities by receiving coins or bills from the public as a deposit
    C. withdraw part of their deposit with a Federal Reserve Bank
    D. increase their loans to the public
    E. none of these

11. If the Federal Reserve sells government bonds to the public on a large scale, the following is a LIKELY result:
    A(n)

    A. decrease in interest rates and a rise in total spending (unless spending fails to respond to easier credit conditions)
    B. rise in stock market prices as activity in this market responds to increased activity in the bond market
    C. increase in Reserve Bank credit
    D. contraction of bank reserves and a reduction in bank lending
    E. none of these

12. In a depression, when the Federal Reserve was trying to expand business activity, it would NOT

    A. raise the total of bank reserves
    B. expand the amount of Reserve Bank credit
    C. sell government bonds
    D. lower the legal reserve ratio required of banks with respect to their deposits
    E. none of these

13. Most governments would PROBABLY prefer

    A. unemployment to suppressed inflation
    B. suppressed inflation to unemployment
    C. open inflation to suppressed inflation
    D. open inflation to unemployment
    E. none of these

14. Effective demand as related to general employment may BEST be defined as

    A. greater demand for goods and services
    B. increased demand for higher wages
    C. desire for new and cheaper sources of raw materials
    D. quantity of labor that employers will hire at the prevailing wage rates
    E. none of these

15. According to principles of comparative advantage,

    A. trade is a substitute for international movement of productive factors
    B. the gains from international trade will be evenly divided among the trading nations
    C. a country with absolute advantage in two goods will not import either
    D. world total production of the traded goods is unaffected by trade, for the increases in output by exporters are just offset by the decreases on the part of the importers
    E. none of these

16. A sound economic argument can be advanced in favor of protective tariffs aimed at

    A. giving long-term support to an increasing-cost industry
    B. giving initial support to a decreasing-cost industry
    C. raising the general level of real wages by raising money wages in the protected industries
    D. equalizing the costs of production at home and abroad
    E. none of these

17. The International Monetary Fund

    A. provides long-term loans for development projects
    B. provides short-term credit to stabilize foreign exchange rates
    C. makes loans to foreigners for purchase of U.S. goods only
    D. is a central pool of gold and dollars earned and used by the British Commonwealth countries
    E. none of these

18. The trade policy MOST likely to promote industrialization in an overpopulated agricultural country today is

    A. a tariff on manufactured goods with low initial rates gradually raised over the following years
    B. a tariff on manufactured goods with high initial rates gradually reduced over the following years
    C. a stable rate of tariff on agricultural imports
    D. free trade
    E. none of these

19. Devaluation of the currency by a given country tends directly to

    A. reduce the physical volume of exports
    B. raise the domestic selling price of imported goods
    C. maintain the physical volume of imports for which demand elasticity is unity
    D. decrease the burden of servicing the foreign debt
    E. none of these

20. Expenditures of French tourists in the United States affect the French balance of payments in much the same way as

    A. French imports from the United States
    B. French exports to the United States
    C. American tourists travelling in France
    D. United States loans to France
    E. none of these

21. According to the C.E.D. pamphlet on United States Tariff Policy, wherever an industry would be damaged by tariff reduction, government should

    A. pay a subsidy to the firms in this industry
    B. offer a bonus to displaced workers
    C. promote diversification of industry
    D. not cut the tariff
    E. none of these

22. A factor which did NOT contribute to the Post World War II *dollar shortage* was

    A. frequent depreciation of currencies by the dollar-shortage countries
    B. wartime destruction of productive facilities in Europe and Asia
    C. efforts by Europeans and Asians to live beyond their means
    D. faster technological progress in dollar countries than elsewhere
    E. none of these

23. A tariff for protection against the competition of cheap foreign labor provides a short-run benefit for

    A. the protected workers   B. all workers
    C. all consumers   D. unions
    E. none of these

24. The following transfer payment is excluded from the computation of national income: 24.____
    A. payment for an intermediary good
    B. payment for a service rendered by a soldier to the government
    C. payment of interest on a government bond
    D. payment of interest on a General Motors bond
    E. undistributed corporation profits

25. *Liquidity preference* refers to the 25.____
    A. desire of banks to avoid long-term loans
    B. to the evaluation of cash as against other forms of asset holdings
    C. to the relationship between inventory holdings and the level of consumer demand
    D. the desire to liquidate ownership of producer durables and inventories in the face of declining consumption
    E. the rising trend in the consumption of alcoholic beverages

KEY (CORRECT ANSWERS)

1.	B	11.	D
2.	D	12.	C
3.	A	13.	B
4.	C	14.	D
5.	B	15.	B
6.	C	16.	B
7.	C	17.	B
8.	A	18.	B
9.	D	19.	B
10.	D	20.	A

21. C
22. A
23. A
24. A
25. B

TEST 3

DIRECTIONS: Each question or incomplete statement is followed by several suggested answers or completions. Select the one that BEST answers the question or completes the statement. *PRINT THE LETTER OF THE CORRECT ANSWER IN THE SPACE AT THE RIGHT.*

1. When the American Government borrowed in order to finance World War II, it thereby

    A. shifted the economic burden to future generations who would have to pay the interest and principal
    B. intensified the danger of national bankruptcy
    C. in no sense shifted the burden of the war on future generations
    D. placed the American people, though to a lesser degree, in the same difficult position as the British were placed by the war-time borrowing of their government from the United States and other foreign governments
    E. none of these

2. The existence of a large internally held public debt has

    A. no effect on the nation as a whole
    B. creates the danger of national bankruptcy
    C. has no effect on the nation as a whole, but does affect certain special interest groups
    D. is likely to depress the level of consumption and, hence, lower the equilibrium Net National Product
    E. is likely to make for greater inequality in the distribution of incomes and to dampen work incentive

3. In the course of production of goods by the modern corporation, marginal costs are those costs which

    A. are considered variable costs
    B. are considered fixed costs
    C. result from a one-unit addition to output
    D. are obtained by dividing the total cost of production by the number of units produced
    E. none of these

4. The MAJOR source of local and state tax revenue is _____ tax.

    A. the payroll
    B. highway (gasoline)
    C. sales
    D. individual and corporate income
    E. property

5. A rise in national income induces a further fall.
   This principal is associated with

    A. Joseph Schumpeter
    B. Alvin Hansen
    C. the accelerator
    D. liquidity preference
    E. the *demand-pull*

6. If people do not consume all their income and put the unspent amount into a bank or buy a security with it, in national income and product terms they are

    A. saving but not investing
    B. investing but not saving
    C. both saving and investing
    D. neither saving nor investing
    E. none of these

7. The *marginal propensity to consume* means the

    A. kinds of consumption goods that would be purchased if the family received extra income
    B. amount of income at which family consumption is just equal to family income
    C. average amount of each dollar of income spent on consumption
    D. ratio of extra consumption expenditure to extra income
    E. none of these

8. If Net National Product is rising, which of the following is MOST likely to occur without any discretionary policy decision being involved?
   A(n)

    A. decrease in government spending on goods and services
    B. decrease in social security payments to the aged
    C. increase in tax rates
    D. increase in tax receipts
    E. none of these

9. If the investment-interest curve is nearly vertical, then

    A. a small change in interest rates will have a substantial effect on the level of investment
    B. a tight money policy will be effective, but not an easy money policy
    C. it is very difficult to change Net National Product through monetary policy alone
    D. monetary policy will be effective in stimulating investment demand, but not in choking it off
    E. none of these

10. Assuming a required 20 percent reserve ratio, a small single large city bank which receives a net cash deposit of $1,000 is in a position to lend out an extra

    A. $5,000   B. $4,000   C. $1,000
    D. $800   E. none of these

11. The MAIN purpose of legal reserve requirements is to

    A. make the public's deposits safe and liquid
    B. keep the commercial banks from becoming too profitable
    C. enable the Federal Reserve authorities to control the amount of demand deposits that the Member Banks can create
    D. prevent *bank runs*
    E. none of these

12. A *favorable balance of trade* in a country which is at full employment tends directly to   12._____

    A. raise the level of real income
    B. raise the level of real consumption
    C. reduce inflationary pressures
    D. produce inflationary pressures
    E. none of these

13. A so-called *scientific tariff* which equalizes the cost of all production at home and abroad will   13._____

    A. avoid foreigners' complaints about being unfairly shut out of our market
    B. reduce both imports and exports virtually to zero
    C. force foreign producers to raise their wage levels
    D. assure us the benefits of comparative advantage
    E. none of these

14. Capital formation in underdeveloped areas is NOT made difficult because of   14._____

    A. low incomes
    B. the desire to emulate foreign consumption standards
    C. difficulties in borrowing abroad
    D. the bourgeois ethic stressing frugality and acquisitiveness and the consequent virtue of thrift
    E. none of these

15. Which of the following is NOT among the four factors which certain economists consider MOST important in promoting economic development?   15._____

    A. Productivity   B. Natural resources
    C. Capital formation   D. Technology
    E. None of these

16. Which of the following is NOT among the measures which certain economists urge for the development of industry?   16._____

    A. Established price control as a check against inflation
    B. Raising tariffs to promote industry
    C. Creating a surplus to finance capital formation
    D. Reforming the tax structure to finance *social overhead capital*
    E. None of these

17. The percentage of the world's population living in areas which are classified as underdeveloped is   17._____

    A. one-third   B. one-half   C. two-thirds
    D. three-quarters   E. none of these

18. The optimum economic situation in regard to population in any country is   18._____

    A. that number of people whose labor will produce the largest possible per capita product
    B. the greatest number of people that country has ever had
    C. that time in a country's history of population where there has been developed the highest per capita, income

D. one in which there is a balance between industrial and agricultural workers
E. none of these

19. Our rational objectives in the development of backward areas would be based on the

    A. desire to import from them goods that they can produce more advantageously than we can at home
    B. need to extend markets as an outlet for our exports so that we can avoid slumps
    C. need to offset the appeals of communism in those areas
    D. altruistic and ethical desire to create a more free and humane world society
    E. none of these

19.____

20. Secular stagnation, according to Alvin Hansen, was NOT to be accounted for by

    A. slowing population increase
    B. competition with low-wage foreign labor
    C. high corporate saving
    D. passing of the frontier's free land
    E. bias towards capital-saving invention

20.____

21. In teaching the forms of business organization, which of the following terms would the teacher be LEAST likely to explain?

    A. Limited liability   B. Absentee ownership
    C. Equity capital   D. Reserve ratio
    E. None of these

21.____

22. The statement that imperfect competition prevails in a given industry means that prices in that industry are determined

    A. by government regulation
    B. by a single firm with a monopoly position
    C. solely by conditions in the market
    D. by the competing firms' decisions
    E. none of these

22.____

23. The tax in the United States which MOST closely meets the needs of a sound tax system is the _____ tax.

    A. personal   B. excess profits
    C. death and inheritance   D. excise
    E. none of these

23.____

24. In teaching the topic of exchange, a point of emphasis would be the fact that at least nine-tenths of all transactions (in terms of value) are accomplished by the use of

    A. Federal Reserve notes   B. promissory notes
    C. checks   D. bills of exchange
    E. none of these

24.____

25. The United States Government prefers to sell defense bonds to individuals rather than to banks because the 25.___

    A. average person hoards his high wages in times of prosperity
    B. banks are reluctant to invest large sums of money in such bonds
    C. tendency of such sales is to avert inflation
    D. administration fears the domination of the Government by banking interests
    E. none of these

KEY (CORRECT ANSWERS)

1.	C	11.	C
2.	C	12.	D
3.	C	13.	B
4.	E	14.	D
5.	A	15.	A
6.	A	16.	A
7.	D	17.	C
8.	D	18.	A
9.	C	19.	D
10.	B	20.	B

21. D
22. D
23. A
24. C
25. C

TEST 4

DIRECTIONS: Each question or incomplete statement is followed by several suggested answers or completions. Select the one that BEST answers the question or completes the statement. *PRINT THE LETTER OF THE CORRECT ANSWER IN THE SPACE AT THE RIGHT.*

1. Economics is a social science because

    A. tables and graphs are used
    B. theory and empirical evidence are related
    C. the scientific method is applied to human behavior
    D. it deals with the allocation of scarce resources to material ends
    E. none of the above

1._____

2. The factors of production are USUALLY considered to be
    I. technology
    II. land
    III. labor
    IV. climate
    V. capital

    The CORRECT answer is:

    A. II, III, IV   B. III, IV, V   C. I, II, III
    D. II, III, V   E. I, IV, V

2._____

3. Division of labor is USUALLY defined as

    A. everyone doing the same amount of work
    B. communism
    C. specialization
    D. none of the above
    E. all of the above

3._____

4. Economizing is necessary because

    A. there is not enough money for everybody
    B. resources are scarce in relation to human desires
    C. it is immoral for things to be wasted
    D. all of the above
    E. none of the above

4._____

5. The economist needs to know

    A. only mathematics because economics deals only with quantities
    B. mainly economic theory because economic behavior is common sense
    C. mainly the development of economic thought and institutions
    D. a minimum about human behavior plus economics
    E. as much as possible about the universe including, especially, economics and statistics

5._____

6. Free economic goods are those

    A. which are not important
    B. given to us by our parents
    C. given to us by the government
    D. given to us by nature and requiring no effort to make usable
    E. none of the above

7. The law of diminishing returns means that

    A. the more people work, the less is produced
    B. if one factor of production increases more slowly, eventually there will be a decline in productivity
    C. as population increases geometrically, food production increases arithmetically
    D. as labor increases, production per person declines
    E. all of the above

8. Living standards depend upon the

    A. number of people in an area
    B. ability to produce commodities
    C. ability to utilize commodities
    D. none of the above
    E. all of the above

9. The industrial revolution
    I. had nothing to do with world population increase
    II. did not develop where slavery was the basis of the economy
    III. has not influenced most of the people of the world
    IV. developed first in Britain and spread east and west
    V. all of the above

    The CORRECT answer is:

    A. I, III   B. I, II   C. II, III
    D. II, IV   E. V

10. World population has increased because

    A. the birth rate has risen sharply
    B. the death rate has fallen sharply
    C. people are not practicing birth control
    D. all of the above
    E. none of the above

11. The amount of natural resources is
    I. fixed and unchanging
    II. dependent upon the level of technology
    III. subject to periodic fluctuations
    IV. subject to depletion
    V. all of the above

    The CORRECT answer is:

    A. I, II   B. I, III   C. II, III
    D. II, IV   E. V

12. The accumulation of capital in an economy means the   12.____

    A. amount of money that is saved
    B. growth of output capacity
    C. rise in values on the stock market
    D. none of the above
    E. all of the above

13. The efficiency of production depends upon   13.____

    A. the division of labor and exchange
    B. mass production and mechanization
    C. automation and cybernetics
    D. none of the above
    E. all of the above

14. To increase output, we must do the following: 14.____
        I. increase hours of work
        II. increase the labor force
        III. increase output capacity
        IV. increase leisure time
        V. none of the above
    The CORRECT answer is:

    A. I, II, III   B. I, II, IV   C. I, III, IV
    D. II, III, IV   E. V

15. Our economic system transforms competition into cooperation by   15.____

    A. freedom of contract
    B. intervention of the government
    C. operation of the price system in commodity markets
    D. all of the above
    E. none of the above

16. Arrange the following great economic thinkers chronologically: 16.____
        I. John Maynard Keynes
        II. Adam Smith
        III. Karl Marx
        IV. David Ricardo
        V. Thorstein Veblen
    The CORRECT answer is:

    A. II, III, IV, I, V   B. II, IV, III, V, I
    C. II, III, IV, V, I   D. IV, II, III, I, V
    E. IV, II, III, V, I

17. The price system tells businessmen how much of what to produce if   17.____

    A. workable competition exists in the market
    B. consumers buy on the basis of advertising only
    C. income is equally distributed only
    D. all of the above
    E. none of the above

18. Place these stages of economic development in sequence from the earliest to the latest.
    I. Machine technology and industrial capitalism
    II. Hunting and food-gathering
    III. Plow-agriculture and irrigation
    IV. Pastoralism and digging-stick agriculture
    V. Commercial capitalism
    The CORRECT answer is:

    A. II, III, IV, I, V
    B. II, III, IV, V, I
    C. II, IV, III, V, I
    D. IV, II, III, I, V
    E. IV, II, III, V, I

19. Modern industrial society is based PRIMARILY upon the following:
    I. Forests
    II. Coal
    III. Gold
    IV. Iron ore
    V. Petroleum
    The CORRECT answer is:

    A. I, II, III
    B. II, IV, V
    C. I, III, IV
    D. I, III, V
    E. II, III, IV

20. Inequality of income is needed in an economy
    I. to create an aristocracy of wealth
    II. to make savings available for investment
    III. to persuade people to work harder
    IV. all of the above
    V. none of the above
    The CORRECT answer is:

    A. I, II
    B. I, III
    C. IV
    D. V
    E. II, III

21. Limitations upon freedom of occupational choice in the United States include

    A. inequality of income distribution
    B. discrimination in employment
    C. inequality of educational or training opportunities
    D. inadequate vocational guidance and apprentice training
    E. all of the above

22. The concept of equilibrium involves the idea that

    A. the economy can operate with no fluctuations
    B. fluctuations tend to be self-correcting
    C. there must be perfect competition for it to work
    D. none of the above
    E. all of the above

23. An economic theory is scientific
    I. even if it requires many assumptions and has no relation to the actual operation of the economy
    II. if it is consistent, even if it has little value for forecasting
    III. if it is internally consistent and has a minimum of assumptions
    IV. if it has considerable usefulness in forecasting
    V. all of the above

    The CORRECT answer is:

    A. I, II
    B. I, III
    C. II, III
    D. III, IV
    E. V

24. The fallacy of composition indicates that

    A. if one event follows another, it is caused by it
    B. if someone acts as we would, the action is correct
    C. a knowledge of economics is needed to see economic contradictions
    D. actions of individuals in their own self-interest may lead to results in the aggregate which injure their interest
    E. none of the above

25. Gross national product is the

    A. entire wealth of a country
    B. entire production less depreciation
    C. value of the annual output of all commodities
    D. income of all wage and salary earners

KEY (CORRECT ANSWERS)

1. C
2. D
3. C
4. B
5. E

6. D
7. B
8. E
9. D
10. B

11. D
12. B
13. E
14. A
15. D

16. B
17. A
18. C
19. B
20. E

21. E
22. B
23. D
24. D
25. C

TEST 5

DIRECTIONS: Each question or incomplete statement is followed by several suggested answers or completions. Select the one that BEST answers the question or completes the statement. *PRINT THE LETTER OF THE CORRECT ANSWER IN THE SPACE AT THE RIGHT.*

1. National income consists of the

   A. value of goods and services from the private and government sectors of the economy
   B. income of all factors of production during a year
   C. income that is available to consumers annually
   D. income that producers receive after savings
   E. none of the above

   1.____

2. Net investment can be defined as
   I. the amount of capital goods added to output capacity annually
   II. the amount of stocks and bonds purchased in one year
   III. gross investment minus depreciation
   IV. none of the above
   V. all of the above

   The CORRECT answer is:

   A. I, II   B. I, III   C. II, III
   D. IV   E. V

   2.____

3. As the United States economy developed after the Civil War,

   A. the merger movement among business firms increased
   B. industry began to become more important than agriculture
   C. broader markets led to greater specialization and mass production
   D. industrial capitalists and financiers became more dominant
   E. all of the above

   3.____

4. Gross national product was

   A. smaller in 1929 than 1932
   B. smaller in 1939 than 1929
   C. larger in 1939 than 1945
   D. none of the above
   E. all of the above

   4.____

5. The impact of technology upon the economy would follow which sequence according to Schumpeter:
   I. Innovation
   II. Acceptance of innovation
   III. Invention
   IV. Scientific development
   V. Financing

   The CORRECT answer is:

   5.____

A. I, II, V, IV, III
B. IV, III, I, V, II
C. IV, I, III, V, II
D. III, IV, V, I, II
E. II, IV, III, I, V

6. If productivity grows more rapidly than production,

   A. we may have growing inflation
   B. we may have growing unemployment
   C. we may need more unskilled labor
   D. a larger part of the labor force may be needed in manufacturing
   E. none of the above

7. Inflation means that
   I. the income of stockholders will decline
   II. there is a general rise in the value of money
   III. there is a general rise in the prices of commodities
   IV. the weighted index of wholesale prices rises
   V. the index of physical output rises

   The CORRECT answer is:

   A. I, II
   B. I, III
   C. II, III
   D. III, IV
   E. I, V

8. The advantage of a weighted price index over one that is not weighted consists of the fact that the

   A. weighted index is easier to calculate
   B. data for the unweighted index is harder to find
   C. unweighted index is more complex
   D. unweighted index does not reflect the importance of the component commodities
   E. all of the above

9. The PRINCIPAL forms of specialization today are by
   I. income
   II. vocation
   III. age
   IV. task
   V. geography

   The CORRECT answer is:

   A. I, II, III
   B. I, III, IV
   C. I, III, V
   D. II, III, IV
   E. II, IV, V

10. As the level of prices changes,

    A. it has the same effects on all consumers and producers
    B. the value of money varies inversely with these changes
    C. the value of commodities remains in unvarying relationship to each other
    D. none of the above
    E. all of the above

11. The effect of inflationary policies upon the economy depends on the

    A. percentage of unemployment
    B. balance of international payments

C. marginal propensity to save
D. none of the above
E. all of the above

12. A policy of inflation is necessary to
    I. increase the purchasing power of the dollar
    II. increase living standards
    III. pay off the national debt
    IV. prevent overexpansion at full employment
    V. all of the above
    The CORRECT answer is:

    A. I, II   B. I, III   C. I, IV
    D. II, III   E. V

13. Private property rights are becoming increasingly limited because

    A. specialization is making people more interdependent
    B. the role of the government in the economy is greater
    C. the density of population is rising
    D. stock ownership has become divorced from control
    E. all of the above

14. The profit motive is
    I. the only incentive businessmen have in the modern economy
    II. a manifestation of the spirit of acquisitiveness
    III. transforms private greed into public benefit through competition
    IV. the only motive making people work under private capitalism
    V. responsible for all economic development
    The CORRECT answer is:

    A. I, II   B. I, III   C. I, IV
    D. II, III   E. IV, V

15. Price competition exists when

    A. there is a large number of independent buyers and sellers
    B. the commodities are comparable
    C. both buyers and sellers have reasonable knowledge about the commodities
    D. there is freedom of entry into the market
    E. all of the above

16. Money replaced barter because
    I. as specialization increased trade expanded
    II. as trade expanded barter became too time consuming
    III. people desired precious metals more than other commodities
    IV. the increasing division of labor made commodity payment increasingly difficult
    V. none of the above
    The CORRECT answer is:

    A. I, II   B. I, III   C. II, III
    D. II, IV   E. V

17. Commercial banks are

    A. reservoirs for peoples' savings
    B. creators of most of the money in use
    C. not regulated by any one
    D. in control of interest rates
    E. playing a growing role in the market for corporation bonds

18. Excess reserves are
    I. the excess of deposits over loans
    II. those over legal reserve requirements
    III. loanable funds
    IV. none of the above
    V. all of the above

    The CORRECT answer is:

    A. I, II   B. I, III   C. II, III
    D. IV   E. V

19. The Federal Reserve system can control the volume of check money

    A. by open market operations in government bonds
    B. changing the rediscount rate
    C. altering reserve requirements
    D. none of the above
    E. all of the above

20. The velocity of circulation of money has

    A. nothing to do with the volume of money
    B. been subject to large short-term fluctuations
    C. been subject to large long-term fluctuations
    D. all of the above
    E. none of the above

21. Effective demand for goods and services is

    A. determined by the funds spent for consumption and investment
    B. disposable personal income
    C. the proportion of national income saved
    D. corporation expenditure for expansion
    E. all of the above

22. As income for the consumer rises,

    A. consumption rises as rapidly
    B. savings increases more slowly
    C. consumption rises more rapidly
    D. savings rises more rapidly
    E. none of the above

23. Businessmen invest when

    A. they want to increase their firm's efficiency
    B. expected profits are larger than the going interest rate

C. demand for their commodity exceeds their output capacity
D. none of the above
E. all of the above

24. Money consists of
   I. legal tender only
   II. generally acceptable symbols of claims upon commodities
   III. only gold and silver
   IV. a medium of exchange and measure of value
   V. currency but not checks
   The CORRECT answer is:

   A. I, III   B. I, V   C. II, IV
   D. III, V   E. I, IV

25. Pre-Keynsian thinking among most economists considered that full employment was the rule because
   I. according to Say's law, *supply creates its own demand*
   II. prices and wages were becoming less flexible
   III. the interest rate in a free market tends to equalize saving and investment
   IV. barriers to trade were growing after World War I
   V. none of the above
   The CORRECT answer is:

   A. I, III   B. I, II   C. II, IV
   D. II, III   E. V

KEY (CORRECT ANSWERS)

1. B
2. B
3. E
4. D
5. B

6. B
7. D
8. D
9. E
10. B

11. E
12. C
13. E
14. D
15. E

16. D
17. B
18. C
19. E
20. B

21. A
22. D
23. E
24. C
25. A

EXAMINATION SECTION
TEST 1

DIRECTIONS: Each question or incomplete statement is followed by several suggested answers or completions. Select the one that BEST answers the question or completes the statement. *PRINT THE LETTER OF THE CORRECT ANSWER IN THE SPACE AT THE RIGHT.*

1. It is an ESSENTIAL characteristic of a theoretical situation of pure competition that all producers of a given product
    A. offer identical units of the product
    B. pursue a vigorous but truthful advertising program
    C. pursue independent price policies
    D. engage in vigorous price competition

    1.____

2. Which one of the following laws in economics is INCORRECTLY stated?
    A. Gresham's Law – Cheap money dives out dear money.
    B. Engel's Law – The greater the family income, the greater the proportion of this income is spent on food.
    C. Law of Monopoly Price – Price which will yield the highest net return.
    D. Law of Diminishing Returns – Increasing investments of one agent of production combined with constant quantities of other agents will result in less than a proportionate return, sooner or later.

    2.____

3. Which one of the following is NOT an argument for free trade?
    A. It permits a nation to control and to manage its currency to maximum advantage.
    B. It permits a nation to achieve maximum productivity.
    C. It accumulates surplus purchasing power abroad.
    D. It permits foreigners to buy goods produced at lowest cost.

    3.____

4. Which one of the following is in the CLOSEST accord with the spirit of the Doctrine of Comparative Costs?
    A. Rationing of foreign exchange
    B. Government monopoly of trade in key commodities
    C. Quantitative import quotas
    D. International division of labor

    4.____

5. Which one of the following was NOT suggested by the mercantilists to foster a favorable balance of trade?
    A. Encouragement of home manufactures
    B. Imposition of low customs duties on imported goods
    C. Establishment of colonies
    D. Encouragement of the fishing and shipping industries

    5.____

6. Which of the following statements are CORRECT?
   I. Monopoly price is always high price.
   II. Elasticity or inelasticity of demand largely determines whether monopoly price will be high or low.
   III. A monopoly of an industry with inelastic demand would probably prove more profitable than a monopoly of an industry with elastic demand.
   IV. The costs of production under pure monopoly are always less than under pure competition.

   The CORRECT answer is:
   A. I, II B. I, III C. II, III D. III, IV

7. Which one of the following statements is NOT true under competition?
   A. In the long run, prices are influenced by the cost of production of the marginal producer.
   B. The selling price of a commodity cannot long rise above the cost of production.
   C. Improvements in technique retard the working of the principle of increasing costs.
   D. If the amount produced in any plant is doubled, the total costs of production are doubled.

8. Which is the CORRECT chronological order in which the following laws were enacted?
   I. The Federal Trade Commission Act
   II. The Robinson-Patman Act
   III. The National Industry Recovery Act
   IV. The Sherman Act

   The CORRECT chronological order is:
   A. IV, I, III, II B. II, I, IV, III C. IV, I, II, III D. II, IV, I, III

9. Which one of the following pairs is NOT properly grouped?
   A. Single proprietorship – personal liability for losses of business
   B. Partnership – impermanence
   C. Corporation – special income taxes
   D. Cooperatives – special tax treatment on patronage dividends

10. The value of money varies
    A. *inversely* with the supply of money
    B. *directly* with the supply of money
    C. *directly* with the general level of prices
    D. *directly* with the velocity of its circulation

11. Which one of the following is NOT designed to act as a prop under business to prevent recession?
    A. Tax cuts will release large sums to individuals and corporations.
    B. Unemployment insurance will absorb shock of job losses.
    C. Long-term amortized mortgages will prevent foreclosures.
    D. Credit will be carefully rationed and money kept relatively dear.

11.____

12. An 8% sales tax on every purchase of any kind would be, in effect,
    A. proportional
    B. inelastic
    C. progressive
    D. regressive

12.____

13. *Negative savings* implies that
    A. annual savings for those family units have passed the thousand dollar mark
    B. the family unit had to borrow to keep going
    C. savings come from a relatively small number of families in the higher-income groups
    D. savings are made by institutions rather than family units

13.____

14. During deflation, unearned benefits come to
    A. farmers
    B. businessmen
    C. persons with savings
    D. debtors

14.____

15. Which of the following were *post-war* MAJOR problems in Italy?
    I. Insufficient agricultural production
    II. Religious disputes with the Vatican
    III. Restoration of colonies
    IV. Unemployment
    V. Unfavorable balance of trade

    The CORRECT answer is:
    A. I, II, III   B. I, IV, V   C. II, III, IV   D. II, III, V

15.____

16. The Colombo Project was MOST similar in its aims to the
    A. Yangtze Plan
    B. Point IV Program
    C. St. Lawrence Seaway Project
    D. Tennessee Valley Authority

16.____

17. Of the following, which were related to the control of production of atomic energy?
    I. Lilienthal-Acheson Plan
    II. Gromyko Plan
    III. McMahon Act
    IV. Baruch Plan
    V. Monnet Plan

    The CORRECT references are:
    A. I, II, III, V   B. III, IV, V   C. I, II, III, IV   D. I, II, IV, V

17.____

18. Which SIGNIFICANT development in our foreign trade occurred during recent years?
    A. Imports increased to a new high figure in our history.
    B. Exports continued at the peak volumes of previous years.
    C. Dollar shortages disappeared over the world.
    D. Import and exchange restrictions were cancelled by European countries.

19. Of the following items, the one with the LOWEST degree of elastic demand is
    A. sirloin steak   B. beef   C. food   D. meat

20. A college teacher listed the following Supreme Court cases on the board:
    Munn v. Illinois
    New State Ice Co. v. Liebmann
    Tyson v. Banton
    Nebbia v. New York
    What subject was his class studying?
    A. Public utilities   B. Interstate commerce
    C. Reasonable rate   D. Regulation of monopolies

21. All of the following factors may account for the strengthening of the British pound EXCEPT
    A. decreased imports of gold
    B. increased British exports
    C. decreased imports from the dollar area
    D. increasing interest rates

22. A function of the International Monetary Fund is to
    A. grant loans of a self-liquidating nature to underdeveloped countries
    B. provide stability in foreign exchange rates while allowing freedom of action in coping with domestic problems
    C. grant loans for relief and rehabilitation to members of the United Nations who sustained extensive damage during World War II
    D. prevent the flight of capital from countries with unstable currencies

23. The Randall Commission, during the first Eisenhower administration, recommended
    A. higher protective tariffs   B. Buy-American program
    C. extension of reciprocal tariffs D. removal of tariffs

24. THE AGE OF THE MOGULS, a contemporary book on the great American fortune builders from 1865-1929, was written by
    A. John Kouwenhoven   B. Kendall Smith
    C. James Flexner   D. Stewart Holbrook

25. A contemporary book which is favorable to big business is
    A. C. Wright Mills, WHITE COLLAR
    B. George Soule, ECONOMIC FORCES IN AMERICAN HISTORY
    C. David Lilienthal, BIG BUSINESS: A NEW ERA
    D. Harold U. Fulkner, DECLINE OF LAISSEZ-FAIRE

KEY (CORRECT ANSWERS)

1. A
2. B
3. A
4. D
5. B

6. C
7. D
8. A
9. D
10. A

11. D
12. D
13. B
14. C
15. B

16. B
17. A
18. A
19. C
20. A

21. A
22. B
23. C
24. D
25. C

TEST 2

DIRECTIONS: Each question or incomplete statement is followed by several suggested answers or completions. Select the one that BEST answers the question or completes the statement. *PRINT THE LETTER OF THE CORRECT ANSWER IN THE SPACE AT THE RIGHT.*

1. Which one of the following is wholly a program of the states? 1.____
    A. Old age pensions
    B. Old age and survivors' insurance
    C. Workmen's compensation
    D. Unemployment insurance

2. Life insurance in New York can be purchased at low rates in 2.____
    A. commercial banks
    B. trust companies
    C. investment banks
    D. savings banks

3. Which one of the following is LEAST based on the ability to pay theory of taxation? 3.____
    A. Corporate income tax
    B. Sales tax
    C. Personal income tax
    D. Estate tax

4. Which one of the following is the MOST common form of money in circulation in the U.S. today? 4.____
    A. United States notes
    B. Federal Reserve Bank notes
    C. Federal Reserve notes
    D. National Bank notes

5. In which one of the following ways can the Federal Reserve Banks loosen credit? By 5.____
    A. raising the rediscount rate
    B. rediscounting member banks' notes
    C. sending warnings to member banks
    D. selling notes in open market

6. The legal reserves of a member bank with the Federal Reserve Bank are 6.____
    A. the cash it deposits with the Federal Reserve Bank
    B. till money
    C. the accounts which it keeps at the Federal Reserve Bank
    D. cash deposited with correspondent banks

7. Which one of the following is in violation of the provisions of the Taft-Hartley Law? 7.____
    A. Refusal to bargain with a certified union because of the existence of a strike
    B. The union shop
    C. A statement by management to the workers on labor matters
    D. Liability of unions for damage suits in jurisdictional strikes

8. Which title and author are INCORRECTLY paired?
   A. Henry George – PROGRESS AND POVERTY
   B. Thorstein Veblen – THEORY OF THE LEISURE CLASS
   C. Joseph A. Schumpeter – CAPITALISM, SOCIALISM AND DEMOCRACY
   D. Wesley C. Mitchell – GENERAL THEORY OF EMPLOYMENT, INTEREST AND MONEY

8.____

9. In a corporation, there is
   A. *unlimited* liability of stockholders
   B. *limited* liability of stockholders
   C. *unlimited* liability of stockholders and of the corporation
   D. *unlimited* liability of stockholders and *limited* liability of the corporation

9.____

10. Which of the following aspects of the Federal Social Security system are administered by the states?
    I. Old age pension
    II. Unemployment insurance
    III. Aid to dependent children
    IV. Aid to the needy aged

    The CORRECT answer is:
    A. I, III, IV   B. II, III   C. I, II   D. II, III, IV

10.____

11. Which of the following types of social insurance are provided by MOST state governments in the United States?
    I. Old age insurance
    II. Workmen's compensation
    III. Unemployment insurance
    IV. Health insurance

11.____

12. Labor unions in the United States have a legal right to
    A. compel employers to hire only union members
    B. force an employer to bargain collectively
    C. refuse to bargain collectively with employers
    D. require an employer to pay for work not actually performed

12.____

13. Economists are in general agreement that a monopolist
    A. controls demand for his products and maximizes his profit
    B. sells more cheaply than competitive enterprise can in the same field
    C. considers the elasticity of demand for his product in fixing his price
    D. ignores demand for his product and sets his price at the highest possible level

13.____

14. The real wages of workers depend upon money wages and
    A. bonuses
    B. the price level
    C. deductions for Social Security and income taxes
    D. working hours

14.____

15. The U.S. Bureau of Standards sets standards
    A. for products purchased by the government
    B. for government grading meats
    C. for grade labeling of canned goods
    D. of purity for drug products

15.____

16. Which one of the following is NOT a basic principle of consumers' cooperatives?
    A. Distributing earnings to consumers in proportion to buyers' purchases
    B. Opening membership to all consumers regardless of race, color, or creed
    C. Permitting each member only one vote, regardless of shares owned or purchases made
    D. Selling to members at special discounts in order to keep profits down

16.____

17. Modern economic principles of international trade support the view that
    A. American tourists traveling in Europe help European countries to pay their debts to the United States
    B. creditor nations under normal conditions should seek to have favorable balances of trade
    C. a nation like England cannot import more merchandise than it exports without losing gold
    D. no nation can gain by international trade because imports must be paid for by some kind of exports

17.____

18. Under the present system of federal deposit insurance,
    A. all savings bank deposits are fully insured
    B. all savings bank deposits are fully insured but commercial bank deposits are insured to a limited amount
    C. savings bank deposits are insured to a limited amount
    D. deposits in national banks only are insured

18.____

19. Which one of the following is NOT a device for achieving minority control of corporations?
    A. The holding company
    B. Non-voting stock
    C. The voting trust
    D. The joint-stock company

19.____

20. Which of the following ACCURATELY contrasts a corporation and a consumers' cooperative?
    A. One vote per share; one vote per member
    B. Chartered by the state; no charter of incorporation
    C. Profits paid out as dividends; profits eliminated by charging low prices
    D. Issues stock; no stock issued

20.____

21. The capital of a corporation is represented by $400,000 of 5% bonds and $200,000 of common stock. The corporation goes into bankruptcy, and its assets yield $100,000. The amount so realized is distributed as follows: _____ to bondholders; _____ to stockholders.
    A. $80,000; $20,000
    B. Nothing; $100,000
    C. $50,000; $50,000
    D. $100,000; nothing

21.____

22. In the following paired items, the pair that contains examples of items from the two sides of a balance sheet is
    A. inventory and good will
    B. accounts receivable and surplus
    C. notes payable and capital stock
    D. cash and operating expenses

22.____

23. The International Ladies Garment Workers Union is
    I. an industrial union
    II. a vertical union
    III. affiliated with the C.I.O.
    IV. an independent union

    The CORRECT answer is:
    A. I, II
    B. I, II, III
    C. I, III, IV
    D. II, III

23.____

24. Each of the following agencies has the authority to fix some price or rate EXCEPT the
    A. Board of Governors of the Federal Reserve System
    B. SEC
    C. ICC
    D. Public Service Commission

24.____

25. In the matter of appraising the value of public utilities for purposes of rate regulation, the Supreme Court has
    A. adopted the theory of prudent cost less depreciation
    B. favored the theory of reproduction cost
    C. given no clear-cut support to either doctrine
    D. ruled that each state ma set up its own guides for its public service commissions

25.____

KEY (CORRECT ANSWERS)

1.	C	11.	B
2.	D	12.	B
3.	B	13.	C
4.	C	14.	B
5.	B	15.	A
6.	C	16.	D
7.	A	17.	A
8.	D	18.	C
9.	B	19.	D
10.	D	20.	A

21.	D
22.	B
23.	A
24.	B
25.	C

TEST 3

DIRECTIONS: Each question or incomplete statement is followed by several suggested answers or completions. Select the one that BEST answers the question or completes the statement. *PRINT THE LETTER OF THE CORRECT ANSWER IN THE SPACE AT THE RIGHT.*

1. The risks due to speculative production tend to be INCREASED by
   A. improved transportation
   B. improved market information
   C. monopoly
   D. the roundabout method of production

2. The equation $\dfrac{MV + M'V'}{T} = P$
   A. was formulated to explain why wages lag behind prices
   B. is related to the quantity theory of money
   C. obviates the need for index numbers in measuring price changes
   D. was evolved by Adam Smith

3. Indicate by reference to the groupings below which of the following statements are TRUE about wages:
   I. Wages are determined in accordance with the same general principles which apply to all prices.
   II. An increase in the supply of capital tends to raise wages.
   III. The current level of wages is a determinant of the demand for labor.
   IV. Wage differentials result from the existence of non-competing groups.

   The CORRECT answer is:
   A. I, III   B. II, IV   C. I, III, IV   D. I, II, III, IV

4. Profits
   I. in a large corporation go primarily to owners and not to management
   II. are the most variable part of the national income
   III. are partly a matter of luck
   IV. are automatically disbursed as dividends

   The CORRECT answer is:
   A. I, II   B. III, IV   C. I, II, III   D. I, IV

5. Inflationary tendencies are ENHANCED when the government
   A. borrows from the general public   B. balances its budget
   C. sells bonds to banks   D. exports gold

6. To check inflation, the Federal Reserve System might
   A. buy government bonds   B. lower its discount rate
   C. sell securities in the open market   D. devaluate the dollar

7. If the United States sold more goods to Great Britain than it bought from Great Britain, which of the following would REDUCE the resulting drain on Great Britain's dollar resources?
   I. Expenditures by American tourists in Great Britain
   II. Use of British merchant marine facilities by American shippers
   III. Payment of dividends to American holders of British securities
   IV. Allocations to Great Britain under the European Recovery program

   The CORRECT answer is:
   A. IV only   B. I, II, III   C. I, II, IV   D. III, IV

8. Machine industry
   I. was practically underdeveloped before 1750
   II. tends to make the economy dynamic
   III. decreases the risks of business
   IV. is a major basis for specialization

   The CORRECT answer is:
   A. I, II   B. I, III, IV   C. I, II, IV   D. II, IV

9. Value theory is related to
   I. the indifference curve technique
   II. equilibrium theory
   III. the multiplier principle
   IV. marginalism

   The CORRECT answer is:
   A. I, II, III   B. I, II, IV   C. II. III, IV   D. III, IV

10. In which of the following pairs are the items LEAST clearly related?
    A. Distribution – marginal productivity theory
    B. Interest – liquidity preference theory
    C. Price – oligopolistic practices
    D. Monopoly – compensatory policy

11. An American economist who held that the worst social evils arose from land speculation and land monopoly was
    A. Henry George   B. Sumner Slichter
    C. John M. Clark   D. E.R.A. Seligman

12. Henry C. Carey, who began as a disciple of the English classical school and as a free trader, was forced by his environment to change his views. In this change he resembles
    A. List   B. Cobden   C. Muller   D. Sismondi

13. Of the following, the economist who FIRST included the element of time within the scope of his analysis is
    A. Rexford Tugwell   B. Adam Smith
    C. Simon Patten   D. Alfred Marshall

14. John Bates Clark's role, importance, and place in the history of American economic thought can BEST be likened to the role of
    A. Alfred Marshall in England
    B. Francois Quesnay in France
    C. Gustav Cassell in Sweden
    D. V. Pareto in Italy

14.____

15. The founders of modern utility doctrine in economics are
    A. Jevons, Menger, Walras
    B. Ricardo, Roscher, List
    C. Marshall, Walras
    D. J.B. Clark, Boehm-Bawerk

15.____

16. The economist who is BEST remembered for his theory of non-competing groups of workers is
    A. J. E. Cairnes
    B. J. S. Mill
    C. J. B. Say
    D. F. A. Fetter

16.____

17. The abstinence theory of interest was FIRST advanced by
    A. John Stuart Mill
    B. John Bates Clark
    C. William Nassau Senior
    D. Frank A. Fetter

17.____

18. The Keynesian savings-investment approach to employment theory is based in part upon an analysis of
    A. the propensity to consume
    B. the velocity of circulation of money
    C. residual returns
    D. opportunity costs

18.____

19. Which one of the following has NOT been in close association with the others in the formulation of government policies in recent years?
    A. L. H. Keyserling
    B. S. Slichter
    C. E. G. Nourse
    D. J. D. Clark

19.____

20. Peter Drucker's CONCEPT OF THE MODERN CORPORATION is a(n)
    A. description of the operation of General Motors
    B. history of the development of corporations
    C. analysis of the 200 largest industrial corporations
    D. study of the effect of the giant corporation on competition

20.____

21. Which of the following economists whose writings on the business cycle contain a minimum of theorizing as to basic causes and a maximum of the institutional. descriptive approach?
    A. W. C. Mitchell
    B. J. M. Keynes
    C. A. C. Pigou
    D. Karl Marx

21.____

22. Which of the following advocated doctrines with relation to foreign trade that can be included under the heading of *economic nationalism*?
    I. Thomas Mun
    II. Alexander Hamilton
    III. Adam Smith
    IV. Friedrich List
    V. Richard Cobden

    The CORRECT answer is:
    A. I, III, IV   B. II, IV, V   C. I, II, IV   D. I, II, V

23. Adam Smith believed that:
    I. Nations should refrain from manufacturing items which can be imported more cheaply.
    II. Foreign trade should be planned to produce a favorable balance of trade.
    III. Agriculture is more productive than industry and commerce.
    IV. The interest of the producer is secondary to that of the consumer.
    V. The importation of manufactured goods that compete with home products should be restricted.

    The CORRECT answer is:
    A. I, II, IV   B. III, IV, V   C. I, II, III   D. I, III, IV

24. Which of the following pairs does NOT properly associate the economist with the field in which he made a major contribution?
    A. Veblen – Pecuniary aspects of American culture
    B. J. M. Clark – Overhead costs
    C. Sismondi – Marginal utility
    D. Keynes – Propensity to consume

25. According to the Mature Economy Thesis of the Keynes-Hansen school of economics, three of these items are causes and one the effect. Which is the EFFECT? The
    A. end of the frontier and of geographic expansion
    B. declining rate of population growth
    C. decline in investment opportunities
    D. change in capital needs of new industries of today

KEY (CORRECT ANSWERS)

1. D
2. B
3. D
4. C
5. C

6. C
7. C
8. C
9. B
10. D

11. A
12. A
13. D
14. A
15. A

16. A
17. C
18. A
19. B
20. A

21. A
22. C
23. D
24. C
25. C

TEST 4

DIRECTIONS: Each question or incomplete statement is followed by several suggested answers or completions. Select the one that BEST answers the question or completes the statement. *PRINT THE LETTER OF THE CORRECT ANSWER IN THE SPACE AT THE RIGHT.*

1. Which authors would PROBABLY appear in a bibliography of works on the structure and control of the modern corporation?
   - I. Adolph Berle
   - II. John R. Commons
   - III. Arthur S. Dewing
   - IV. William J. Ripley
   - V. Frank Taussig

   The CORRECT answer is:
   - A. II, III, IV
   - B. I, III, IV
   - C. I, IV, V
   - D. I, II, V

2. A teacher of economics recommends reading the important works of the following authors: Frank Fetter, Arthur Burns, E. H. Chamberlin. The class is studying in the field of
   - A. competition and monopoly
   - B. labor history
   - C. money and banking
   - D. consumer problems

3. Which of the following agencies for economics research or investigation might PROPERLY be labeled *private* as distinct from *governmental*?
   - I. National Industrial Conference Board
   - II. Committee for Economic Development
   - III. National Bureau of Standards
   - IV. National Bureau of Economic Research
   - V. Temporary National Economic Committee

   The CORRECT answer is:
   - A. I, IV, V
   - B. I, II, III, IV
   - C. II, III
   - D. I, II, IV

4. In a college class, a teacher listed the following authors on the blackboard for supplementary reading: Werner, Sombart, R. H. Tawney, Max Weber, Henri See. From this grouping, it is evident that the class was studying
   - A. the Renaissance
   - B. Origins of Capitalism
   - C. Development of Modern Transportation
   - D. Neomercantilism

5. The ruling form of business organization in the industrial markets of the United States today is
   - A. competition
   - B. bi-lateral monopoly
   - C. duopoly
   - D. oligopoly

6. Which combination BEST explains the reasons for vertical integration?
   I. Decline of price competition in previously purchased articles
   II. Fear of unduly high prices for raw materials in the future
   III. Fear of failure of supplies in necessary quantities
   IV. Avoidance of stock transfer taxes
   V. Decline of competition among buyers of a product

   The CORRECT answer is:
   A. I, II, IV   B. I, IV, V   C. I, II, III, V   D. II, III, V

7. Which are ACCEPTABLE reasons for the decentralization of management in the canning industry?
   I. The raw material is perishable in nature.
   II. Canning is a seasonal industry.
   III. Markets are chiefly concentrated in the large cities.
   IV. Weather conditions are uncertain.
   V. There are many individual farmers to be bargained with.

   The CORRECT answer is:
   A. I, II, III   B. I, II, IV, V   . III, IV, V   D. I, II, III, IV, V

8. Which of the following statements about a trade acceptance is NOT true? It
   A. is two-name paper
   B. is drawn on a blank agreed upon by both buyer and seller
   C. gives some indication in itself of the transaction out of which it grows
   D. compels the buyer to be ready to pay it at a definite date

9. In which of these instances would market conditions MOST CLOSELY approximate pure competition?
   A. Selling of many types of unprocessed farm products
   B. Mild distribution
   C. Meat packing
   D. Selling of many types of unprocessed mineral resources

10. The market value of all goods and services produced by business and the government is referred to as
    A. net national income
    B. gross national product
    C. net personal and corporate income
    D. gross national income

11. Which of the following statements about price discrimination is TRUE?
    A. Its usual effect is to eliminate mass production.
    B. It is possible only under conditions of monopolistic competition.
    C. It is possible only when the commodity cannot easily be sold by one class of buyers to another.
    D. It is unlikely to be found where a product has several different uses.

12. The demand for an article is likely to be ELASTIC if
    A. money spent on it represents a large percentage of consumers' total expenditures
    B. there are no satisfactory and less expensive substitutes
    C. used articles of the same kind already possessed can neither be used longer nor repaired
    D. the cost of the article represents only a small part of the expense of a larger article of which it is a part

13. Which of the following statements concerning differences between quotas and import duties are TRUE?
    I. Import duties favor only the marginal firms.
    II. Under quotas the balance of international payments becomes more rigid.
    III. Under a quota there may develop wide differences in prices between the exporting and importing country.
    IV. Quotas tend to stabilize imports.
    V. Quotas lend themselves more readily to discrimination among exporting countries.

    The CORRECT answer is:
    A. I, III, IV   B. II, III, IV, V   C. I, II   D. I, II, III, IV, V

14. Which one of the following CORRECTLY describes the effect of U.S. tariffs on U.S. farmers?
    A. They reduce the amount of exchange with which foreigners can buy our agricultural products.
    B. Their effect on the price of manufactured goods needed by farmers is negligible.
    C. They provide a greater home-market by leading to increased wages in protected industries.
    D. They have no effect.

15. Which of the following common arguments for tariffs are ECONOMICALLY JUSTIFIABLE? They
    I. prevent intermittent or predatory dumping
    II. safeguard domestic wage standards
    III. enhance purchasing power at home
    IV. equalize costs of production
    V. offset a corresponding excise tax

    The CORRECT answer is:
    A. I, II, V   . I, V   C. II, IV, V   D. I, II, IV

16. According to a recent Federal Trade Commission report, there is need for legislation to close the major loophole in the Clayton Act, which has permitted the formation of
    A. holding companies   B. mergers
    C. trusts   D. pools

17. From which of the following laws does the Federal Trade Commission derive its authority and powers?
    I. Trade Commission Act of 1914
    II. Clayton Act of 1914
    III. Patman Act of 1936
    IV. Wheeler-Lea Act of 1938
    V. Interstate Commerce Act of 1887

    The CORRECT answer is:
    A. I, III   B. I, II, III, IV   C. II, IV, V   D. I, II, III, IV, V

18. Which of the following are at present under the jurisdiction of the Interstate Commerce Commission?
    I. Cable, telegraph, and telephone
    II. Interstate bus and truck transport
    III. Ocean shipping to foreign ports
    IV. Pipelines carrying oil
    V. Interstate water transportation

    The CORRECT answer is:
    A. I, II, III, IV   B. II, IV, V   C. I, III, V   D. I, II, III, IV, V

19. Which of the following are generally considered ESSENTIALS of a full gold coin standard?
    I. A definite quantity of gold of a certain fineness is used as the standard unit for measuring values.
    II. Gold coin is acceptable as full legal tender.
    III. All government or central bank credit money and all legal tender money are redeemable at par in gold coin on demand.
    IV. Gold can be coined without limit and without substantial seigniorage for all who bring it to the mint.
    V. No restrictions are imposed on the import or export of gold in any form.

    The CORRECT answer is:
    A. I, II, IV   B. II, III, V   C. III, IV, V   D. I, II, III, IV, V

20. In a commercial bank's balance sheet or financial statement, which of the following items will appear in the *liabilities* column?
    I. Cash in vault   II. Capital stock   III. Demand deposits
    IV. Surplus   V. Loans made

    The CORRECT answer is:
    A. II, III, IV   B. I, III, IV   C. II, III, V   D. I, II, IV

21. What authority does the Federal Reserve System give to the Board of Governors? To
    A. create a demand for bank credit
    B. control the volume of bank reserves
    C. control the use of bank reserves
    D. place a limit on the movement of gold to this country from abroad

22. Which one of the following is NOT among the purposes and activities of the International Monetary Fund? To
    A. promote exchange rate stability among nations
    B. manage henceforth the bulk of foreign exchange transactions
    C. permit orderly changes in exchange rates among nations
    D. create a revolving fund upon which members may draw in need of foreign exchange

23. The concept of the U.S. as a nation that is developing a "laboristic" economy which lies somewhere between a capitalistic and a socialistic economy, was developed in a book written by
    A. S. Harris   B. S. Slichter   C. S. Kuznets   D. D. H. Carr

24. The MOST important institutional influence on labor supply and on wage rates comes from
    A. the organization of labor
    B. the organization of capital
    C. federal legislation
    D. state and local legislation

25. Which are causes of jurisdictional disputes? The
    I. extremely complex nature of modern industry
    II. continually changing processes of modern industry
    III. existence of unions in narrow craft forms
    IV. desire of each union to control as much work as possible
    V. discontent with geographical boundaries set by international unions

    The CORRECT answer is:
    A. I, II, III, IV   B. I, III   C. II, IV, V   D. I, II, III, IV, V

KEY (CORRECT ANSWERS)

1.	B	11.	C
2.	A	12.	A
3.	D	13.	B
4.	B	14.	A
5.	D	15.	B
6.	C	16.	B
7.	B	17.	B
8.	B	18.	B
9.	A	19.	D
10.	B	20.	A

21.	B
22.	B
23.	B
24.	A
25.	A

ECONOMICS

EXAMINATION SECTION
TEST 1

DIRECTIONS: Each question or incomplete statement is followed by several suggested answers or completions. Select the one that *BEST* answers the question or completes the statement. *PRINT THE LETTER OF THE CORRECT ANSWER IN THE SPACE AT THE RIGHT.*

1. What would be the *net balance* of international payments of a nation with the following credits and debits?
   Value of commodity imports..500 units
   Value of commodity exports...500 units
   Cost of use of foreign merchant vessels... 500 units
   Credits sent abroad by resident aliens...500 units
   Interest on investments in foreign nations.......................................500 units
   Expenditures made by citizens traveling abroad............................. 500 units

   A. A net debit of 1,000 units B. A net debit of 500 units
   C. No net debits or credits   D. A net credit of 500 units
   E. A net credit of 1,000 units

   1._____

2. Which of the following descriptions is *MOST* consistent with *a favorable balance of trade?*

   A. Goods and services available for domestic use exceed the value of domestic production.
   B. Domestic holdings of gold increase.
   C. Domestic exports of merchandise exceed imports of merchandise.
   D. Net foreign investment is negative.
   E. More merchandise traded is carried in domestic ships than in foreign ships.

   2._____

3. Nor will it be easy with per capita incomes as low as they are in southern Asia to raise the rate of savings and investment. These countries are caught in something like a vicious circle of poverty. Not much can be saved from low incomes; but since not much is saved and consequently invested in production equipment, income continues to remain low. It has been estimated that with population increasing at current Indian rates a net saving of 5 percent of the national income would be just about sufficient to maintain per capita incomes at their present level.
   Given an output-capital ratio of 1:3, the rate of population increase in India must be *approximately*

   A. 1/3%   B. 1%   C. 1 2/3%   D. 3%   E. 5%

   3._____

Questions 4-5.

DIRECTIONS: Questions 4-5 are based on the following terms which are often used to describe different points or portions of a demand curve.

   A. Perfectly elastic   B. Elastic   C. Having unit elasticity
   D. Inelastic   E. Perfectly inelastic

93

4. Which is *MOST* suitable as a description of the demand curve facing a firm in perfect competition?

4.____

5. If an imported commodity is reduced in price, and more is purchased for smaller total expenditure, how would the demand be described?

5.____

Questions 6-7.

DIRECTIONS: Questions 6-7 are based on the following production-possibility schedules:

For Country A

Food	50	40	30	20	10	0
Clothing	0	6	12	18	24	30

For Country B

Food	100	80	60	40	20	0
Clothing	0	18	36	54	72	90

6. *Both* schedules indicate

6.____

   A. decreasing costs
   B. constant costs
   C. increasing costs
   D. first decreasing costs, then increasing costs
   E. first increasing costs, then decreasing costs

7. If there are no restrictions on trade between the two countries, it is *most likely* that

7.____

   A. both countries will produce both commodities
   B. no trade will take place
   C. Country A will produce only food; Country B will produce both commodities
   D. Country A will produce only food; Country B will produce only clothing
   E. Country B will produce only food; Country A will produce only clothing

Questions 8-9.

DIRECTIONS: Questions 8-9 are based on the following data for a hypothetical economy.

If income* is	Scheduled consumption* is	Scheduled investment* is
300	258	43
320	275	45
340	291	48
360	306	50
380	320	50

*In billions of dollars.

8. The equilibrium level of income is

8.____

   A. 300   B. 320   C. 340   D. 360   E. 380

9. If people decided to save 3 billion more at *every* level of income, the equilibrium level of income would

   A. fall by more than 3 billion
   B. fall by 3 billion
   C. be unchanged
   D. rise by 3 billion
   E. rise by more than 3 billion

Questions 10-11.

DIRECTIONS: Questions 10-11 are based on the following diagram.

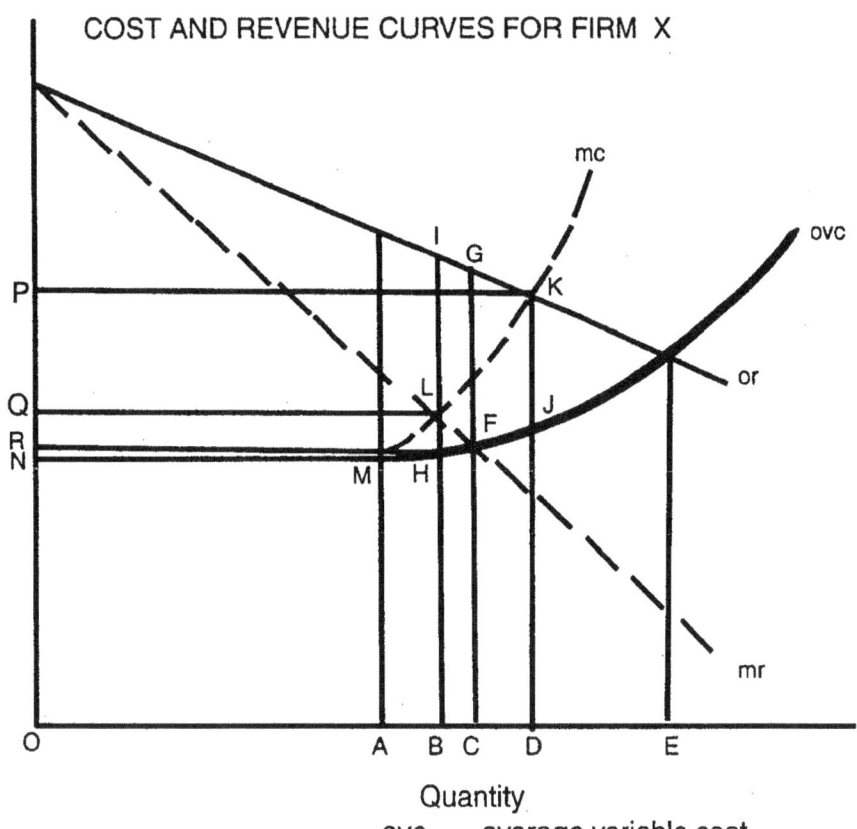

avc = average variable cost
mc = marginal cost
ar = average revenue
mr = marginal revenue

10. The *MOST* profitable output for Firm X to produce is

   A. OA   B. OB   C. OC   D. OD   E. OE

11. If a tax per unit of output were levied, the price per unit for Firm X would

   A. rise by the amount of the tax
   B. rise by more than the tax
   C. rise by less than the tax
   D. fall by less than the tax
   E. be unaffected

Questions 12-13.

DIRECTIONS: Questions 12-13 are based on the following choices:
- A. Consignment
- B. Assignment
- C. Conditional sale
- D. Short sale
- E. None of these

12. The seller retains possession of the merchandise until the payment is complete. 12.___

13. The seller expects the market price to decline during the intervening period between the date of contract and the actual delivery of the commodity. 13.___

14. The conversion of bonds into common stock by a corporation will *most likely INCREASE* the 14.___

   A. income taxes of the corporation
   B. degree of leverage in the capital structure of the corporation
   C. book value per share of the common stock of the corporation
   D. total assets of the corporation
   E. dividends per share of common stock

15. We can't afford depreciation this year. Sales and profits are down, we're short of cash, and we'll have to wait until things improve before we can have any more depreciation in our income statement.
    This statement by a business executive is *BEST* described as 15.___

   A. *wrong,* because depreciation is not a cash expense
   B. *wrong,* because depreciation is a source of cash
   C. *wrong,* because the income tax laws fix the percentage to be taken as depreciation for tax purposes, without reference to a company's state of affairs
   D. on balance, *justified,* because the tax saving from depreciation does not outweigh the expense
   E. *consistent* with good accounting practices

16. If Country I can produce Commodity A with 1 unit of input and Commodity B with 3 units of input, and Country II can produce Commodity A with 5 units of input and Commodity B with 10 units of input, it would be *most likely* that 16.___

   A. Country I would produce both commodities and Country II neither
   B. no trade would take place between the two countries
   C. Country II would gain from trade, Country I would not
   D. Country I would gain from trade, Country II would not
   E. each country would gain by trading with the other

17.   ASSETS

Cash.. $1,200
90-day Government bills 350
Inventory... 1,600
Receivables.. 1,250
Investment in affiliated company................ 400
Plant... 1,100
Equipment.. 2,000
Goodwill and patents.................................. 100
   Total... 8,000

LIABILITIES

Accounts payable....................................... $1,250
Short-term notes payable........................... 1,000
Taxes payable.. 500
Deferred taxes.. 500
Long-term debt... 1,000
Common stock... 2,000
Capital surplus 1,000
Retained earnings 750
   Total... 8,000

Which of the following is the CORRECT amount of the XYZ Corporation's working capital, according to the above balance sheet?

A. $1,150   B. $1,650   C. $3,750   D. $4,400   E. $8,000

Questions 18-20.

DIRECTIONS: Questions 18-20 are based on the following choices:

A. Specific tariffs   B. Ad valorem tariffs
C. Compound tariffs (specific or ad valorem, whichever is lower)
D. Quotas   E. None of the above tariffs

18. If both domestic prices and the prices of imports fall, they tend to be more protective than before.

19. When import prices rise, they give greater protection than before.

20. They do not provide an incentive for exporting countries to decrease their prices.

21. Which of the following is a form of governmental action that restricts trade?

   A. Allocation by cartels
   B. A corporate franchise agreement
   C. An unfavorable trade balance
   D. An exchange control
   E. Limitation of balance of payments

22. All of the following are in general use as payment arrangements between a U.S. seller and a foreign buyer EXCEPT

   A. bills of exchange   B. open accounts
   C. consular invoices   D. cash
   E. letters of credit

23. A consumer survey was made with a sample of 1,000 in an area with a population of 1,000,000 and the results were considered precise enough for the purpose. A similar survey is being considered for a larger area with a population of 10,000,000. It is assumed that conditions are similar to the earlier survey except for the size of the universe.
To assure the SAME degree of accuracy in the second study, the sample size should be

    A. 100   B. 1,000   C. 10,000   D. 100,000   E. 1,000,000

24. A calculation of maximum possible sales opportunities for all sellers of a good or a service during a stated period is known as

    A. market potential
    B. market analysis
    C. market segmentation
    D. market share
    E. none of the above

25. If annual output per employee in the iron and steel industry is 200 tons of finished steel, capital invested per employee is $20,000, and the rate of profit on invested capital is 10 percent, the industry earns a profit on each ton of steel of

    A. $4.50   B. $10.00   C. $20.00   D. $100.00   E. $2,000.00

KEY (CORRECT ANSWERS)

1. A
2. C
3. C
4. A
5. D

6. B
7. D
8. B
9. A
10. B

11. C
12. E
13. D
14. A
15. A

16. E
17. B
18. A
19. B
20. D

21. D
22. C
23. C
24. A
25. B

TEST 2

DIRECTIONS: Each question or incomplete statement is followed by several suggested answers or completions. Select the one that BEST answers the question or completes the statement. PRINT THE LETTER OF THE CORRECT ANSWER IN THE SPACE AT THE RIGHT.

1. Assume that you are reviewing the balance sheet and income statement of the ABC Manufacturing Corp.

1._____

BALANCE SHEET OF ABC MANUFACTURING CORP.
AS OF DECEMBER 31, 2018
(millions of dollars)

Assets
Current Assets
  Cash   5
  Accounts Receivable   5
  Inventories   10
    Total Current Assets   20
Fixed Assets
  Gross Plant   140
  Depreciation Reserve   60
    Net Plant   80
Total Assets   100
Liabilities
Current Liabilities
  Accounts Payable   3
  Taxes Payable   2
    Total Current Liabilities   5
  Long-term Debt   15
Net Worth
Common Stock (par value $10 per share)*   10
Retained Earings   70
Total Liabilities and Net Worth   100
*Market value $100 per share

INCOME STATEMENT FOR CALENDAR
YEAR 2018 AS COMPARED TO CALENDAR
YEAR 2017
(millions of dollars)

	2018	2017
Sales	100	90
Cost of Goods Sold	70	63
Depreciation	10	5
Selling and Administrative Expense	10	9
Operating Profit	10	13
Federal Taxes	5	6.5
Net Profit	5	6.5

On the basis of these statements, the BEST measures of the current ratio and the debt-equity ratio for the company, respectively, are
A. 1:4 and 3:2
B. 2:1 and 3:2
C. 2:1 and 3:20
D. 4:1 and 3:2
E. 4:1 and 3:20

2. If the marginal revenue associated with a given decline in price is *negative,* it can be concluded that

   A. the demand for the product is inelastic with respect to price in this price range
   B. the product is an inferior good
   C. in this price range the coefficient of price elasticity of demand is greater than unity
   D. the demand for the product is inelastic with respect to income
   E. the price decline will increase the firm's profits

3. The *PRIMARY* function of legal reserve requirements of the Federal Reserve Board today is to

   A. protect depositors from asset depreciation
   B. provide commercial banks with liquidity
   C. force commercial banks to lend money to the Federal Reserve System
   D. encourage commercial banks to save part of their deposits
   E. allow the central bank to control the creation of money

4. A profitable corporate business in the United States wishes to do business in a foreign country where it anticipates that operations will be unprofitable for a number of years. Which type of organization is likely to be *MORE* favorable from the standpoint of United States income taxes during these years? A

   A. subsidiary incorporated in the foreign country
   B. United States sister corporation organized specifically to carry on the operation
   C. branch of the present United States company
   D. Western Hemisphere Trade Corporation
   E. corporate joint venture

5. Which of the following is a *CORRECT* statement concerning international commodity agreements? They

   A. mark a movement in the direction of less government involvement in international trade
   B. indicate that agricultural price stabilization programs are internationally unacceptable
   C. have been exclusively the work of exporting nations
   D. tend to stabilize somewhat the erratic foreign exchange earnings of less-developed countries
   E. have resulted primarily from Russian initiatives

6. The Colossal Oil Company is a fully integrated United States company which owns and operates producing, refining, and distribution facilities throughout the world. It is company policy to earn its lowest profit margins in its distribution (i.e., consumer marketing) operations.
   Which of the following is *MOST* helpful in explaining this policy?

   A. Colossal wishes to discourage new companies from entering the oil distribution business.
   B. Competitive pressures give Colossal's management no other pricing alternative.
   C. Refined petroleum products cannot be differentiated in the mind of the consumer.
   D. This policy is consistent with the Robinson-Patman pricing laws.
   E. Colossal's distributing facilities require it.

7. Which of the following BEST describes the relationship between the United States balance-of-payments deficit and the persistence of relatively high unemployment levels in the United States during the Obama administration?

   A. The balance-of-payments deficit caused the unemployment.
   B. The low level of employment caused the deficit.
   C. The excess of imports over exports caused the deficit and the low level of economic activity.
   D. The tools which the United States could use to mitigate unemployment might aggravate the deficit.
   E. Inflation, in the United States caused both the deficit and the unemployment.

8. The public deposits $1,000,000 in currency in demand deposits in the banking system. Legal reserve requirements are 20 percent. After maximum expansion, the money supply will have risen by

   A. $1,000,000   B. $4,000,000   C. $5,000,000
   D. $10,000,000   E. none of the above

9. Under a system of floating exchange rates, an *increase* in a country's prices would tend to

   A. improve its balance of payments
   B. lead to a depreciation of its exchange rate
   C. worsen its balance of payments
   D. have an indeterminate effect on its balance of payments
   E. lead to a suspension of convertibility

10. As chief economist of a multi-national corporation, you are asked to rank the projects shown below on the basis of purely market tests in order to determine whether or not they should be financed by aid from one of your companies in the United States. Each project involves the same investment outlay.
    Which is the CORRECT ranking, starting with the highest rank *first* except where otherwise specified?

	Net Profit			
	First Year	Second Year	Third Year	Fourth Year
Project I	$110	$110	$0	$0
Project II	105	115	0	0
Project III	55	55	55	55

    A. I, II, III
    B. II, I, III
    C. I and II are of equal rank and both are higher than III
    D. I and II are of equal rank and both are lower than III
    E. I, II, and III are of equal rank

11. A manufacturer of engines in a foreign country is thinking about the possibility of exporting them. Assuming other factors remain constant, a currency devaluation in this foreign country would

    A. make his engines less competitive with engines manufactured elsewhere
    B. make his engines more competitive with engines manufactured elsewhere
    C. not affect the competitiveness of the engines he manufactures
    D. cause possible buyers to lose confidence in his engines
    E. have none of the above consequences

12.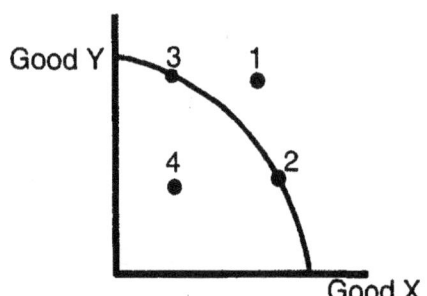

Which of the following statements is CORRECT concerning the production-possibilities frontier for the economy shown above?

A. Point 1 is the maximum output at full employment.
B. The economy is better off at point 3 than at point 2.
C. The economy is better off at point 2 than at point 3.
D. Production at point 2 involves substantial unemployment.
E. Production at point 4 involves substantial unemployment.

13. Which of the following would *probably NOT* be considered for inclusion in a fiscal program designed to combat a recession in the United States economy?

A. The reduction or elimination of federal excise taxes
B. An increase in the level of spending for public works
C. A reduction in corporation and personal income tax rates
D. A gradual reduction of the national debt
E. An extension of the term or enlargement of the benefits of unemployment compensation

14. If a competitive firm is faced with an increase in the ad valorem sales tax on its product, it is *most likely* to

A. *shift* the entire increase to the consumer if the elasticity of demand is *infinite*
B. *shift* the entire increase to the consumer if the elasticity of demand is *zero*
C. *bear* the entire increase itself if the elasticity of demand is *zero*
D. *bear* the entire increase itself if the elasticity of demand is *one*
E. *shift* the entire increase to the consumer if the elasticity of demand is *one*

15. Historically, patterns of population change during the process of industrialization *generally* have shown that

A. the birth rate drops markedly and is followed by decreases in the death rate
B. the birth and death rates show marked and simultaneous reductions
C. the death rate falls initially and is followed by reductions in the birth rate
D. both birth and death rates remain fairly constant until very high levels of material prosperity are achieved
E. the death rate falls and is followed by a rise in the birth rate

Questions 16-18.

DIRECTIONS: Questions 16-18 refer to the diagram below.

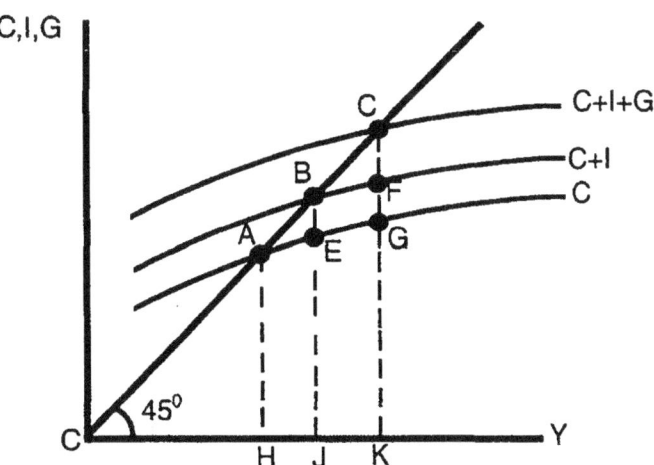

16. Equilibrium national income would be

    A. OK   B. BJ   C. FK   D. OJ   E. OE

17. Savings plus taxes would be

    A. FG   B. BE   C. CG   D. AH   E. BC

18. Consumption at equilibrium income would be

    A. GK
    D. OK
    B. AH
    E. none of the above
    C. EJ

19. A flow of capital investment from the United States to a foreign country can do *all* of the following *EXCEPT*

    A. provide the foreign country with a greater volume of goods and services than it could produce internally
    B. permit the level of investment to exceed the level of saving in the recipient country
    C. increase the supply of foreign exchange available to the foreign country
    D. increase the tax base of the foreign country
    E. decrease the marginal productivity of labor in the foreign country

Question 20.

DIRECTIONS: Question 20 is based on the graph below.

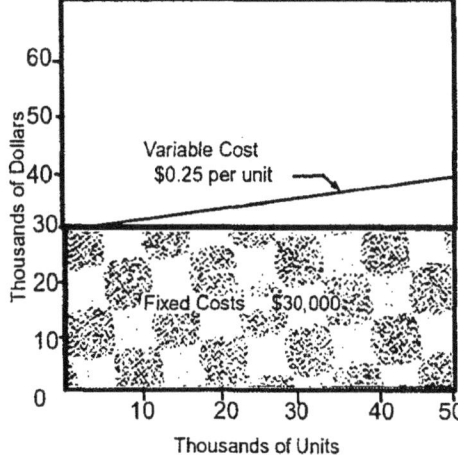

20. At a retail price of $2.00, the manufacturer would net at the mill $1.00 per unit. How many units would he have to sell to recover all costs?

   A. 20,000   B. 30,000   C. 35,000   D. 40,000   E. 60,000

Questions 21-23.

DIRECTIONS: Questions 21-23 are based on the following information.

A consumption function for a certain developed country is estimated by ordinary least squares regression over the period 1998-2018 to be:

$C = 150 \ + \ 0.8\ Y_d$ where Y_d is disposable income and the numbers
$\ \ \ \ (178)\ \ \ \ \ (0.2)$ in parentheses under the constant and coefficient are their respective standard deviations.

21. The income multiplier is

   A. 0.2   B. 0.8   C. 5.0   D. 30.0   E. 120.0

22. If Y_d = $2 billion in 2018 and is growing at 10 percent per annum, consumption in 2021 will be *approximately*

   A. $1.60 billion   B. $2.00 billion   C. $2.13 billion
   D. $2.42 billion   E. $2.66 billion

23. The standard deviations indicate which of the following?

   A. The constant and the coefficient are statistically significant at the 95% confidence level.
   B. The constant is statistically significant but the coefficient is not at the 95% confidence level.
   C. The coefficient is statistically significant but the constant is not at the 95% confidence level.
   D. Neither the constant nor the coefficient is statistically significant at the 95% confidence level.
   E. The constant and the coefficient are statistically significant at the 90% confidence level.

24. A country considering both devaluation of its currency and additional import barriers should consult with which of the following? (Assume that it is a member.)

   A. The International Monetary Fund and the General Agreement on Tariffs and Trade
   B. The Bank for International Settlements and the United Nations Economic and Social Council
   C. The International Bank for Reconstruction and Development and the Organization for Economic Cooperation and Development
   D. The International Monetary Fund and the United Nations Economic and Social Council
   E. None of the above

25. The UNCTAD II meeting proposed that developed nations should allocate what percent of their gross national product to official and private assistance to the developing world?

   A. 0.5%   B. 1.0%   C. 5.0%   D. 7.5%   E. 10.0%

KEY (CORRECT ANSWERS)

1.	E	11.	B
2.	A	12.	E
3.	E	13.	D
4.	C	14.	B
5.	D	15.	C
6.	A	16.	A
7.	D	17.	C
8.	B	18.	A
9.	B	19.	E
10.	A	20.	D

21. C
22. C
23. C
24. A
25. B

TEST 3

DIRECTIONS: Each question or incomplete statement is followed by several suggested answers or completions. Select the one that *BEST* answers the question or completes the statement. *PRINT THE LETTER OF THE CORRECT ANSWER IN THE SPACE AT THE RIGHT.*

1. An economic report *clearly* indicates that the LEAST important factor (on the basis of percentage increase since 2009) in the enlargement of markets and employment during the last decade, has been

   A. individual consumer buying
   B. business purchases of equipment
   C. Government outlays
   D. imports from foreign countries
   E. exports to foreign countries

   1.___

2. Which combination of statements presents the MOST ACCURATE comparison of current affairs of our federal government with those of states and municipalities?
   I. Whereas the major source of federal government revenie is income taxes, municipalities generally derive most of theirs from property taxes.
   II. The total amount of the public debt of all municipalities is second in size only to that of the federal government.
   III. Income taxes furnish fifty states generally with a greater percentage of their total revenue than the federal income tax does our national government.
   IV. Although it is not true of the federal government, at least 10 percent of the revenue of both municipalities and States is derived from grants of other governmental units.
   V. The public debt of all units of state and local governments last year was greater than the annual income of the federal government during that year

   The CORRECT combination is:

   A. II, III, IV, V   B. I, III, V   C. I, II, IV
   D. I, II, III, IV   E. I, II, III, IV, V

   2.___

3. A basic difference between The Brookings Institution and the National Bureau of Economic Research is:

   A. Brookings studies offer conclusions concerning policy, while the National Bureau tends to confine its studies to assembling and analyzing data.
   B. The studies of the National Bureau offer conclusions concerning policy, while Brookings tends to confine its studies to assembling and analyzing data.
   C. As an agency of the Federal government, the studies of the National Bureau are concerned primarily with fiscal policy.
   D. Wesley C.Mitchell's long association with Brookings has tended to center its interest on problems of business cycles.
   E. All of the above.

   3.___

4. Which two of the following theories of wages were MOST similar in their basic approach to the problem?
   I. Francis A.Walker—residual claimant theory
   II. F.W.Taussig—discounted marginal productivity theory
   III. John Davidson—bargaining theory
   IV. Karl Marx—exploitation theory

   The CORRECT combination is:

   A. I, II   B. II, III   C. III, IV   D. I, IV   E. I, III

   4.___

5. Which of the following is author of a book that develops the theoretical aspects of corporate activity?

   A. N.S. Buchanan B. A.A. Berle C. W.Z. Ripley
   D. J.T. Flynn E. E. J. William Fulbright

6. The standard twentieth-century work, on which much of the study of incidence and shifting of taxes has since been based, was written by

   A. Harold M. Groves   B. Edwin R.A. Seligman
   C. William H. Steiner D. Hartley L. Lutz
   E. John K. Galbraith

7. Theoretical justification for social security legislation can be found in the theory of the causes of unemployment as stated by
   I. A.H. Hansen
   II. J.M. Keynes
   III. J.B. Say
   IV. Alfred Marshall
   The CORRECT combination is:

   A. I, II, III   B. III, IV   C. II, III   D. I, II   E. I, III

KEY (CORRECT ANSWERS)

1. E
2. C
3. A
4. A
5. B
6. B
7. D

ECONOMICS

EXAMINATION SECTION
TEST 1

DIRECTIONS: Each question or incomplete statement is followed by several suggested answers or completions. Select the one that BEST answers the question or completes the statement. *PRINT THE LETTER OF THE CORRECT ANSWER IN THE SPACE AT THE RIGHT.*

1. A tax on land rent is USUALLY

   A. passed on to the tenant in higher rent, but does not raise the price of products grown on the land
   B. passed on to the final consumer in the form of higher prices for the products of land
   C. paid by the owner of the land; it cannot be passed on to tenants or consumers
   D. paid by reduction in the wages earned by farm labor
   E. paid by increase in the wages earned by farm labor

   1.____

2. If a 10 percent tax were placed on any rent earned from land planted to tomatoes, but not on rent earned from any other crop, the result would tend to be

   A. a rise in the price of tomatoes
   B. a rise in the price of other crops
   C. increased tomato production
   D. higher rent per acre devoted to other crops
   E. higher rent per acre devoted to tomatoes

   2.____

3. In the manufacture of glass containers, production workers' wages make up half of the variable cost. This suggests that a 10 percent wage increase tends to raise the prices of glass containers by about _____ percent.

   A. 5   B. 10   C. 15   D. 20   E. 25

   3.____

4. The *games of chance* that were previously widely adopted in gasoline retailing

   A. reduce the differentiation among gasoline brands and contribute to lower prices
   B. increase customer loyalty to particular brands and contribute to higher prices
   C. constitute a clear violation of the NLRA
   D. constitute a possible violation of the Sherman Act
   E. decrease customer loyalty to particular brands and contribute to lower prices

   4.____

5. The long-run effect of competition is to force prices to the point where

   A. only variable costs can be covered
   B. product innovation is impossible
   C. markups are only high enough to break even
   D. further price reductions reduce, rather than increase, total sales revenue
   E. further price reductions increase, rather than reduce, total sales

   5.____

6. A CENTRAL goal of antitrust policy is to

    A. balance giant firms off against one another
    B. strengthen labor unions against employers
    C. promote competition and discourage monopoly
    D. outlaw product differentiation
    E. foster the growth of small businesses

7. Markups tend to be HIGHER in industries where

    A. marginal costs are higher
    B. high concentration makes firms aware of their influence on each other
    C. low concentration keeps firms from becoming aware of their influence on each other
    D. the absence of advertising keeps volume low
    E. the presence of advertising keeps volume high

8. Grocers' bags are a nearly homogeneous product, sold to business buyers who are acutely price-conscious. Bottled soft drinks are highly differentiated products, sold to households. The ratio of price to marginal cost in one industry is 1.98. In the other, it is 1.10.
    The markup on grocers' bags is

    A. 1.98
    B. 1.10
    C. 1.10/1.98
    D. 1.98/1.10
    E. cannot be determined from the information given

9. Considering the market for grocers' bags, it would be safe to predict that the industry-wide introduction of a labor-saving method of producing them would increase output and

    A. increase the total amount of labor employed in their production
    B. reduce the total amount of labor employed in their production
    C. increase or decrease the amount of labor employed, depending on the price of grocers' bags
    D. increase or decrease the amount of labor employed by the grocers' bag industry, but we can't tell which from the data given
    E. nothing else

10. Production worker payrolls constitute only about 15 percent of the marginal cost of producing grocers' bags. Taking this into account, we could SAFELY conclude that the industry-wide introduction of a labor-saving method of product would increase the output of bags and

    A. increase the total amount of labor employed in their production
    B. decrease the total amount of labor employed in their production
    C. increase or decrease the amount of labor employed, depending on the price of grocers' bags
    D. increase or decrease employment in the industry, but we can't tell which from the information given
    E. nothing else

11. Judging from the characteristics of the grocers' bags industry (in the preceding three questions), it would appear that an industry-wide labor union would

    A. be in a position to raise wages with a minimum reduction in employment
    B. be in a vulnerable position because of the high elasticity of demand for labor in the industry
    C. find it impossible to bargain with firms in the industry because of the inelastic demand for these products
    D. find it possible to raise wages without forcing up the price of bags
    E. be in a position to raise wages with a maximum reduction in employment

12. A STANDARD goal of union wage policy is to

    A. maximize total employment in the industry
    B. maximize earnings per employee in the industry
    C. maximize the total wage bill paid by the industry
    D. minimize the total wage bill paid by the industry
    E. do none of the above

13. The percentage of all wage and salary workers who are now union members is ABOUT _____ percent.

    A. 35 B. 25 C. 15 D. 10 E. 5

14. One of the IMPORTANT reasons for antitrust legislation is that

    A. markups in highly concentrated industries depend on buyer sensitivity to prices of the firm's own brand or product rather than on that for the market as a whole
    B. fixed costs in monopoly industries tend to be higher than those on competitive products
    C. monopoly contributes disproportionately to social costs
    D. high monopoly prices in relation to cost restrict output and force labor into less important jobs
    E. fixed costs in monopoly industries tend to be lower than those on competitive products

15. One reason for government subsidy of higher education is that

    A. students benefit more from universities than the public does
    B. the public gains two or three times as much as students do
    C. although most of the benefit of education accrues to students, there is some *spill over* of benefits onto the public at large
    D. higher education could not be provided by private enterprise without subsidy
    E. higher education could be provided by private enterprise with subsidy

16. In the last 25 years, the real earnings of labor have increased by 35 percent. The PRINCIPAL cause of this rise was the

    A. rising productivity of labor
    B. increased militance of organized labor in pressing for wage gains
    C. increased power given unions by the Taft-Hartley Act
    D. steady increases in the legal minimum wage
    E. decreasing productivity of labor

17. At one time, according to estimates, when Chrysler was making $500 a car, General Motors' profit was $3,000 per car.
This suggests

    A. that General Motors was exerting its monopoly to hold its prices above those of its competitors
    B. that General Motors was undercutting the prices of other manufacturers
    C. that the automobile industry is characterized by overt collusion on prices
    D. all of the above
    E. none of the above

17.____

18. An industry in which the bulk of production is concentrated in a few large firms is USUALLY characterized by

    A. high responsiveness of demand to changes in national income
    B. high ratios of price to marginal cost
    C. low rates of product innovation
    D. great price flexibility and frequent price changes
    E. small price flexibility and infrequent price changes

18.____

19. In setting prices, a monopolist tends to

    A. reduce prices when production costs are reduced
    B. exert its monopoly power to hold prices up even when costs fall
    C. keep prices proportional to average total costs, regardless of marginal cost
    D. keep prices proportional to the average price level, regardless of cost
    E. raise prices when production costs are reduced

19.____

20. Unlike bargaining by private employees, collective bargaining by public employees

    A. must proceed without the assistance of a labor relations law since the NLRA applies only to private employees
    B. involves an employer agency that does not have the power to raise the revenue needed to meet the wages agreed to
    C. involves workers whose services to the community are essential
    D. involves only white collar professionals
    E. has little effect in government

20.____

21. In the United States, cigarettes are subject to special taxes that amount to about half the price of the final product.
One IMPORTANT result of this high tax is that

    A. the demand for labor in cigarette manufacturing is less elastic than it would otherwise be
    B. cigarette prices are more responsive to changes in production costs than they would otherwise be
    C. cigar and pipe tobacco sales are smaller than they would be if there were no special cigarette tax
    D. fewer different brands of cigarettes are available than would be true without the tax
    E. cigarette prices are less responsive to changes in production than they would otherwise be

21.____

22. A bill introduced into the Congress proposed an embargo restricting the export of logs from the United States. If the embargo were enacted, it would tend to

    A. increase domestic lumber prices
    B. raise the profits of United States lumber manufacturers at the expense of United States loggers
    C. raise the profits of the United States logging industry at the expense of foreign lumber producers
    D. benefit the foreign lumber consumer at the expense of United States lumber buyers
    E. decrease domestic lumber prices

23. If passed, the embargo on logs (in the preceding question) would ALSO help to

    A. encourage the use of aluminum in place of wood siding on houses
    B. encourage the use of cinderblock instead of structural timber
    C. check the rising use of aluminum window frames in place of wood
    D. expand the quantity of wood pulp imported from Canada
    E. decrease the quantity of wood pulp imported from Canada

24. One thing which is NOT likely to result from a United States tariff on steel imports is that

    A. there will be an inflationary effect on the United States price level
    B. foreign countries may retaliate by placing tariffs on some United States products
    C. employment in the steel industry will be lower than it would be without the tariff
    D. foreign cars will tend to be more effective competitors in the United States auto market
    E. foreign cars will tend to be less effective competitors in the United States auto market

25. Since the 1930's, most union organization has been in the form of industrial unions rather than craft unions LARGELY because

    A. it is easier to organize the whole company or factory than it is just one department or skill
    B. if all the workers in a company join together to bargain, they can get a larger wage increase than if the different crafts bargain separately
    C. the National Labor Relations Board tended to favor the formation of large jurisdictional units in representation elections
    D. most crafts were not organized and the skilled workers were the only ones left
    E. most crafts were already organized and the unskilled workers were the only ones left

KEY (CORRECT ANSWERS)

1.	C	11.	A
2.	A	12.	E
3.	A	13.	C
4.	B	14.	D
5.	C	15.	C
6.	C	16.	A
7.	B	17.	E
8.	B	18.	B
9.	B	19.	A
10.	B	20.	B

21. A
22. B
23. C
24. C
25. E

TEST 2

DIRECTIONS: Each question or incomplete statement is followed by several suggested answers or completions. Select the one that BEST answers the question or completes the statement. *PRINT THE LETTER OF THE CORRECT ANSWER IN THE SPACE AT THE RIGHT.*

Questions 1-7.

DIRECTIONS: Questions 1 through 7 are to be answered on the basis of the following information.

Costs of a small manufacturer of steel cans are:
Fixed Cost $4,000,000
Variable Cost per box
  Labor $ 2.70
  Materials, power, etc.   11.30
  Marginal Cost $14.00
(These costs apply at operating rates up to 1,500,000 boxes per year. Higher rates are possible, working overtime and using older stand-by equipment.)

1. The most profitable price is $21.
   This represents a markup of ABOUT

   A. .67   B. 1.2   C. 1.5   D. 2.0   E. 3.6

2. The firm sells 800,000 boxes per year at $21, resulting in a

   A. profit of $6,400,000   B. profit of $3,200,000
   C. profit of $1,600,000   D. profit of $800,000
   E. loss

3. If, given the level of demand (800,000 boxes sold at $21, the most profitable price), the firm should raise its price to $23.10, sales volume would decline to ABOUT

   A. 350,000 to 449,000   B. 450,000 to 549,000
   C. 550,000 to 649,000   D. 650,000 to 749,000
   E. 750,000 to 800,000

4. If demand declined by 50 percent from the level above (Question 3), the firm could PROFITABLY

   A. reduce price to expand sales volume
   B. raise price to cover the rise in average fixed cost as volume shrinks
   C. reduce price to maintain the most profitable gross margin as total cost declines
   D. shut down to avoid the $1,200,000 loss
   E. do none of the above

5. If demand doubled from its initial level (Question 3), the firm would find it MOST profitable to

   A. increase prices
   B. reduce prices
   C. leave price unchanged

115

D. increase or reduce prices, depending on whether fixed cost rises or falls
E. increase or reduce prices, depending on whether operating cost rises or falls

6. At this higher level of demand, the firm's MAXIMUM profit would be

   A. less than $4,800,000
   B. $4,800,000 to $5,300,000
   C. $5,400,000 to $6,500,000
   D. more than $6,500,000
   E. less than $6,500,000

7. At the initial level of demand (Question 3), the public relations department reports that a new advertising and selling program would increase sales by 200,000 boxes per year. It would be profitable to undertake the program even if it cost as much as

   A. $2,600,000   B. $2,100,000   C. $1,900,000
   D. $1,200,000   E. $1,000,000

Questions 8-14.

DIRECTIONS: Questions 8 through 14 are to be answered on the basis of the following information.

Figures published by an outside source during a recent year allegedly showed prices and costs of a number of items manufactured by the Ford Motor Co. to be as follows:

	Ford Cost	Price to Dealer	Suggested Retai Price
Ford Crown Victoria	$16,030	$18,720	$26,760
Automatic Transmission/Luxury Pkg.	560	1,360	1,850
Optional V8 engine (extra cost)	190	750	1,050
Power pkg.	290	660	950
Ford - JBL Sound System	220	400	570

8. Since the Ford *cost* figures presumably include allowances for fixed costs, they correspond MOST closely to _____ cost.

   A. average fixed   B. average variable
   C. average total   D. marginal
   E. direct

9. Most fixed costs can be assigned to individual products only arbitrarily, and it is reasonable to suppose that each of the Ford *cost* items includes about the same proportion of fixed costs.
   On this basis, it would appear that the LOWEST manufacturing markup is represented by the

   A. Crown Victoria
   B. automatic transmission/luxury package
   C. power package
   D. radio system
   E. optional V8 engine

10. The comparison between the markup on the Crown Victoria and that represented by the automatic transmission is   10.____

    A. the opposite of what normally would be expected from the relationship between the products
    B. in general agreement with what would normally be expected from the relationship between the products
    C. in partial agreement with what would normally be expected from the relationship between the products
    D. independent of the relationship between the products and might just as well be the other way around
    E. impossible to determine from the information given

11. The suggested retail price of the Ford represents a dealer's GROSS margin of about _____ percent.   11.____

    A. 16   B. 25   C. 30   D. 43   E. 50

12. A certain dealer sold 100 Crown Victorias during the year. If the figures are correct, the dealer netted a PROFIT of about   12.____

    A. $900,000
    B. $800,000
    C. $700,000
    D. $600,000
    E. profit cannot be determined from data given

13. The relationship between the $190 extra manufacturing cost of a V8 engine and the $1,050 difference in retail price suggests that   13.____

    A. few people want the optional V8 engine
    B. most people want the V8 engine
    C. people who want the V8 engine are relatively insensitive to its price
    D. people who want the V8 engine are relatively sensitive to its price
    E. the optional V8 engine is overpriced compared to its actual value to the consumer

14. The outside source also suggested that present auto price increases represent an attempt by the industry to pass off the 10 percent (corporate profits) tax surcharge on to the consumer.   14.____
    Since the tax is on corporate profits, auto companies can pass the surcharge on ONLY if

    A. automobile companies include normal profits as part of fixed cost
    B. auto prices were kept below the most profitable level during the year
    C. the price increases raise the break-even point of auto production
    D. the demand for automobiles has become more elastic
    E. the demand for automobiles has become inelastic

15. Forty years ago, United States farmers harvested almost 340,000 tons of green peas, of which 40 percent was sold for fresh use and 60 percent was sold to processors. Today, although the harvest is up to about 650,000 tons, practically the entire crop goes to processors. Only 3 percent is sold for fresh use.   15.____
    There are a combination of causes for this change in allocation, one of which is the

A. introduction of frozen food technology and the consequent shift of household demand from fresh to processed peas
B. normal reallocation of a larger crop between elastic demand in the fresh market and the inelastic demand of processors
C. normal reallocation of the crop resulting from equal percentage expansion of an inelastic demand for fresh use and an elastic demand for processing
D. steady growth of processing costs as wages rose throughout the post-war period
E. steady growth of wages as processing costs declined throughout the post-war period

16. A contributing cause of the reallocation of the green pea crop (refer to Question 15) was the

    A. rising labor productivity in food processing
    B. rising family incomes permitting families to consume more fresh food
    C. soil bank program to control agricultural prices
    D. declining labor productivity in food processing
    E. declining family incomes permitting families to consume less fresh food

17. Another contributing cause to the allocation of the green pea crop was PROBABLY the

    A. increasing proportion of working wives
    B. introduction of the mechanical cotton picker
    C. replacement of rayon by nylon
    D. increased output per acre of wheat and corn
    E. decreased output per acre of wheat and corn

Questions 18-21.

DIRECTIONS: Questions 18 through 21 are to be answered on the basis of the following information.

The price and allocation of the United States strawberry crop in two consecutive recent years are shown.

Year	Price per pound	Total	Millions of pounds bought for fresh use	for processing
1	20	500	300	200
2	22	400	270	130

18. Since the price response was typical, the elasticity of demand for the total strawberry crop must be in the range of

    A. zero to 0.49   B. 0.5 to 0.99   C. 1.0 to 1.49
    D. 1.5 and over   E. 2.0 and over

19. Given the strawberry crop, a 20 percent increase in the total demand for strawberries would tend to raise price by _____ percent.

    A. 36 to 40   B. 26 to 35   C. 16 to 25
    D. 11 to 15   E. less than 11

20. In the data above, the GREATEST response to price was shown by 20.____

    A. buyers for fresh use
    B. buyers for processing
    C. all buyers combined
    D. none of the above
    E. cannot be determined from the data given

21. In addition, the figures suggest that, perhaps, 21.____

    A. processors can easily pass on higher prices for strawberries with small loss in sales
    B. processed strawberries are highly perishable
    C. the fruit is only a small part of the cost of the product and exerts a correspondingly small influence on price
    D. processed strawberries must be sold in competition with many other types of frozen and preserved fruit, jam, etc.
    E. processor cannot pass on higher prices for strawberries without large loss in sales

22. 22.____

United States Peaches

	Price per	Billions of Pounds		
Year	pound	Used fresh	Canned	Total Crop
2002	$.045	1.4	1.6	3.0
2003	.055	1.1	1.9	3.0

Which of the following is MOST consistent with all the data presented above? 22.____

    A. The large stocks of canned peaches that had been already on hand when the 2002 crop arrived had been reduced by 2003.
    B. Canners' demand remained stable, but consumers' demand declined from 2002 to 2003, releasing peaches for canning.
    C. Neither demand shifted; rising inflation drove up prices and reallocated the crop.
    D. The price of other fruits that consumers substitute for fresh peaches rose from 2002 to 2003.
    E. The price of other fruits that consumers substitute for fresh peaches declined from 2002 to 2003.

Questions 23-24.

DIRECTIONS: Questions 23 and 24 are to be answered on the basis of the following data.

One of the following commodities is watermelons; the other is onions. To further disguise them, their prices and quantities are expressed as percentages of 2002 levels.

	Commodity A		Commodity B	
Year	Price	Quantity	Price	Quantity
2002	100	100	100	100
2003	120	80	150	90

The responses are typical of demands for the respective products.

23. Given the crop, a 10 percent expansion of demand for Commodity B would tend to raise its price by

    A. about 10 percent
    B. considerably more than 10 percent
    C. considerably less than 10 percent
    D. considerably less than 5 percent
    E. an amount that cannot be estimated from the data given

23.____

24. The BEST guess as to the identity of the commodities is that

    A. Commodity A is onions
    B. Commodity A is watermelons
    C. Commodity A is as likely to be onions as watermelons
    D. Commidity B is as likely to be onions as watermelons
    E. their identity cannot be determined from the information given

24.____

25. When two items are close substitutes for each other (for example, aluminum beverage cans and disposable bottles), a cheaper method of manufacturing one tends, in the short run, to

    A. increase the average total cost of manufacturing the other
    B. reduce the average total cost of the other
    C. leave the average total cost of the other unaffected, but increase the demand for it
    D. leave the demand for the other unaffected, but increase its total cost
    E. be indeterminable from the information given

25.____

KEY (CORRECT ANSWERS)

1. C
2. C
3. D
4. E
5. A

6. D
7. D
8. C
9. A
10. B

11. C
12. E
13. C
14. B
15. A

16. A
17. A
18. D
19. E
20. B

21. D
22. A
23. B
24. B
25. A

TEST 3

DIRECTIONS: Each question or incomplete statement is followed by several suggested answers or completions. Select the one that BEST answers the question or completes the statement. *PRINT THE LETTER OF THE CORRECT ANSWER IN THE SPACE AT THE RIGHT.*

1. During World War II, price ceilings were set on most products and producers were forbidden to charge more than the ceiling.
   Unable to adjust their prices, producers found it most profitable to restrict operating rates so that

   A. output volume was a minimum
   B. average total cost was the least
   C. average total cost equaled the ceiling price
   D. demand elasticity was lowest
   E. marginal cost equaled ceiling price

   1.____

2. In recent years, aluminum cans have become important competitors for steel.
   The further replacement of steel cans by aluminum would PROBABLY be speeded up by

   A. sharp reduction in steel production costs by wider use of the oxygen reduction process
   B. a decline in demand for automobiles, since automobiles are an important user of steel
   C. granting the steel industry's request for quotas to cut the import of foreign steel into the United States
   D. increasing the rate at which aluminum is used in place of steel for automobile bodies, engine blocks, and transmissions
   E. all of the above

   2.____

3. The practice whereby manufacturers of cigarettes were permitted to set the minimum price to be charged by retailers has been abolished in England.
   The move is reported to have delighted British owners of supermarkets, but displeased small retailers and the three major cigarette manufacturers because

   A. manufacturers see their demand as relatively elastic, but that facing individual supermarkets is relatively inelastic
   B. manufacturers see their demand as relatively inelastic, but that facing individual supermarkets is relatively elastic
   C. manufacturers produce with constant marginal costs, while supermarkets tend to have increasing marginal costs
   D. English supermarkets do not sell cigarettes
   E. English supermarkets do sell cigarettes

   3.____

4. Suppose that the elasticity of demand for oranges is .3. Because of good weather, the orange crop is expected to be 20% greater than it was last year.
   The change in price will probably be ABOUT a

   A. 67% increase   B. 33% increase
   C. 33% decrease   D. 67% decrease
   E. none of the above

   4.____

121

5. The price of cocoa futures has risen sharply.
   This is PROBABLY related to

   A. unusually good weather in cocoa-growing areas
   B. unusually bad weather in cocoa-growing areas
   C. unusually good weather in coffee-growing areas
   D. unusually bad weather in coffee-growing areas
   E. a strike at the Hershey Chocolate Company

6. Suppose a razor manufacturer produced a new super blade which gave close shaves but would never cause nicks or bleeding. This replaced its old super blade which gave close shaves bud did not give immunity to nicks.
   The company would PROBABLY

   A. lower its markup in order to sell more
   B. raise its markup because marginal revenue was greater than marginal cost
   C. raise its markup because the elasticity of demand for its product was lower
   D. lower its markup because the elasticity of demand for its product was higher
   E. raise its markup in order to sell more

7. Retail gross margins for food tend to be higher in city slums than in suburban communities because of all of the following reasons EXCEPT

   A. suburban stores have lower costs
   B. suburban housewives are more likely to watch the newspapers for announcements of sales than slum housewives
   C. suburban housewives tend to have better facilities for storing food
   D. suburban housewives are more likely to have access to an auto
   E. many slum stores carry special food items like collards and chitterlings

8. The marginal cost of producing a football is $12. The elasticity of demand for them is 3. What is the MOST profitable price?

   A. $16   B. $18   C. $24   D. $36   E. $40

Questions 9-10.

DIRECTIONS: Questions 9 and 10 are to be answered on the basis of the following information.

The elasticity of demand for automobiles has been estimated to be about 0.8, and the elasticity of demand for individual makes of automobiles has been estimated to be about 4.0, provided other manufacturers did not match price changes.

9. The auto industry increased car prices by an average of 1.8 percent.
   The number of cars sold would be expected to _____ by about _____ percent.

   A. increase; 1.5   B. increase; 7   C. reduce; 7
   D. reduce; 5   E. reduce; 1.5

10. Chrysler announced a price increase averaging $890 per car or about 4 percent. Had the other manufacturers left their prices unchanged, Chrysler would probably have lost sales of ABOUT _____ percent.

    A. 2.4   B. 3.6   C. 6   D. 12   E. 16

11. According to a recent report, a member of the New York Port Authority has suggested that higher bridge and tunnel tolls during rush hours would encourage people to leave their cars at home and ride railroad, subway, or bus to work.
    The proposal is likely to work ONLY if

    A. many people can choose whether to drive their own cars or not
    B. there is little or no relationship between subway and bus travel on the one hand and bridge or tunnel tolls on the other
    C. subways, tunnels, and bridges are usually used jointly
    D. there is little or no relationship between bridge and tunnel use and the level of tolls
    E. there is a close relationship between bridge and tunnel use and the level of tolls

11.____

12. If the toll proposal (referred to in the preceding question) were successful, which of the following is the MOST likely result?

    A. Reduced revenues from bridge and tunnel tolls
    B. Increased rental for parking space
    C. Reduced rush hour traffic
    D. Reduced total cost of subway operation
    E. Increased total cost of subway operation

12.____

13. Even if the higher tolls (referred to in the preceding two questions) fail to increase the use of other modes of travel, they might

    A. force up bus fares
    B. force down bus fares
    C. force up subway fares
    D. end the incentive for some New York firms to allow employees to report to work and leave for home after the peak of rush traffic
    E. encourage car pools

13.____

14. Speculation on grain markets tends to

    A. magnify price swings so that speculators can make huge profits
    B. stabilize the amount of the crop allocated to current use, regardless of the size of the crop
    C. divide the crop between current and future use on the basis of the expected priorities for the two
    D. force flour millers and other grain processors to assume the risk created by speculative price movements in both cash grain and future markets
    E. minimize price swings so that speculators cannot make huge profits

14.____

15. It has recently been announced that, beginning next year, auto tolls on a certain bridge will be substantially reduced. As part of the arrangement, the state legislature is to appropriate 12 million dollars to add to bridge revenue.
    The need for the appropriation suggests that

    A. the demand for services of the bridge are inelastic
    B. less bridge traffic is expected despite the toll reduction
    C. bridge operating costs will greatly be swollen by the increase in traffic expected next year
    D. the new price will be below marginal cost
    E. the new price will be above marginal cost

15.____

16. Which of the following is an IMPORTANT barrier to new firms trying to enter a number of industries? 16.___

    A. High unit labor cost compared to average fixed cost
    B. Product homogeneity
    C. Economics of large scale production
    D. Low fixed cost
    E. Product heterogeneity

17. Land on which carrots are grown is also excellent for onions. 17.___
    As a result, a fall in the demand for carrots tends to

    A. raise carrot prices
    B. reduce the output of onions
    C. reduce rent from land planted to onions
    D. raise rent on land planted to carrots
    E. reduce rent on land planted to carrots

18. Over the last twenty years, the yield of onions has grown from 8 tons per acre to 16 tons per acre. Considering the nature of onion demand, it is hardly surprising that during the same period total acreage planted to onions 18.___

    A. almost doubled
    B. increased only fifty percent
    C. remained almost constant
    D. decreased about twenty-five percent
    E. decreased more than fifty percent

Questions 19-20.

DIRECTIONS: Questions 19 and 20 are to be answered on the basis of the following data.

Product	Bottled Soft Drinks	Newspapers
Elasticity of Demand	1.2	0.1
Labor as percent of marginal cost	15%	25%

19. These data suggest that 19.___

    A. unions in the soft drink industry can push up wages with less employment loss than those in the newspaper industry
    B. newspaper unions can push up wages with less employment loss than those in the soft drink industry
    C. unlike the newspaper industry, whose union demands are strongly resisted, union gains are welcomed in the soft drink industry because they add to profit through the markup
    D. the advantages of bargaining with the entire industry rather than with a single firm are greater in the newspaper industry than in the soft drink industry
    E. the newspaper industry is more elastic than the soft drink industry

20. According to the above data, application of labor-saving methods would tend to   20.____
    A. increase employment in the soft drink industry but reduce it in newspapers
    B. increase employment in the newspaper industry but reduce it in soft drinks
    C. increase employment in both industries
    D. reduce employment in both industries
    E. have little or no effect on either industry

21. A major steel company announced a 22 percent price reduction in hot rolled sheets. One reason for the reduction was that   21.____

    A. the company recognized it could expand its sales by undercutting other steel producers
    B. the company expects its prices to be supported by the rest of the industry to take advantage of low elasticity of demand for steel
    C. the company needs to increase its volume because of higher wage costs from recent wage negotiations
    D. elasticity of demand for domestic steel has risen due to increasing low priced imports
    E. elasticity of demand remained relatively unchanged

22. A large part of the apparel and piece goods sold in this country are *price lined,* that is, they are sold at traditional prices such as $89.50 dresses, $249 suits, and so on. The fact that these prices are fixed means that   22.____

    A. the industry operates by price collusion
    B. producers tend to raise the quality of their products whenever production costs decline
    C. the firms in these industries are not maximizing profits
    D. the industry is characterized by conscious parallel action rather than effective competition
    E. the industry operates by pure competition

23. In setting prices, a monopolist - for example, ALCOA between 1900 and 1940 - tends to   23.____

    A. reduce prices when production costs are reduced
    B. exert his monopoly power to hold prices up even when costs fall
    C. keep prices proportional to the average price level, regardless of costs
    D. charge the same high price to buyers who can easily substitute something else for the monopolized product as he charges buyers who find the product essential
    E. conform to the prevailing mode

24. According to estimates, at the very time Chrysler was making a profit of less than $400 per car, General Motors' profit was almost $3,000 per car. This suggests   24.____

    A. General Motors was exerting its monopoly power to hold its prices above those of its competitors
    B. General Motors was unfairly undercutting the prices of other automobile manufacturers
    C. the automobile industry was characterized by overt collusion on prices
    D. all of the above
    E. none of the above

25. Nonprice competition - that is, competition in quality, styling, advertising, and the like - is MOST frequently found in industries 25.____

    A. producing homogeneous products like chemicals
    B. where output is spread over many firms like cotton manufactures
    C. where sales are concentrated in a few large firms producing highly differentiated products
    D. with high fixed and low variable costs
    E. with low fixed and high variable costs

KEY (CORRECT ANSWERS)

1.	E	11.	A
2.	C	12.	C
3.	B	13.	E
4.	D	14.	C
5.	B	15.	A
6.	C	16.	C
7.	A	17.	C
8.	B	18.	D
9.	E	19.	B
10.	E	20.	D

21.	D
22.	B
23.	A
24.	E
25.	C

TEST 4

DIRECTIONS: Each question or incomplete statement is followed by several suggested answers or completions. Select the one that BEST answers the question or completes the statement. *PRINT THE LETTER OF THE CORRECT ANSWER IN THE SPACE AT THE RIGHT.*

1. An IMPORTANT underlying cause of the shift of cotton production from New England to the South was that

    A. Southern mills saved on transportation cost by being closer to raw cotton supplies
    B. since there was lower industrialization in the South, more investment funds were available there
    C. Northern mills had to compete with other industries for scarce labor while Southern mills had to compete mainly with agriculture for labor that was being forced off farms anyhow
    D. the national minimum wage law offset the natural advantages of location in the North and forced mills to move
    E. the national minimum wage law actually favored the North more than the South

1.____

2. The appearance of cheap synthetic fabrics on the market in competition with cotton fabrics tends to

    A. force cottonseed oil out of uses where it is easily replaced by soy, corn, or other vegetable oils, since cottonseed is produced in proportion to cotton
    B. force cotton out of surgical and other non-fabric uses where synthetics are poor substitutes
    C. raise cotton prices and accelerate the replacement of cotton by synthetic fabrics
    D. contribute to a reduction in the quality of all-cotton garments by reducing the weight of cotton fabrics used and by changing patterns to save material
    E. lower cotton prices and slow the replacement of cotton by synthetic fabrics

2.____

3. The MOST important thing to consider in evaluating government expenditure for space exploration is

    A. how much the space program will cost in taxes
    B. whether the space program will add to the national debt
    C. how any potential gains from the space program compare to other things we might accomplish with the same resources
    D. whether the space program produces technological *spin-offs* that can be applied by private enterprise to reduce costs of production
    E. how much the space program will cost in capital funds

3.____

4. The income remaining to a small private businessman after he has deducted taxes, depreciation, and current expenses from his business revenue is LIKELY to consist of

    A. rent
    B. profit
    C. interest
    D. income from his own labor
    E. a combination of all the above

4.____

5. Probably the MOST important contribution of labor unions to the welfare of labor as a whole has been to

   A. raise average real wages
   B. enable workers to participate in decisions about working conditions and other matters that affect their daily lives
   C. introduce feather-bedding practices and other methods of controlling the application of automation and other labor-saving methods
   D. channel worker opinion into a united and politically effective vote
   E. magnify the gross national product (GNP)

6. The three principal products of Hawaii are pineapples, sugar cane, and tourist services. The farm price of pineapple tends to rise when

   A. the government reduces the quota on sugar, restricting the amount that can be imported into the United States from abroad
   B. Louisiana farmers increase their planting of sugar beets
   C. the yield per acre of pineapples rises
   D. Hawaiian pineapple canners have to pay higher prices for cans
   E. none of the above

7. After the Stock Market crash in 1987, the Federal Reserve Board did something that helped stabilize the market, which was completely opposite of its actions after the 1929 crash.
   What was it that the Federal Reserve Board did?

   A. Guaranteed all municipal obligations
   B. Greatly reduced the M1 and M2 money supply
   C. Increased liquidity in the M1 and M2 money supply
   D. Reduced then increased M1 and M2
   E. Purchased shares on the open market

8. When the prices of farm crops fall, it is MOST profitable for farmers to

   A. use more fertilizer to raise yield and make up for lower prices by greater volume
   B. use less fertilizer despite the further reduction in yield that would result
   C. replace fertilizer by additional hired labor to keep yield from declining
   D. use both more fertilizer and more labor to get a double increase in yield to make up for lower prices
   E. depend on government subsidies

9. Money set aside by a company to redeem its bonds, debentures, and/or preferred shares periodically as specified in the indenture or charter is known as a(n)

   A. debenture trust
   B. sinking fund
   C. accelerated pay fund
   D. serial bond
   E. money market fund

10. A declining dollar value vs. the Japanese Yen (i.e., $1 = ¥114 vs. = ¥150$) will have which effect on Japanese exports to the United States?

    A. The final price of Japanese goods will increase.
    B. There will be no visable difference.
    C. The NIKKEI average on the Tokyo exchange will cycle downward.

D. Inflation in Japan will run out of control.
E. None of the above.

11. The historic re-unification of Germany has unified a highly industrial and technologically advanced West Germany with a less advanced East Germany.
Fear of inflation as a result of this action caused the Bundesbank to

    A. keep real interest rates relatively high
    B. restructure the Deutschmark to reconcile the value of the East German currency
    C. devalue the mark
    D. impose a moratorium on consumer price adjustments
    E. restrict trading activity on the DAX in Bonn

11.____

12. Short-term options granted to existing shareholders of a company to purchase new issues of stock, generally at a reduced price level, is a(n)

    A. put option
    B. arbitrage transaction
    C. pre-emptive right
    D. round lot trust
    E. special situation

12.____

13. During World War II, most prices were subject to legal *ceilings* that kept them below their equilibrium levels.
This tended to

    A. make the quantities bought exceed the amount sold
    B. create shortages that required rationing
    C. cause surpluses of goods to accumulate and to create pressure for further price reductions
    D. stimulate production and hence to contribute to needed war production
    E. depress production and hence fail to contribute to needed war production

13.____

14. Union power over wages is SEVERELY limited when

    A. buyers of the product are unresponsive to price increases
    B. the product is nondurable
    C. unionization is limited to the highly skilled workers in the industry
    D. the product is durable
    E. non-union firms produce good substitutes for the output of the unionized firms

14.____

15. It has been estimated that a 10 percent increase in automobile prices reduces sales about 8 percent below what they would otherwise be. Union wages constitute about 10 percent of variable costs of automobile manufacturing. Since the new automobile contracts provide for wage and labor-related costs to rise about 20 percent during the next 3 years, they should tend to reduce employment in automobile production below what it would be with no wage increases at all by ABOUT, over the three-year period, _____ percent.

    A. 16
    B. 8
    C. 5
    D. 3
    E. less than 2

15.____

16. Some UAW members in the skilled trades think they could do better for themselves by splitting off from the UAW and establishing their own union to bargain for them. This is for the reason that

16.____

A. the skilled trades are a small but essential part of automobile labor
B. if workers in skilled trades don't get satisfactory terms from the automobile industry, they can always get good jobs elsewhere
C. the change would narrow the scope of the seniority unit for skilled workers who tend to be older and need the extra protection
D. their investment in skill is substantially greater than that of the semi-skilled machine operator or the unskilled worker
E. all of the above

17. Over an 18-year period, average hourly earnings of manufacturing workers rose from $3.60 to $7.50 while the consumer price index rose from 80 to 100.
The REAL buying power of an average hour of manufacturing work

   A. declined greatly (50 percent or more)
   B. declined somewhat (less than 50 percent)
   C. rose somewhat (less than 50 percent)
   D. rose greatly (50 percent or more)
   E. remained unchanged

18. Under the Taft-Hartley Act, it is ILLEGAL for a collective bargaining agreement to require management to

   A. hire only workers who are already union members
   B. make all workers join the union as a condition of employment by the firm
   C. extend union benefits to all employees whether union members or not
   D. employ more workers than would normally be needed according to the accepted technical standards of the industry
   E. do any or all of the above

19. The answer to this question is: *It increases or decreases depending on the elasticity of demand.*
What is the question?

   A. What would you expect to happen to the number of shirts a manufacturer could sell if he raised prices?
   B. What would you expect to happen to the total sales revenue if shirt prices were cut?
   C. What would you expect to happen to the price of shirts when a new and cheaper material becomes available?
   D. What would you expect to happen to the quality of shirts when materials get cheaper?
   E. None of the above

20. Consumers are more responsive to changes in prices of some things than of others. They tend to be MOST responsive to changes in prices of

   A. necessities, like wheat
   B. products that are small components of larger things, like spark plugs in an automobile
   C. products that have many close substitutes that will serve the same purpose
   D. products that are already very cheap
   E. necessities of any kind

21. A taxpayer preparing his income tax return has $4,500 in capital losses on some stock transactions.
How much of this loss can be taken for that particular tax year?

    A. The entire $4,500
    B. $3,000 - for that particular year with $1,500 carried forward to the next year
    C. $2,250 - for that particular tax year and $2,250 carried forward to the next tax year
    D. $3,000 - for that particular tax year with no carry forward
    E. Under TRA '86, no capital loss is allowed.

22. Since 1980, trade union membership has

    A. remained constant
    B. decreased
    C. increased
    D. increased during the 1980's, then dropped
    E. none of the above

23. The MOST important fact about income distribution is that

    A. there's only so much to go around - if somebody gets more, somebody else gets less
    B. the incomes people get are largely a matter of luck
    C. some high incomes are a reward for innovation, so that allowing one person to get more often results in more for all of us
    D. since incomes are just costs in another form, holding down costs reduces real income
    E. there is no equality

24. True profits, that is, profits as distinguished from interest on invested capital or from wages for the work effort contributed by the owner, arise when

    A. workers are exploited, that is, their wages are kept below the value of their product
    B. unemployment and excess labor supply keeps wages below the value of labor's product
    C. new products and new methods enable labor to produce more than before, and the difference temporarily goes to the innovator
    D. the cost of producing labor (subsistence) is below the value of the products that labor produces
    E. prices and wages achieve a relative equilibrium

25. According to recent reports, a certain bridge authority proposes to reduce toll rates on a bridge from $3.75 per car to $1.50 per car.
Considering the nature of traffic on the bridge, which is the sole connection between two states, the proposed toll cut will PROBABLY

    A. increase annual bridge revenue more than 50 percent
    B. increase annual bridge revenue 25 to 50 percent
    C. increase annual bridge revenue somewhat, but less than 25 percent
    D. increase annual bridge revenue
    E. reduce annual bridge revenue

KEY (CORRECT ANSWERS)

1.	C	11.	A
2.	A	12.	C
3.	C	13.	B
4.	E	14.	E
5.	B	15.	E
6.	A	16.	A
7.	C	17.	D
8.	B	18.	A
9.	B	19.	B
10.	A	20.	C

21. B
22. B
23. C
24. C
25. E

ECONOMICS
EXAMINATION SECTION
TEST 1

DIRECTIONS: Each question or incomplete statement is followed by several suggested answers or completions. Select the one that BEST answers the question or completes the statement. *PRINT THE LETTER OF THE CORRECT ANSWER IN THE SPACE AT THE RIGHT.*

1. The concept of equilibrium involves the idea that

   A. the economy can operate with no fluctuations
   B. fluctuations tend to be self-correcting
   C. there must be perfect competition for it to work
   D. the economy can operate with fluctuation
   E. the economy can operate even in a state of monopoly

1.____

2. Limitations upon freedom of occupational choice in the United States include

   A. inequality of income distribution
   B. discrimination in employment
   C. inequality of educational or training opportunities
   D. inadequate vocational guidance and apprentice training
   E. all of the above

2.____

3. Inequality of income is needed in an economy to
   I. create an aristocracy of wealth
   II. make savings available for investment
   III. persuade people to work harder
   IV. provide a strong national defense
   V. make a nation self-sufficient

   The CORRECT answer is:

   A. I, II   B. I, III   C. I, III, V
   D. III, IV, V   E. II, III

3.____

4. Modern industrial society is based PRIMARILY upon which of the following?
   I. Forests
   II. Coal
   III. Gold
   IV. Iron ore
   V. Petroleum

   The CORRECT answer is:

   A. I, II, III   B. II, IV, V   C. I, III, IV
   D. I, III, V   E. II, III, IV

4.____

133

5. Place these stages of economic development in sequence from the EARLIEST to the LATEST:
    I. Machine technology and industrial capitalism
    II. Hunting and food-gathering
    III. Plow-agriculture and irrigation
    IV. Pastoralism and digging-stick agriculture
    V. Commercial capitalism

   The CORRECT answer is:

   A. II, III, IV, I, V
   B. II, III, IV, V, I
   C. II, IV, III, V, I
   D. IV, II, III, I, V
   E. IV, II, III, V, I

6. The price system tells businessmen how much of what to produce if

   A. workable competition exists in the market
   B. consumers buy on the basis of advertising only
   C. income is equally distributed only
   D. income is unequally distributed
   E. workable competition does not exist in the market

7. Arrange the following great economic thinkers chronologically:
    I. John Maynard Keynes
    II. Adam Smith
    III. Karl Marx
    IV. David Ricardo
    V. Thorstein Veblen

   The CORRECT answer is:

   A. II, III, IV, I, V
   B. II, IV, III, V, I
   C. II, III, IV, V, I
   D. IV, II, III, I, V
   E. IV, II, III, V, I

8. Our economic system transforms competition into cooperation by

   A. freedom of contract
   B. intervention of the government
   C. operation of the price system in commodity markets
   D. all of the above
   E. none of the above

9. *Induced investment* refers to

   A. changes in investment which result from a change in the Net National Product (NNP)
   B. the fact that increased saving may sometimes result in increased investment
   C. investment made as a result of government orders
   D. an increase in investment which results from technological change
   E. an increase in investment which results from demographical change

10. The *paradox of thrift* means

    A. positive saving will always mean unemployment
    B. if changes in investment are induced by changes in Net National Product (NNP), then a decision on the part of people to save more might result in their actually saving less
    C. if the economy is at full employment, a decision on the part of people to save more might produce an inflationary gap
    D. saving stimulates investment spending so as to worsen an inflationary spiral
    E. saving must always equal investment

11. *Liquidity preference* refers to the

    A. desire of banks to avoid long-term loans
    B. evaluation of cash as against other forms of asset holdings
    C. relationship between inventory holdings and the level of consumer demand
    D. desire to liquidate ownership of producer durables and inventories in the face of declining consumption
    E. rising trend in the consumption of alcoholic beverages

12. Which of the following transfer payments is EXCLUDED from the computation of national income?

    A. Payment for an intermediary good
    B. Payment for a service rendered by a soldier to the government
    C. Payment of interest on a government bond
    D. Payment of interest on a General Motors bond
    E. Undistributed corporation profits

13. A tariff for protection against the competition of cheap, foreign labor provides a short-run benefit for

    A. the protected workers   B. all workers
    C. all consumers   D. unions
    E. the government

14. A factor which did NOT contribute to the postwar *dollar shortage* was the

    A. frequent depreciation of currencies by the dollarshortage countries
    B. wartime destruction of productive facilities in Europe and Asia
    C. efforts by Europeans and Asians to live beyond their means
    D. faster technological progress in dollar countries than elsewhere
    E. rebuilding of war-torn countries

15. Which of the following statements is FALSE?

    A. Tax reduction tends to stimulate income.
    B. Tax reduction tends to increase personal consumption.
    C. Tax reduction tends to increase personal saving.
    D. Whatever else tax reduction does, the increases in personal consumption resulting from tax reductions must stimulate income.
    E. If tax reductions cause personal saving to increase, then Net National Product will fail.

16. If the level of spending increases, with the quantity of money held constant, then   16.___

    A. the velocity of circulation of money must have increased
    B. the amount of real national output must have increased
    C. either the velocity of money circulation or the amount of real national output must have increased, or both
    D. the amount of real national output must have decreased
    E. either the velocity of money circulation must have increased, or the amount of real national output must have decreased, or both

17. If the Federal Reserve authorities wished to pursue an expansionary monetary policy, it would be CORRECT for them to   17.___

    A. raise the discount rate to discourage hoarding by the public
    B. raise reserve requirements to eliminate any excess reserves held by the Member banks
    C. raise margin requirements to discourage wasteful speculation
    D. sell securities on the open market to drive interest rates down
    E. do none of the above

18. An expansionary monetary policy adopted by a central bank will be UNSUCCESSFUL if   18.___

    A. prices do not increase
    B. saving on the part of the public does not decrease
    C. investment spending is not changed by a change in the interest rate
    D. the inflationary tendency which prompted this policy is not checked
    E. no decrease in the price of government bonds occurs

19. The C plus I plus G schedule would tend to be shifted up by   19.___

    A. an increase in taxes
    B. a decrease in government spending
    C. an increase in interest rates
    D. open-market sales by the central bank
    E. none of the above

20. MOST of the very large United States federal debt outstanding arose as the result of   20.___

    A. war
    B. depressions
    C. borrowing to meet interest charges on previous debts
    D. borrowing from abroad
    E. welfare payments

21. In the following table, indicate the number showing the interval in which demand is elastic.   21._____

	P	q
	1	100
I.	3	60
II.	8	30
III.	15	10
IV.	30	5
V.	50	4

    The CORRECT answer is:

    A. I   B. II   C. III   D. IV   E. V

22. Using the same table as in the above question, indicate the number showing the interval in which demand is of unitary elasticity.   22._____
    The CORRECT interval is:

    A. I   B. II   C. III   D. IV   E. V

23. When the American Government borrowed in order to finance World War II, it thereby   23._____

    A. shifted the economic burden to future generations who would have to pay the interest and principal
    B. intensified the danger of national bankruptcy
    C. in no sense shifted the burden of the war on future generations
    D. placed the American people, though to a lesser degree, in the same difficult position as the British were placed by the war-time borrowing of their government from the United States and other foreign governments
    E. lessened the danger of national bankruptcy

24. The existence of a large internally held public debt has   24._____

    A. no effect on the nation as a whole
    B. creates the danger of national bankruptcy
    C. has no effect on the nation as a whole, but does affect certain special interest groups
    D. is likely to depress the level of consumption and, hence, lower the equilibrium Net National Product (NNP)
    E. is likely to make for greater inequality in the distribution of incomes and to dampen work incentive

25. The risks due to speculative production tend to be increased by   25._____

    A. improved transportation
    B. improved market information
    C. monopoly
    D. the roundabout method of production
    E. none of the above

KEY (CORRECT ANSWERS)

1.	B	11.	B
2.	E	12.	A
3.	E	13.	A
4.	B	14.	A
5.	C	15.	E
6.	A	16.	A
7.	B	17.	E
8.	D	18.	B
9.	A	19.	E
10.	B	20.	A

21. C
22. D
23. C
24. C
25. D

TEST 2

DIRECTIONS: Each question or incomplete statement is followed by several suggested answers or completions. Select the one that BEST answers the question or completes the statement. *PRINT THE LETTER OF THE CORRECT ANSWER IN THE SPACE AT THE RIGHT.*

1. To increase output, we MUST do which of the following? Increase
    I. hours of work
    II. the labor force
    III. output capacity
    IV. leisure time
    V. fringe benefits
   The CORRECT answer is:

   A. I, II, III
   B. I, II, IV
   C. I, III, V
   D. II, III, IV
   E. I, II, III, IV, V

1.____

2. The efficiency of production depends upon

   A. the division of labor and exchange
   B. mass production and mechanization
   C. automation and cybernetics
   D. all of the above
   E. none of the above

2.____

3. The accumulation of capital in an economy means the

   A. amount of money that is saved
   B. growth of output capacity
   C. rise in values on the stock market
   D. amount of money that is invested
   E. rise in values on the realty market

3.____

4. The amount of natural resources is
    I. fixed and unchanging
    II. dependent upon the level of technology
    III. subject to periodic fluctuations
    IV. subject to depletion
    V. proportional to government investment and subsidy
   The CORRECT answer is:

   A. I, II, V
   B. I, III
   C. II, III
   D. II, IV
   E. II, V

4.____

5. World population has increased because

   A. the birth rate has risen sharply
   B. the death rate has fallen sharply
   C. people are not practicing birth control
   D. abortion is illegal in almost all countries
   E. there are more multiple births today due to special drugs

5.____

6. The industrial revolution   6.____
    I.   had nothing to do with world population increase
    II. did not develop where slavery was the basis of the economy
    III. has not influenced most of the people of the world
    IV. developed first in Britain and spread East and West
    V.   has, to all practical purposes, ceased
   The CORRECT answer is:

   A. I, III, V   B. I, II   C. II, III
   D. II, IV   E. II, III, IV, V

7. Living standards depend upon   7.____

   A. the number of people in an area
   B. the ability to produce commodities
   C. the ability to utilize commodities
   D. all of the above
   E. none of the above

8. The law of diminishing returns means that   8.____

   A. the more people work, the less is produced
   B. if one factor of production increases more slowly, eventually there will be a decline in productivity
   C. as population increases geometrically, food production increases arithmetically
   D. as labor increases, production per person declines
   E. as labor decreases, production per person rises

9. The United States Government prefers to sell defense bonds to individuals rather than to banks because the   9.____

   A. average person hoards his high wages in times of prosperity
   B. banks are reluctant to invest large sums of money in such bonds
   C. tendency of such sales is to avert inflation
   D. administration fears the domination of the Government by banking interests
   E. interest rate will be lower

10. In teaching the topic of exchange, a point of emphasis would be the fact that at least nine-tenths of all transactions (in terms of value) are accomplished by the use of   10.____

    A. Federal Reserve notes   B. promissory notes
    C. checks   D. bills of exchange
    E. certificates of deposit

11. The tax in the United States which MOST closely meets the needs of a sound tax system is the _____ tax.   11.____

    A. personal income   B. excess profits
    C. death and inheritance   D. excise
    E. sales

12. Money consists of
    I. legal tender *only*
    II. generally acceptable symbols of claims upon commodities
    III. only gold and silver
    IV. a medium of exchange and measure of value
    V. currency but not checks
    The CORRECT answer is:

    A. I, III   B. I, IV   C. II, IV
    D. III, V   E. I, IV

13. Pre-Keynesian thinking among most economists considered that full employment was the rule because
    I. according to Say's law, *supply creates its own demand*
    II. prices and wages were becoming less flexible
    III. the interest rate in a free market tends to equalize saving and investment
    IV. barriers to trade were growing after World War I
    V. prices and wages were becoming more flexible
    The CORRECT answer is:

    A. I, IV, V   B. I, II   C. II, IV
    D. II, III   E. I, III, V

14. Free economic goods are those

    A. which are not important
    B. given to us by our parents
    C. given to us by the government
    D. given to us by nature and requiring no effort to make usable
    E. all of the above

15. The economist needs to know

    A. only mathematics because economics deals only with quantities
    B. mainly economic theory because economic behavior is common sense
    C. mainly the development of economic thought and institutions
    D. a minimum about human behavior plus economics
    E. as much as possible about the universe including, especially, economics and statistics

16. Economizing is necessary because

    A. there is not enough money for everybody
    B. resources are scarce in relation to human desires
    C. it is immoral for things to be wasted
    D. standards of value must be established
    E. it is necessary to distribute the wealth more evenly

17. Division of labor is USUALLY defined as

    A. everyone doing the same amount of work
    B. compartmentalization
    C. specialization
    D. every one doing the same kind of work
    E. mechanization

18. The factors of production are USUALLY considered to be
    I. technology
    II. land
    III. labor
    IV. climate
    V. capital

    The CORRECT answer is:

    A. II, III, IV   B. III, IV, V   C. I, II, III
    D. II, III, V   E. I, IV, V

19. Economics is a social science because

    A. tables and graphs are used
    B. theory and empirical evidence are related
    C. the scientific method is applied to human behavior
    D. it deals with the allocation of scarce resources to material ends
    E. none of the above

20. In terms of numbers, the form of business unit MOST frequently found in the United States today is the

    A. individual, or single, proprietorship
    B. partnership
    C. small corporation
    D. giant corporation
    E. middle corporation

21. The term *limited liability* is frequently used in describing the characteristics of a corporation.
    It means the following:

    A. Any officer of the corporation is strictly limited in his ability to speak for the corporation and commit it to any liability
    B. Once a shareholder has paid for his stock, he has no further financial obligation, regardless of how much trouble the corporation gets into
    C. The corporation's liability to pay dividends to its stockholders is a limited one since it is required to pay them only if it has earned a profit
    D. There are certain obligations which a corporation can legally refuse to pay
    E. The corporation has only a limited obligation to meet claims made by any single person or firm against it (provided it has acted within the scope of its charter) so that there is some protection for its assets and financial position

22. A corporation's obligation to pay interest on bonds it has issued may be PROPERLY described as follows:

   A. Interest must be paid regardless of whether a profit has been earned or not
   B. Interest must be paid whenever a profit has been earned
   C. Interest need not be paid even if a profit has been earned, but it must be paid before any dividend is paid
   D. Normally, interest ranks ahead of dividends, but there are some circumstances in which a dividend can be paid without payment of bond interest
   E. Interest ranks behind dividends and is paid only after dividends have been paid in full

23. The MAIN reason why indirect or *capital-using* methods of production have not displaced direct methods in economically underdeveloped areas of the world is:

   A. The governments of such areas have not issued enough money to finance indirect methods
   B. People do not realize that the indirect methods would produce more consumption goods
   C. There are no indirect methods that would actually produce more consumption goods
   D. Such areas do not have a properly functioning price system
   E. The adoption of such indirect methods would involve a sacrifice of present consumption

24. The economic problem of how goods shall be produced is that of

   A. finding out how much product will be obtained when given quantities of factors of production are put to work together in the most effective known manner
   B. having a mechanism that will somehow reveal what goods people really want to be produced
   C. getting the existing factors of production distributed among different occupations to best produce whatever goods the community wants
   D. deciding how the goods that have been produced shall be distributed among the people who made those goods
   E. none of the above

25. An economic theory is scientific
   I. even if it requires many assumptions and has no relation to the actual operation of the economy
   II. if it is consistent, even if it has little value for forecasting
   III. if it is internally consistent and has a minimum of assumptions
   IV. if it has considerable usefulness in forecasting
   V. it is internally consistent and has a maximum of assumptions

   The CORRECT answer is:

   A. I, II, V   B. I, III   C. II, III
   D. III, IV   E. III, IV, V

KEY (CORRECT ANSWERS)

1. A
2. D
3. B
4. D
5. B

6. D
7. D
8. B
9. C
10. C

11. A
12. C
13. A
14. D
15. E

16. B
17. C
18. D
19. C
20. A

21. B
22. A
23. E
24. E
25. D

TEST 3

DIRECTIONS: Each question or incomplete statement is followed by several suggested answers or completions. Select the one that BEST answers the question or completes the statement. *PRINT THE LETTER OF THE CORRECT ANSWER IN THE SPACE AT THE RIGHT.*

1. The *accelerator* principle of the business cycle means that

    A. a slight increase in demand will step up a much larger increase in production
    B. an increase in production, followed up by efficient advertising techniques, will accelerate an increase in demand
    C. the severity of a depression will be accelerated if the government does not step in with a public works program
    D. the upward trend of business depends upon a quickened activity in the sale of stocks and bonds

1.____

2. In a free economy, the volume of investment in a given period is determined by the

    A. demand for consumer goods and the volume of savings
    B. level of national income and the volume of money
    C. average return on investment and the volume of savings
    D. marginal efficiency of capital and the interest rate

2.____

3. The principle of comparative cost applies to

    A. pricing under conditions of imperfect competition
    B. determination of economic profit
    C. the analysis of marginal productivity
    D. analyses of international trade

3.____

4. The concept of the multiplier in economic analysis refers to the effect of

    A. increased demand on investment
    B. the interest rate on saving
    C. increased investment on income
    D. increased income on the propensity to consume

4.____

5. A significant increase in the liquidity preference will tend to have the effect of

    A. encouraging investment
    B. raising the interest rate
    C. increasing the marginal efficiency of capital
    D. reducing the supply of money

5.____

6. Which one of the following statements is INCORRECT with regard to holding companies?

    A. Holding companies are subject to more serious legal restrictions than are other forms of combination.
    B. Public utility holding companies above the second level are forbidden by federal law.

6.____

C. Holding companies allow companies in a combination to retain their separate identities.
D. Holding companies can exercise control over subsidiaries without outright ownership of their assets.

7. The statement, *Industry-wide collective bargaining tends to take wages and working conditions out of competition,* refers to the effect of such bargaining on the possibility of

   A. sanctioning featherbedding in contracts
   B. introducing new machinery and improved processes
   C. reducing production costs for all employers
   D. passing increased labor costs along to consumers

8. Which one of the following is NOT used in the computation of the gross national product?

   A. Personal consumption expenditures
   B. Gross private domestic investment
   C. Income of unincorporated businesses
   D. Government purchases of goods and services

9. Under a system of flexible farm price supports,

   A. only the so-called *basic* commodities receive price support
   B. price supports are applied when marketing quotas are inapplicable
   C. acreage allotments, as a production control device, are abandoned
   D. price support levels are fixed in relation to supply levels of products

10. Which one of the following economic problems will result when dollars pumped into the economy of an underdeveloped country are changed into local currency?

    A. The effect will be inflationary unless compensated for by exports from that country.
    B. Economic development will be curbed unless aid is offered on a grant rather than on a loan basis.
    C. No real contribution to economic development will occur unless funds are employed in self-liquidating projects.
    D. The effect will be inflationary unless accompanied by additional imports into that country.

11. Which one of the following pairs of economists is INCORRECTLY associated as having similar viewpoints on economic theory?

    A. Edward Chamberlain - Joan Robinson
    B. John Bates Clark - Wesley C. Mitchell
    C. John R. Commons - Thorstein Veblen
    D. William Stanley Jevons - Leon Walros

12. Which one of the following BEST expresses the theme of THE TWENTIETH CENTURY CAPITALIST REVOLUTION by Adolf A. Berle, Jr.?

    A. The present trend toward increased corporate influence in broad problems of community development must be reversed.
    B. The concept of the *soulless* corporation must be replaced by a concept of a corporate conscience.

C. Means should be found to reduce the control exercised over the largest corporate units by the financial market.
D. The absence of competition, in our present system of corporate concentrates, must be corrected.

13. Which author is INCORRECTLY linked with the book which he wrote?

    A. Henry George - PROGRESS AND POVERTY
    B. Gustavus Myers - FRENZIED FINANCE
    C. Frank Norris - THE OCTOPUS
    D. Norbert Wiener - THE HUMAN USE OF HUMAN BEINGS

14. Joan Robinson, Edward H. Chamberlin, and Robert Triffin are noted CHIEFLY for their contributions in the areas of

    A. monopolistic or imperfect competition
    B. money and banking
    C. international trade
    D. public and private finance

15. In which of the following items is the public policy NOT correctly associated with the name of the economist?

    A. Welfare state - John A. Hobson
    B. Laissez-faire - John Ruskin
    C. Labor legislation - John R. Commons
    D. Tariffs - Henry Carey

16. Henry Hazlett's ECONOMICS IN ONE LESSON is MOST accurately described as

    A. a socialist critique of capitalism
    B. non-Keynesian advocacy of laissez-faire
    C. criticism of ideas presented by the Keynesian school
    D. a popularization of Keynesian theory

17. Thorstein Veblen, to the extent that he could be said to be part of a group, was CLOSEST to which of the following?

    A. Max Weber, Somart, Schmoller
    B. Marshall, Pigou, Mill
    C. Von Wieser, Bohm-Bawerk, Menger
    D. Davenport, Patten, John Bates Clark

18. W.C. Mitchell, A.F. Burns, F.C. Mills, and Simon Kuznets were associated in the work of the

    A. Council of Economic Advisers
    B. National Bureau of Economic Research
    C. Committee for Economic Development
    D. Brookings Institution

19. The view of Karl Marx on the economic position of labor was that labor

    A. could not be considered a commodity
    B. was a commodity just like any other
    C. was a commodity of a unique type
    D. was sometimes a commodity and sometimes not, depending on the circumstances

20. Which of the following business cycle theorists is INCORRECTLY paired with a theory?

    A. W.S. Jevons - Sunspot theory
    B. J.M. Keynes - Savings-Investment theory
    C. J. Schumpeter - Innovation theory
    D. J.A. Hobson - Monetary theory

21. Marginalism in economics is MOST closely based on the psychology of

    A. Darwin   B. Bentham   C. Koffka   D. James

22. The acceleration principle in the business cycle theory refers to the fact that

    A. the demand for productive agents fluctuates more sharply than does the demand for ultimate products
    B. unemployment spreads more rapidly as recession continues
    C. new investment will increase the total national income by more than the amount of the new investment
    D. inventories fluctuate more widely than does output

23. Which of the following are characteristics of monopolistic competition?
    I. Division of sales territory
    II. Product differentiation
    III. Price leadership
    IV. Relatively few producers
    V. Cartel agreements
    The CORRECT answer is:

    A. I, II, III   B. I, IV, V
    C. II, III, IV   D. III, V

24. A term which has come into frequent use in recent economic theory is *the multiplier*. This refers to the

    A. inflationary spiral
    B. relationship between oligopolistic industry and the price level
    C. relationship between changes in investment and consequent changes in consumption
    D. relationship between technological progress in an industry and the level of individual production

25. J. Kenneth Galbraith's reference to the so-called *countervailing force* in the American economy referred to the

    A. rise of the C.I.O. in the 1930's and 40's that stimulated a phenomenal growth in the labor movement
    B. trust-busting campaign of Theodore Roosevelt, stemming the growth towards bigness
    C. passage of the Taft-Hartley Act, tilting the scales backward for the benefit of the employer
    D. force, unleashed by the New Deal through its sympathy for labor, that brought about a redistribution of national income

25._____

KEY (CORRECT ANSWERS)

1.	A	11.	B
2.	D	12.	B
3.	D	13.	B
4.	C	14.	A
5.	B	15.	B
6.	A	16.	B
7.	D	17.	A
8.	C	18.	B
9.	D	19.	C
10.	D	20.	D

21.	B
22.	A
23.	C
24.	C
25.	D

TEST 4

DIRECTIONS: Each question or incomplete statement is followed by several suggested answers or completions. Select the one that BEST answers the question or completes the statement. *PRINT THE LETTER OF THE CORRECT ANSWER IN THE SPACE AT THE RIGHT.*

1. The basing point system of fixing prices refers to the practice among producers in the same industry of charging

   A. the same price and adding freight charges from a common point, regardless of actual freight costs
   B. the same price and adding freight costs based on the average distance from all mills to the delivery point
   C. the F.O.B. price based on the average cost of production in all mills
   D. a competitive price and adding freight charges from a common point, regardless of actual freight costs

   1._____

2. The characteristics of a free competitive market are BEST illustrated in the case of a(n)

   A. organized exchange
   B. well-advertised product
   C. large number of companies
   D. auction

   2._____

3. The fact that Switzerland undersells the United States in watch movements in spite of the existence of equally skilled watchmakers is an illustration of the law of _____ costs.

   A. comparative   B. diminishing
   C. absolute   D. increasing

   3._____

4. The effect of deficit financing by the federal government is to

   A. increase idle cash balances in the hands of the public
   B. increase unemployment in the short run
   C. increase the total amount of United States Notes outstanding
   D. maintain or increase the national income

   4._____

5. In which of the following pairs did the second statute legalize acts previously prohibited by the first?
   I. Sherman Anti-Trust Act - Webb-Pomerene Act
   II. National Industrial Recovery Act - Public Utility Holding Company Act
   III. Norris-LaGuardia Anti-Injunction Act - National Labor Relations Act
   IV. Clayton Anti-Trust Act - Miller-Tydings Act
   The CORRECT answer is:

   A. I, IV   B. II, IV
   C. I, II, III   D. I, II, III, IV

   5._____

6. The status of American agriculture during and after World War II differed MOST from that of the period of World War II in the   6.____

   A. reasons for the advance of agricultural prices
   B. extent of increase in farm mortgage debt
   C. changes in agriculture prices in the postwar years
   D. behavior of the foreign market for American farm products

7. Under flexible or variable price supports for farm commodities, the MAXIMUM support level would be approached when   7.____

   A. the ratio of total supplies to normal supplies fell
   B. the export market expanded
   C. overproduction increased
   D. marketing quotas were disapproved

8. To meet the problem of surplus commodities, states have attempted to overcome the constitutional prohibition on interstate tariffs by   8.____

   A. promoting a constitutional amendment
   B. utilizing their police powers
   C. advertising state specialities on a national scale
   D. passing legislation to curtail production

9. Unemployment is likely to be low if   9.____

   A. consumer demand remains stable
   B. employers grant wage increases as demanded by unions
   C. the price level drops gradually in response to increasing productivity
   D. no inflationary gap develops

10. MOST of the controversy in the courts in regard to utility rates has centered around   10.____

    A. what rate of profit is fair
    B. how the properties of a public utility should be valued
    C. how to determine the reasonableness of operating expenses
    D. the division of power between federal and state agencies

11. Which one of the following was a factor in the development of the other three?   11.____

    A. Growing surpluses of capital in the United States
    B. Tendency of producers of American staples to deal directly with foreign markets rather than through European brokers
    C. Change in the status of the United States from a debtor to a creditor nation
    D. Rise of New York as a rival of London as an international transactions center

12. Which of the following factors in the development of shipbuilding apply MORE to Great Britain than to the United States?   12.____

    A. Mass production of standardized ships
    B. Existence of rivers with wide, open estuaries
    C. Relative importance of foreign trade in the nation's economy
    D. Proximity to areas of steel production

13. Which one of the following statements is TRUE concerning the production of gold? It(s)

    A. fluctuations in the past two decades have responded to changes in the legally established price
    B. has no influence on purchasing power of countries in international trade
    C. is a currently important factor in causing fluctuations in the price level in the United States
    D. is influenced by the fact that it is mined in close association with other metals

14. The McGuire Act increased the effectiveness of state fair trade laws as compared with their former status by

    A. adding liquor and drugs to the list of items in which fair trade contracts can be enforced
    B. making it possible to bind non-signers as well as signers of fair trade contracts
    C. adding interstate price-fixing agreements to the Miller-Tydings Law's provision for intrastate price fixing
    D. reaffirming the Supreme Court's 1950 decision as to the status of price-fixing agreements

15. Which of the following were characteristic of United States tariff legislation of the period 1934-1953?
    I. The abolition of the Tariff Commission
    II. The granting of greater tariff-making powers to the President
    III. The elimination of unconditional most-favored-nation clauses
    IV. The abandonment of the *Buy American* Act

    The CORRECT answer is:

    A. II *only*
    B. I, II
    C. II, III
    D. III, IV

16. MOST of the loans made by the International Bank for Reconstruction and Development come from

    A. sale of its bonds
    B. its earnings
    C. funds raised from its parent body (the UN)
    D. assessments paid by member nations

17. Cost of production will have the GREATEST influence on the price of a commodity in the case of

    A. classical paintings in the hands of an art dealer
    B. fresh strawberries in a retail store
    C. antiques offered for sale at an exhibition
    D. shoes sold by a manufacturer

18. Monopolistic competition is

    A. a contradiction in terms
    B. cut-throat competition preliminary to the formation of complete monopoly
    C. competition among monopolized industries
    D. characterized by product differentiation in the same market

19. Which one of the following is NOT a characteristic of industries generally considered to be public utilities?   19.____

    A. The proportion of labor to material agents is large.
    B. They are frequently decreasing cost industries.
    C. There are usually no close substitutes.
    D. Duplication of service may lead to ineffiency or inconvenience to customers.

20. The *Pittsburgh plus* system of quoting steel prices was an example of   20.____

    A. monopsony
    B. the basing point principle
    C. agreement not to absorb freight charges
    D. assuring the same net prices to all steel mills

21. Which of the following government agencies is MOST concerned with granting direct subsidies to the industry involved?   21.____

    A. Maritime Commission
    B. Federal Communications Commission
    C. Interstate Commerce Commission
    D. Civil Aeronautics Authority

22. The CHIEF reason for the striking gains in American agricultural production during the past two decades has been the increase in   22.____

    A. total acreage   B. productivity
    C. number of farm workers   D. imports

23. The trend toward the abandonment of the one-crop system of agriculture in the southern states has led to   23.____

    A. an increase in the number of family-sized farms
    B. heavy migration of Black farm workers from the northern to the southern states
    C. relatively less reliance on federal price supports for the *basic* commodities
    D. substantial decline in the production of cotton

24. Which of the following trends is a result of the other three?   24.____

    A. Shift of population away from rural areas
    B. Increased mechanization of agriculture
    C. Depletion of soil fertility
    D. Improvement in general business conditions

25. Which one of the following groupings includes laws which were CLOSELY related to each other?   25.____

    A. Social Security Act, Wheeler-Rayburn Act, Fair Labor Standards Act
    B. National Labor Relations Act, Taft-Hartley Law, Webb-Pomerene Act
    C. Sherman Anti-trust Act, Clayton Act, Robinson-Patman Act
    D. Walsh-Healey Act, Federal Reserve Act, Glass-Steagall Act

KEY (CORRECT ANSWERS)

1.	A	11.	A
2.	A	12.	C
3.	A	13.	D
4.	D	14.	B
5.	A	15.	A
6.	B	16.	A
7.	A	17.	D
8.	B	18.	D
9.	C	19.	A
10.	B	20.	B

21. A
22. B
23. C
24. A
25. C

TEST 5

DIRECTIONS: Each question or incomplete statement is followed by several suggested answers or completions. Select the one that BEST answers the question completes the statement. *PRINT THE LETTER OF THE CORRECT ANSWER IN THE SPACE AT THE RIGHT.*

1. Which one of the following objections to a steadily increasing public debt involves a fallacy:

    A. Fear of the debt may deter investment.
    B. Interest must be paid by taxes or further borrowing.
    C. Our generation is spared at the expense of future generations.
    D. Expenditure may be wasteful if no ceiling to the debt is enforced.

    1._____

2. When a nation devalues its currency, the tendency is to

    A. increase imports
    B. decrease its tourist trade
    C. reduce its dollar shortage
    D. lower prices in Great Britain

    2._____

3. Which one of the following is NOT a plan for alleviating the effects of the business cycle?

    A. The Social Credit Program
    B. The compensated dollar
    C. Pump priming
    D. The International Stabilization Fund

    3._____

4. A law office purchases a new computer system and decides to take a depreciation deduction. The computer was purchased in January 1992.
Which system of depreciation will be used?

    A. Straight Line Depreciation (SLD)
    B. Accelerated Cost Recovery System (ACRS)
    C. Modified Accelerated Cost Recovery System (MACRS)
    D. Real Property Cost Depreciation (RPD)

    4._____

5. The idea of conspicuous consumption was FIRST set forth by

    A. Karl Marx   B. Thorstein Veblen
    C. John Stuart Mill   D. Wesley C. Mitchell

    5._____

6. In the history of horizontal combinations for the purpose of eliminating competition, the form which developed LAST was the

    A. community of interest   B. trust
    C. holding company   D. pool

    6._____

7. Which of the following would tend to cause inflation?
Increase in
   I. the supply of gold
   II. production
   III. the supply of credit
   IV. the velocity of circulation of money
The CORRECT answer is:

   A. I, II, III, IV
   C. I, III, IV
   B. II, III, IV
   D. II, IV

8. The corporate form of business organization is popular in small family enterprises because

   A. corporations decentralize management
   B. corporations are subject to less government regulation than individual entrepreneurs
   C. the tax rate for corporations is less than that of individual owners
   D. the corporation provides for limited liability

9. Which of the following will result from an increase in loans to businessmen by a bank?
A
   I. rise in the deposits of the bank
   II. rise in the profits of the bank
   III. rise in the assets of the bank
   IV. decrease in the cash on hand of the bank
The CORRECT answer is:

   A. I, II, IV
   C. I, II, III
   B. I, III, IV
   D. II, IV

10. Of the following, the one LEAST likely to affect consumption would be

   A. the expectation of changes in prices
   B. a change in the distribution of the national income
   C. the expectation of changes in supply
   D. changes in income tax rates for higher incomes

11. In general, statistics indicate MOST consistently that as the family income rises, the percentage of the income spent on

   A. food increases
   C. food decreases
   B. rent decreases
   D. luxuries decreases

12. Of the following, the one which is a RESULT of the other three is:

   A. Stockholders are numerous and scattered throughout the world
   B. Stockholders generally consider themselves as investors rather than active partners in a firm
   C. The large corporation is often controlled by minority stockholders
   D. Many corporations permit voting by proxy

13. The theory that wages tend to remain at a level which is barely sufficient to support a worker and his family is known as the _____ theory.   13.____

    A. wages fund
    B. marginal productivity
    C. subsistence
    D. commodity

14. Which of the following pairs does NOT contain an employee and an employer weapon or tactic?   14.____

    A. Boycott - injunction
    B. Check-off - blacklist
    C. Open shop - lockout
    D. Closed shop - yellow-dog contract

15. Which one of the following is LIKELY to result from the other three?   15.____

    A. Increasing reserve requirements
    B. Raising the re-discount rate
    C. Contraction of bank credit
    D. Sale of securities in the open market by Federal Reserve Banks

16. Anything becomes money when it   16.____

    A. is backed by a bank
    B. has general acceptability
    C. has intrinsic value
    D. is backed by precious metals

17. The term *national debt* means the   17.____

    A. obligations-to-pay of the federal government
    B. interest-bearing debt of the federal government
    C. sum total of all federal, state, and local debts
    D. sum of all public and private debts

18. The Federal Reserve System is owned   18.____

    A. and controlled by private banks
    B. by the government and controlled by private banks
    C. and controlled by the government
    D. by private banks with control divided between the government and representatives of the banks

19. Anti-trust laws have resulted in which of the following?   19.____
    I. The dissolution of a majority of holding companies in America
    II. The elimination of ruthless practices of great corporations.
    III. The rise of a cartel system in the United States similar to that of Europe
    IV. Government approval of reasonable combinations

    The CORRECT answer is:

    A. I, II, III
    B. II, III, IV
    C. I, II, III, IV
    D. II, IV

20. Which of the following functions do the Federal Reserve Banks perform today?

    I. Making loans
    II. Issuing Federal Reserve Bank Notes
    III. Creating their own credit
    IV. Accepting deposits

    The CORRECT answer is:

    A. II, III
    B. I, II, III
    C. I, III, IV
    D. I, II, IV

21. In recent years, the LARGEST proportion of the income of the federal government has been derived from _____ taxes.

    A. corporation income
    B. individual income
    C. federal excise
    D. estate and gift

22. Which of the following factors explain the failure of the cooperative movement in the United States to keep pace with the movement in other countries?

    I. It has been marked by many conspicuous failures and bankruptcies.
    II. Our marketing system is relatively more efficient than that of most countries.
    III. The large geographical area of the country serves as a deterrent to cooperation.
    IV. The individualistic character of the average American bodes no good for cooperation.

    The CORRECT answer is:

    A. I, II, III
    B. II, III, IV
    C. I, III
    D. I, II, III, IV

23. Which one of the following does NOT tend to result from an overvalued currency?

    A. Export and import prices in the overvalued domestic currencies are low.
    B. The supplies available to the domestic economy are reduced.
    C. The sale of goods abroad is discouraged.
    D. Inflationary pressures are lessened.

24. Which one of the following does NOT correctly state a contrast between price competition and monopolistic competition?

    A. In price competition, capital tends to be fully utilized whereas in monopolistic competition it is not.
    B. Price competition usually results in wide price swings whereas, in monopolistic competition, there is usually price lethargy.
    C. Price competition has cyclical price flexibility whereas monopolistic competition has little cyclical price flexibility.
    D. In price competition, it usually pays the vendor to divert effort to selling and advertising whereas, in monopolistic competition, it does not.

25. Which of the following statements concerning pricing factors are TRUE?
    I. When buyers feel that competing products are different, demand elasticities are lowered.
    II. Where a low price is regarded as a sign of inferiority, the price elasticity of demand will be low.
    III. Coordination of business policies in oligopolistic markets may exist without direct contacts among firms.
    IV. Oligopoly is most often found in industries fabricating raw materials from farms.
    V. The profitability in discrimination in pricing rests upon differences in the elasticities of demand of different groups.

    The CORRECT answer is:

    A. II, III, IV, V
    B. I, III, V
    C. I, II, III, V
    D. I, II, IV

KEY (CORRECT ANSWERS)

1.	C	11.	C
2.	C	12.	C
3.	D	13.	C
4.	B	14.	C
5.	B	15.	C
6.	C	16.	B
7.	C	17.	B
8.	D	18.	D
9.	C	19.	D
10.	D	20.	C

21.	B
22.	B
23.	B
24.	D
25.	C

A SURVEY OF THE IDEAS OF THE GREAT ECONOMISTS

ADAM SMITH (1723-1790)

In the Wealth of Nations, first published in 1776, Adam Smith was concerned with an analysis of two broad problems: the market mechanism which holds society together, and the dynamic movement of society over time.

1. MARKET MECHANISM: Smith's laws of the free market demonstrate how the interaction of self-interest among individuals results in competition, which in turn provides society with those goods and services it wants, at the prices society is willing to pay, and in the quantities society desires. This comes about in the following manner:

(a) Self-Interest: Adam Smith assumed that all individuals are motivated by self-interest. The desire to get ahead and advance economically is part of the make-up of all persons, causing them to work in whatever capacity society is willing to pay for. Smith asserted that "it is not from the benevolence of the butcher, the brewer, or the baker, that we expect our dinner, but from regard to their own self-interest. We address ourselves not to their humanity, but to their self-love, and never talk to them of our necessities but of their advantages."

(b) Competition: Self-interest is regulated by competition, the logical outcome of the free play of conflicting self-interests. Each person trying to maximize his own gain is in competition with similarly motivated individuals, which prevents each one's self-interest from getting out of hand. If a shopkeeper charges too much for his goods, in the hope of making excessive profits, he will lose business to his competitors, who will undersell him. If he refuses to pay acceptable wages, his employees will find work elsewhere, at higher wages, and he will be left without workers. Collusive agreements to fix prices will be broken by an independent producer, selling below the monopolistic price. The laws of the market not only insure a competitive price, but also see to it that the goods produced are in the quantities desired by society. If there is a surplus of radios and a shortage of television sets, the price of the former will fall and the price of the latter will rise. Workers will be released from the radio industry, cutting down the output of the radios, as a result of the decline in profits. These temporarily unemployed workers will be absorbed by the increased demand for labor in the television industry. The ultimate result of these shifts will be exactly what society wants: an increase in television production and a decrease in radio production. The interaction of supply and demand in the free market also regulates the incomes of the productive factors. If the wages of steel workers are out of line with wages in comparable occupations, there will be a shift of workers to the steel industry, causing wages there to fall. In conclusion, *Adam Smith's laws of the market, assuming self-interest and competition exist, provide society with a self-regulating mechanism.*

2. DYNAMIC MOVEMENT OF SOCIETY: The wealth and standard of living of society increase over the years. This is partly the result of the market mechanism, which propels men to work, to innovate, and to take risks. Smith believed that the increase in productivity of society was the result of two additional factors. First, capital

accumulation, generated by the profits of the system, led to more machinery and equipment, expanding the division of labor and leading to greater riches. This increased the demand for labor, which increased wages and reduced the source of accumulation (profits). The second factor, the growth of population in response to the increased demand for workers, reduced wages, restored profits, and led to further capital accumulation.

3. CONCLUSION: The workings of the market mechanism, which beneficially harnesses the self-interests of individuals, and the natural trend of the nation's standard of living led Adam Smith to favor a governmental policy of *laissez-faire*. Smith was against the government meddling with the free market mechanism. He was protesting against the many government economic regulations in 18th century England.

DAVID RICARDO (1772-1823)

Ricardo amassed a fortune early in life as a stockbroker, which enabled him to retire from business at an early age and to devote himself to intellectual pursuits. The Principles of Political Economy and Taxation, published first in 1817, is his most important work. In this book Ricardo was interested primarily in the theory of value and distribution. Ricardo's theory is best understood by dividing it into three sections: the theory of value; the theory of wages, profit and rent; and the theory of economic development.

1. THE THEORY OF VALUE: The relative value of commodities (i.e. exchange value) is determined according to Ricardo from scarcity of labor. Great art works are valued not by the quantity of labor bestowed upon them, but by their scarcity. However, most commodities in a capitalist system are capable of infinite reproduction. The comparable value of these commodities is determined by the quantity of labor contained in them. Thus, if good X contains four hours of labor and good Y contains two hours of labor, good X will be worth twice as much as good Y. In advanced economies, Ricardo argued that not only present but also past labor, embodied in machinery, tools, buildings, etc., determine the relative value of commodities. In this case, the worker's remuneration is less than the value of the commodity, the difference being the capitalist's profit.

2. THE THEORY OF WAGES, PROFIT AND RENT: Ricardo distinguished between two types of wages: the natural price of labor and the market price of labor. The former is that which is "necessary to enable the laborers, one with another, to subsist and to perpetuate their race, without either increase or diminution." The latter is determined by the current market conditions in accordance with supply and demand; but it will gravitate towards the natural price. If wages are above the subsistence level (i.e., the natural price), population will increase, primarily, as a result of a decline in the mortality rate of infants and young children, and the wages of labor will fall. Ricardo's theory of wages is often called the *iron law of wages*.

The return to capital, which Ricardo called the profit rate, is set by the interaction of supply and demand. In this connection, Ricardo pointed out that competition among capitalists tends to establish a uniform profit rate. For example, when the profit rate of an industry is relatively high, capital will be attracted into the industry, bringing down the profit rate.

Ricardo believed that rent is derived from differences in the fertility of soil. The market price of an agricultural product must be sufficient to cover its cost of production on the poorest soil. Thus, on the least fertile land the cost of production will equal the price of the product. However, a surplus or profit will appear on better quality land since the cost of production will be less than the market price. This surplus will be extracted by the landowner from the tenant farmer due to competition among tenants for better land. Ricardo argued that in the course of time poorer quality lands would be cultivated in order to feed the rising population, resulting in larger surpluses which would increase the rentier's share of national income relative to the labor and capitalist class. This conclusion of Ricardo's *differential theory of rent* provided the rising industrialist class with a powerful weapon against the landed interests.

3. THE THEORY OF ECONOMIC DEVELOPMENT: In the future, progressively poorer lands will be cultivated, leading to higher food prices. This in turn will force upward money wages to enable the working class to maintain its subsistence level. Since Ricardo alleged that profits and wages are inversely related, capital accumulation, which directly depends upon profits, will fall and hence future economic progress will be restricted. Ricardo's analysis of economic development means that the interest of the landlord is opposed to the general welfare of society, as well as the interest of the capitalist and labor classes. The theory of differential rent is at the heart of Ricardo's pessimistic interpretation of the natural course of economic progress. However, Ricardo overlooked the fact that improved technology would offset the increasing use of less fertile lands, causing future food prices to fall.

THOMAS MALTHUS (1772-1834)

Malthus's most significant contribution to economic thought is contained in his Essay on the Principle of Population, published first in 1798. In this work Malthus alleged that population tended to increase in a geometrical progression (1, 2, 4, 8, 16, 32...) while the subsistence level of food output tended to increase in an arithmetical progression (1, 2, 3, 4, 5, 6...). The tendency for population to outrun the food supply would be checked by two methods: positive and preventive. Positive checks such as famines, diseases and wars increased the death rate. Preventive checks, on the other hand, such as moral restraint, diminished the birth rate. Malthus, who was a parson, naturally advocated moral restraint, by which he meant abstention from marriage until one was financially able to support a family. Malthus was against poor relief because it aggravated the problem by encouraging the poor to have children.

1. BASIS FOR POPULATION THEORY: Both Malthus' theory of population and Ricardo's theory of differential rent are based on the famous law of diminishing returns. The increase in differential rent over time, postulated by Ricardo, arises because the cultivation of inferior land means that the cost of a unit of agricultural output increases as output is expanded (i.e. diminishing returns), making it progressively more difficult to provide subsistence for a growing population. Malthus and Ricardo both underestimated the powerful effects the opening up of new areas and the improvement in technology would have on the world's food supply.

JOHN STUART MILL (1806-1873)

In 1848 Mill published his <u>Principles of Political Economy</u>, which surveyed the whole field of economics, retracing and updating many of the principles on rent, wages, profits, prices and taxes previously analyzed by Smith, Ricardo and Malthus. However, Mill made a very important contribution of his own by pointing out the applicability of economic laws to production and to distribution.

1. PRODUCTION: Economic laws only apply to production. These impersonal laws are not arbitrary but are closely related to limits nature imposes on productivity (i.e. diminishing returns in agriculture). They tell us how to maximize output given the relative scarcity of resources.

2. DISTRIBUTION: The distribution of output is unrelated to the laws of economics. Mill argued that "the laws and conditions of the production of wealth partake of the character of physical truths. There is nothing optional or arbitrary in them ... It is not so with the Distribution of Wealth. That is a matter of human institution solely. The things once there, mankind, individually or collectively, can do with them as they like ... The Distribution of Wealth, therefore, depends on the laws and customs of society." This conclusion permitted Mill to favor laissez-faire in the sphere of production, and at the same time advocate reforms aimed at redistributing income in favor of the poor. Even if the natural course of real wages is downward, society could alter this natural result by taxing income and subsidizing the low-income families. Mill argued that there are no economic forces to justify the sharing of society's wealth. Thus, Mill's recognition that distribution was determined solely by human action allowed him to view the world optimistically, hoping that mankind, guided by reason, would progress and improve social welfare.

KARL MARX (1816 -1883)

Marx was a revolutionist who used the study of economics as a theoretical mechanism to condemn a social system which he despised. Two great forces influenced Marx's thinking. The first was the new industrial society of the 19th century, and the second was the philosophy of Hegel. From Hegel's dialectic principle, Marx drew his notion of contradiction as the cause of social change.

1. DIALECTIC MATERIALISM: Society sets up a particular economic structure (i.e. the ownership of the means of production) to enable society to utilize to the fullest its productive powers. However, the continual increase in productive power brings society into a conflict with the economic structure it has created. The economic structure and the productive power are out of line. The former has not kept pace with the latter, and as a result the economic structure of society is inappropriate for its productive powers. To illustrate, the earliest economic structure was characterized by common ownership of the means of production, which at that time was merely land. As productive powers improved, society was able to produce a surplus above the subsistence level. This surplus was appropriated by individuals, making private property an integral part of the economic structure. The first form of private property, Marx argued, was the ancient slave states in which private ownership included man himself. When slave states became inadequate, they gave way to feudalism, and this in turn was replaced by capitalism. To the latter Marx also applies the concept of dialectic materialism and,

therefore, he viewed capitalism and its system of private property in historical perspective as being a temporary phase of economic development. The inherent contradiction in capitalism, forcing it to give way to another economic structure, is the conflict between the interests of the proletariat and the interests of the capitalists. The struggle between capital and labor is the inevitable outcome of the economic structure, where the former owns the means of production and the latter owns nothing but labor power.

2. THE LABOR THEORY OF VALUE: Workers sell their labor to capitalists for exactly what it is worth (its value). This saleable value is the wage the worker needs in order to subsist. In other words, the value of labor is equivalent to a wage that will keep the laborer alive. If the wage of labor is $.50 per hour and four hours work per day is necessary for the worker to subsist, the value of labor or its worth is $2.00 a day. However, the worker does not contract to work merely four hours each day, but agrees to work a ten- or twelve-hour day. Thus, profits accrue to the capitalist because he obtains the produce of twelve hours worth of value, which he sells in the market, at a cost of four. Marx terms the portion of unpaid work surplus value. The worker gets paid his true value, but at the same time he is cheated for he must work longer than the hours required to subsist. This situation arises because the capitalist, by owning the means of production, can refuse a worker a job (i.e. his means of subsistence) unless he agrees to work a full day.

3. COMPETITION AMONG THE CAPITALISTS: Motivated by the desire to accumulate, capitalists are always trying to increase the scale of their operations. This leads to an increased demand for the services of labor, which bids up their wages and hence lowers surplus value. Smith and Ricardo also argued that profits would be narrowed by rising wages. However, they alleged that profits would be restored by the tendency of the working class to increase their numbers with every increase in wages. Marx could not accept the Malthusian answer to the profit problem because it viewed the proletariat, the future rulers of society, as being shortsighted and ignorant. For Marx, the capitalist meets the dilemma of rising wages by introducing labor-saving machinery into his factory. As a consequence, workers thrown out of jobs form an "Industrial Reserve Army," which leads to greater competition for jobs, lowering wages to their former subsistence level. The introduction of labor-saving machinery means that the capitalist is substituting non-profitable means of production for profitable ones which ultimately must lead to a reduction in profits. Unemployment appears again as capitalists continue their drive for accumulation. These crises worsen with the introduction of more non-profitable means of production, and eventually the system is overthrown by the workers.

4. THE FUTURE: The successor to capitalism would be a classless state where private property would be eliminated and the means of production would be owned by society. A proletariat dictatorship would be set up during a transitional period which would evolve into pure communism.

ALFRED MARSHALL (1842-1924)

Marshall was determined that economics should continue as a productive science which would guide statesmen and influence policy. His theoretical analysis was aimed at maintaining this contact between economic theory and policy. Marshall's major work is his Principles of Economics, published originally in 1890. Some of Marshall's more important contributions are provided below.

1. VALUE: Marshall argued that the forces behind supply and demand determine value. They are visualized as two blades of a pair of scissors, making it impossible to ascertain which one fixes the value of a product. The concept of marginal utility lies behind the demand curve, while the notion of sacrifice (i.e. cost of production) lies behind the supply curve. Marshall, therefore, brings the cost of production into view as a determinant of value.

2. CONSUMER SURPLUS: The concept of consumer surplus is derived from a demand curve as illustrated in figure 5. At point A on the demand curve the marginal utility of the fifth unit of good X is valued at $5.00; at point B the marginal utility of the eleventh unit is $3.00; and at point C the marginal utility of the fourteenth unit is $2.00. If the price is $2.00 per unit, those individuals with a marginal utility (i.e. satisfaction derived from a good X) greater than $2.00 will receive a surplus, indicated by the shaded area, because the monetary satisfaction they derive from the good is greater than its price. Although the idea of consumer surplus is abstract, Marshall was able to use it to demonstrate the effect of taxes on demand curves of different elasticities. And in this manner, Marshall tried to show what forms of government tax policy are desirable.

3. EQUILIBRIUM PERIODS: Marshall distinguished between four different equilibrium periods for supply and demand. They are as follows:

(a) MARKET: The market equilibrium is the immediate situation where the supply of a product is fixed. Thus, a change in demand can only result in an increase in price without any immediate effect on supply.
(b) SHORT RUN: In the short run, supply may be varied slightly by increasing the variable factors (i.e. labor, raw materials, etc.).
(c) LONG RUN: In the long run, the fixed factors of production such as the firm's plant and machinery may be altered to meet changes in demand. In this case the supply curve will be very elastic, which will permit an expansion of output without a change in price.
(d) EXTRA LONG RUN: In this length of time economic variables such as technology, tastes and population are subject to change.

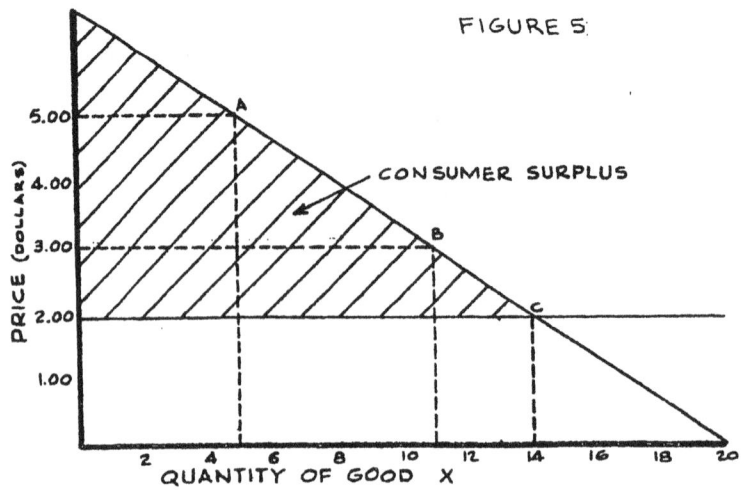
FIGURE 5

JOHN MAYNARD KEYNES (1883-1946)

In 1919, Keynes, after having served as an advisor to the British government at Versailles, published the Economic Consequences of the Peace in which he attacked the Versailles Treaty. He regarded it as impractical and dangerous. On the one hand, it attempted to destroy Germany's economic system, Keynes argued, and on the other hand, it ordered Germany to pay an impossibly large reparation sum for war damage. Keynes correctly foresaw in the consequences of the treaty the resurgence of German nationalism and militarism. In the years following World War I, Keynes wrote A Tract on Monetary Reform (1923) and A Treatise on Money (1930), both of which are particularly concerned with the monetary mechanism and its relationship to economic fluctuations. These works, however, are overshadowed by The General Theory of Employment, Money and Interest (1936), a book which caused a revolution in economic thinking. Written in the time of the greatest depression of the modern era, the General Theory explained how the level of employment and income are determined; and most important, Keynes' theoretical analysis showed that full employment is not necessarily the equilibrium level of employment. In other words, there are no automatic forces existing to pull an economy out of a depression and restore full employment.